THE LIARS' CLUB

'Heart-stopping and horribly funny despatches from the family battlefield – *The Liars' Club* is a bruising, beautiful book'
Christopher Hope

'It would not be presuming too much to suggest that *The Liars' Club*, with its burden of remembered guilt and anguish, was a hideously difficult book to write: this only disposes you to admire it all the more'
Observer

'Every sinew of her embattled childhood is unsentimentally evoked by Karr's mastery of phrase and wit'
The Times

'Bold, blunt, and cinematic, poet Mary Karr's memoir of growing up in Texas in the sixties is nothing short of superb'
Entertainment Weekly

'A devastating new childhood memoir'
Harper's Bazaar

MARY KARR'S memoir, *The Liars' Club*, won the PEN/Martha Albrand Award. A poet and an essayist, she has won Pushcart prizes in both genres. She is the author of the poetry collections *Abacus*, *The Devil's Tour* and *Viper Run*, as well as another memoir, *Cherry*, a sequel to *The Liars' Club*. She lives in New York State and is the Peck Professor of English at Syracuse University.

ALSO BY MARY KARR

memoir

CHERRY

poetry

ABACUS

THE DEVIL'S TOUR

VIPER RUN

MARY KARR

THE LIARS' CLUB

A MEMOIR

PICADOR

First published 1995 by Viking, a division of Penguin Books USA, Inc.

First published in Great Britain 1995 by Picador

This edition published 1996 by Picador
an imprint of Pan Macmillan Ltd
Pan Macmillan, 20 New Wharf Road, London N1 9RR
Basingstoke and Oxford
Associated companies throughout the world
www.panmacmillan.com

ISBN 0 330 34458 7

A portion of this book first appeared as 'Grandma Moore's Cancer' in *Granta*.

Grateful acknowledgement is made for permission to reprint excerpts from
mthe following copyrighted works:
Canto LXXVI from *The Cantos of Ezra Pound*. Copyright © 1938, 1948 by Ezra Pound.
Reprinted by permission of Faber & Faber.
'The Envoy of Mr Cogito' from *Mr Cogito* by Zbigniew Herbert. Copyright © 1974 by Zbigniew Herbert.
Translation copyright © 1993 by John Bogdana Carpenter. First published 1993 by The Ecco Press.
Reprinted by permission.

Photographs from the author's collection.

7 9 8

A CIP catalogue record for this book is available from
the British Library.

Printed and bound in Great Britain by
Mackays of Chatham plc, Chatham, Kent

for Charlie Marie Moore Karr
and J. P. Karr,
who taught me to love
books and stories, respectively

We have our secrets and our needs to confess. We may remember how, in childhood, adults were able at first to look right through us, and into us, and what an accomplishment it was when we, in fear and trembling, could tell our first lie, and make, for ourselves, the discovery that we are irredeemably alone in certain respects, and know that within the territory of ourselves, there can be only our footprints.

—R. D. Laing,
The Divided Self

ACKNOWLEDGMENTS

Amanda Urban, my agent at ICM, first urged me to write the proposal for this book. Nan Graham subsequently bought it for Viking. Her work as editor and dear friend and passionate enthusiast proved invaluable. Ditto for Courtney Hodell, also of Viking. My sister, Lecia Harmon Scaglione, confirmed the veracity of what I'd written. James Laughlin of New Directions also gave me a needed boost. As final readers, Tobias and Catherine Wolff worked quickly and incisively and without recompense. For all these, I'm grateful.

Thanks also to the Mrs. Giles Whiting Foundation for a much-needed Writers Award, and to the Mary Ingraham Bunting Institute of Radcliffe College for a fellowship.

My mother didn't read this book until it was complete. However, for two years she freely answered questions by phone and mail, and she did research for me, even when she was ill. She has been unreserved in her encouragement of this work, though much in the story pains her. Her bravery in this is laudable. Her support means everything.

I. Texas, 1961

nothing matters but the quality
of the affection—
in the end—that has carved the trace in the mind
dove sta memoria

—Ezra Pound, Canto LXXVI

CHAPTER 1

My sharpest memory is of a single instant surrounded by dark. I was seven, and our family doctor knelt before me where I sat on a mattress on the bare floor. He wore a yellow golf shirt unbuttoned so that sprouts of hair showed in a V shape on his chest. I had never seen him in anything but a white starched shirt and a gray tie. The change unnerved me. He was pulling at the hem of my favorite nightgown—a pattern of Texas bluebonnets bunched into nosegays tied with ribbon against a field of nappy white cotton. I had tucked my knees under it to make a tent. He could easily have yanked the thing over my head with one motion, but something made him gentle. "Show me the marks," he said. "Come on, now. I won't hurt you." He had watery blue eyes behind thick glasses, and a mustache that looked like a caterpillar. "Please? Just pull this up and show me where it hurts," he said. He held a piece of hem between thumb and forefinger. I wasn't crying and don't remember any pain, but he talked to me in that begging voice he used when he had a long needle hidden behind his back. I liked him but didn't much trust him. The room I shared with my sister was dark, but I didn't fancy hiking my gown up with strangers milling around in the living room.

It took three decades for that instant to unfreeze. Neighbors and family helped me turn that one bright slide into a panorama. The bed frame tilted against the wall behind the doctor had a scary, spidery look in the dark. In one corner, the tallboy was tipped over on its back like a stranded turtle, its drawers flung around. There were heaps of spilled clothes, puzzles, comics, and the Golden Books I could count on my mom to buy in the supermarket line if I'd stayed in the carriage. The doorway framed the enormous backlit form of Sheriff Watson, who held my sister, then nine, with one stout arm. She had her pink pajamas on and her legs wrapped around his waist. She fiddled with his badge with a concentration too intense for the actual interest such a thing might hold for her. Even at that age she was cynical about authority in any form. She was known for mocking nuns in public and sassing teachers. But I could see that she had painted a deferential look on her face. The sheriff's cowboy hat kept the details of his expression in deep shadow, but I made out a sort of soft half-smile I'd never seen on him.

I had a knee-jerk fear of the sheriff based on my father's tendency to get in fights. He'd pull open the back screen with knuckles scraped and bleeding, then squat down to give instructions to me and Lecia (pronounced, she would have me tell you, "Lisa"). "If the sheriff comes by here, you just tell him you ain't seen me in a few days." In fact, the sheriff never came by, so my ability to straight-faced lie to the law was never tested. But just his presence that night flooded me with an odd sense: *I done something wrong and here's the sheriff.* If I had, that night, possessed a voice, or if anyone nearby felt like listening, that's what I might have said. But when you're a kid and something big is going on, you might as well be furniture for all anybody says to you.

It was only over time that the panorama became animate, like a scene in some movie crystal ball that whirls from a foggy blur into focus. People developed little distinct motions; then the whole scene jerked to smooth and sudden life. Sheriff Watson's jaw dipped into the light and returned to shadow with some regularity as he said things that I couldn't hear to my blond, suddenly cherubic-acting sister. Some firemen wearing canary-colored slickers started to move through the next room, and Dr. Boudreaux's thick fingers came again to rub the edge of my speckled nightgown the way old ladies at the five-and-dime tested yard goods. There must have been an ambulance outside, because at intervals big triangles of red light slashed across the room. I could almost feel them moving over my face, and in the window, through a web of honeysuckle, I saw in my own backyard flames like those of a football bonfire.

And the volume on the night began to rise. People with heavy boots stomped through the house. Somebody turned off the ambulance siren. The back screen opened and slammed. My daddy's dog, Nipper, was growling low and making his chain clank in the yard. He was a sullen dog trained to drink beer and bite strangers. He'd been known to leap from a speeding truck's window to chase down and fight any hound he saw. He'd killed one lady's Chihuahua, then just shook it like a rag while Daddy tried to coax him out of her garage and she hollered and cried. When a voice I didn't know told some sonofabitch to get out of the way, I knew it meant Nipper, who disappeared that night into the East Texas bayou—or more likely, my sister later figured out, the gas chamber at the local pound. Anyway, we never saw him again, which was okay by me. That dog had bitten me more than once.

More door slams, the noise of boots, and some radio static from the cruiser in the road. "Come on, baby," Dr. Boudreaux said, "show me the marks. I'm not about to hurt you." I kept waiting to make eye contact with my sister to get some idea of how to handle this, but she was dead set on that badge.

I don't remember talking. I must eventually have told Dr. Boudreaux there weren't any marks on me. There weren't. It took a long time for me to figure that out for certain, even longer to drive my memory from that single place in time out toward the rest of my life.

The next thing I knew, I was being led away by Sheriff Watson. He still held Lecia, who had decided to pretend that she was asleep. My eyes were belt-level with his service revolver and a small leather sap that even then must have been illegal in the state of Texas. It was shaped like an enormous black tear. I resisted the urge to touch it. Lecia kept her face in his neck the whole time, but I knew she was scudging sleep. She slept like a cat, and this was plenty of hoopla to keep her awake. The sheriff held my left hand. With my free one, I reached up and pinched her dirty ankle. Hard. She kicked out at me, then angled her foot up out of reach and snuggled back to her fake sleep on his chest.

The highway patrolmen and firemen stood around with the blank heaviness of uninvited visitors who plan a long stay. Somebody had made a pot of coffee that laid a nutty smell over the faint chemical stink from the gasoline fire in the backyard. The men in the living room gave our party a wide berth and moved toward the kitchen.

I knew that neither of my parents was coming. Daddy was working the graveyard shift, and the sheriff said that his deputy had driven out to the plant to try and track him down. Mother had been taken Away—he further told us—for being Nervous.

I should explain here that in East Texas parlance the term Nervous applied with equal accuracy to anything from chronic nail-biting to full-blown psychosis. Mr. Thibideaux down the street had blown off the heads of his wife and three sons, then set his house on fire before fixing the shotgun barrel under his own jaw and using his big toe on the trigger. I used to spend Saturday nights in that house with his daughter, a junior high twirler of some popularity, and I remember nothing more of Mr. Thibideaux than that he had a crew cut and a stern manner. He was a refinery worker like Daddy, and also a deacon at First Baptist.

I was in my twenties when Mr. Thibideaux killed his family. I liked to call myself a poet and had affected a habit of reading classical texts (in translation, of course—I was a lazy student). I would ride the Greyhound for thirty-six hours down from the Midwest to Leechfield, then spend days dressed in black in the scalding heat of my mother's front porch reading Homer (or Ovid or Virgil) and waiting for someone to ask me what I was reading.

No one ever did. People asked me what I was drinking, how much I weighed, where I was living, and if I had married yet, but no one gave me a chance to deliver my lecture on Great Literature. It was during one of these visits that I found the Thibideauxs' burned-out house, and also stumbled on the Greek term *ate.* In ancient epics, when somebody boffs a girl or slays somebody or just generally gets heated up, he can usually blame *ate,* a kind of raging passion, pseudo-demonic, that banishes reason. So Agamemnon, having robbed Achilles of his girlfriend, said, "I was blinded by *ate* and Zeus took away my understanding." Wine can invoke *ate,* but only if it's ensorcered in some way. Because the *ate* is supernatural, it releases the person possessed of it from any guilt for her actions. When neighbors tried to explain the whole murder-suicide of the Thibideaux clan after thirty years of grass-cutting and garbage-taking-out and dutiful church-service attendance, they did so with one adjective, which I have since traced to the Homeric idea of *ate:* Mr. Thibideaux was Nervous. No amount of prodding on my part produced a more elaborate explanation.

On the night the sheriff came to our house and Mother was adjudged more or less permanently Nervous, I didn't yet understand the word. I had only a vague tight panic in the pit of my stomach, the one you get when your parents are nowhere in sight and probably don't even know who has a hold of you or where you'll wind up spending the night.

I could hear the low hum of neighbor women talking as we got near the front door. They had gathered on the far side of the ditch that ran before our house, where they stood in their nightclothes like some off-duty SWAT team waiting for orders. The sheriff let go of my hand once we were outside. From inside the tall shadow of his hat, with my sister still wrapped around him in bogus slumber, he told me to wait on the top step while he talked to the ladies. Then he went up to the women, setting in motion a series of robe-tightenings and sweater-buttonings.

The concrete was cold on my bottom through the thin nightgown. I plucked two june bugs off the screen and tried to line them up to race down a brick, but one flew off, and the other just flipped over and waggled its legs in the air.

At some point it dawned on me that my fate for the night was being decided by Sheriff Watson and the neighbor ladies. It was my habit at that time to bargain with God, so I imagine that I started some haggling prayer about who might take us home. *Don't let it be the Smothergills,* I probably prayed. They had six kids already and famously strict rules about who ate what and when. The one time we'd spent the night there, Lecia and I wound up in the bathroom eating toothpaste past midnight. We'd eaten a whole tube, for which we had been switch-whipped in the morning by a gray-faced Mr. Smothergill. He was undergoing weekly chemotherapy treatments for mouth cancer at the time, and every kid in the neighborhood had an opinion about when he would die. Cancer and death were synonymous. His sandpaper voice and bleak disposition scared us more than any whipping. His kids called him Cheerful Chuck behind his back. The oldest Smothergill daughter had been permitted to visit my house only once. (Our house was perceived as Dangerous, a consequence of Mother's being Nervous.) She was so tickled by the idea that we could open the refrigerator at will that she melted down a whole stick of butter in a skillet and drank it from a coffee mug. *Lord, I would rather eat a bug than sleep on that hard pallet at the Smothergills'. Plus in the morning the boys get up and stand around the TV in their underpants doing armpit farts. Let it be the Dillards', and I'll lead a holy life forever from this day. I will not spit or scratch or pinch or try to get Babby Carter to eat doo-doo.* Mrs. Dillard stood with the other ladies in her pale blue zip-front duster, her arms folded across her chest. She made Pillsbury cinnamon rolls in the morning and let me squiggle on the icing. Plus her boys had to wear pajama pants when we were there. But the Dillards had space for only one of us, and that on the scratchy living room sofa. *Maybe Lecia could go to the Smothergills',* I proposed to whatever God I worshiped, *and I could take the Dillards.* I wished Lecia no particular harm, but if there was only one banana left in the bowl, I would not hesitate to grab it and leave her to do without. I decided that if the june bug could be herded the length of a brick before I could count five I'd get what I wanted. But the june bug kept flipping and waggling before it had even gone an inch, and Mrs. Dillard went out of her way, it seemed, not to look at me.

I don't remember who we got farmed out to or for how long. I was later told that we'd stayed for a time with a childless couple who bred birds. Some memory endures of a screened-in breezeway with green slatted blinds all around. The light was lemon-colored and dusty, the air filled with blue-and-green parakeets, whose crazy orbits put me in mind of that Alfred Hitchcock movie where birds go nuts and start pecking out people's eyeballs. But the faces of my hosts in that place—no matter how hard I squint—refuse to be conjured.

Because it took so long for me to paste together what happened, I will leave that part of the story missing for a while. It went long unformed for me, and I want to keep it that way here. I don't mean to be coy. When the truth would be unbearable the mind often just blanks it out. But some ghost of an event may stay in your head. Then, like the smudge of a bad word quickly wiped off a school blackboard, this ghost can call undue attention to itself by its very vagueness. You keep studying the dim shape of it, as if the original form will magically emerge. This blank spot in my past, then, spoke most loudly to me by being blank. It was a hole in my life that I both feared and kept coming back to because I couldn't quite fill it in.

I did know from that night forward that things in my house were Not Right, this despite the fact that the events I have described so far had few outward results. No one ever mentioned the night again. I don't remember any subsequent home visits from any kind of social worker or concerned neighbor. Dr. Boudreaux seemed sometimes to minister to my health with an uncharacteristic tenderness. And neighbors dragged my sister and me to catechism classes and Vacation Bible School and to various hunting camps, never mentioning the fact that our family never reciprocated. I frequently showed up on doorsteps at suppertime;

foraging, Daddy called it. He said it reminded him of his rail-riding days during the Depression. But no one ever failed to hand me a plate, though everybody knew that I had plenty to eat at home, which wasn't always true for the families I popped in on.

The night's major consequences for me were internal. The fact that my house was Not Right metastasized into the notion that I myself was somehow Not Right, or that my survival in the world depended on my constant vigilance against various forms of Not-Rightness. Whenever I stepped into the road at Leechfield's one traffic light, I usually expected to get plowed down by a Red Ball truck flying out of nowhere (unlikely, given the lack of traffic). I became both a flincher and a fighter. I was quick to burst into tears in the middle of a sandlot baseball game and equally quick to whack someone in the head without much provocation. Neighborhood myth has it that I once coldcocked a five-year-old playmate with an army trench shovel, then calmly went back to digging. Some of this explosiveness just came from a naturally bad temperament, of course. But some stems from that night, when my mind simply erased everything up until Dr. Boudreaux began inviting me to show him marks that I now know weren't even there.

The missing story really starts before I was born, when my mother and father met and, for reasons I still don't get, quickly married.

My mother had just arrived in Leechfield. She'd driven down from New York with an Italian sea captain named Paolo. He was fifty to her thirty, and her fourth husband. My mother didn't date, she married. At least that's what we said when I finally found out about all her marriages before Daddy. She racked up seven weddings in all, two to my father. My mother tended to blame the early marriages on her own mother's strict Methodist values, which didn't allow for premarital fooling around, of which she was fond. She and Paolo had barely finished the honeymoon and set up housekeeping in Leechfield, where he was fixing to ship out, than they began fighting.

So it was on a wet winter evening in 1950 that she threw her dresses, books, and hatboxes in the back of an old Ford and laid rubber out of Leechfield, intending never to return. She was heading for her mother's cotton farm about five hundred miles west. Just outside of Leechfield, where Highway 73 yields up its jagged refinery skyline to bayous and rice fields, she blew a tire. She was about twenty yards from the truck stop where Daddy happened to be working. He had a union job as an apprentice stillman at Gulf Oil, but he was filling in at the station that night for his friend Cooter, who'd called him in desperation from a crap game in Baton Rouge where he was allegedly on a roll.

All Mother's marriages, once I uncovered them in my twenties, got presented to me as accidents. Her meeting Daddy was maybe the most unlikely. Had Cooter not gotten lucky with the dice in a Baton Rouge honky-tonk, and had Paolo not perturbed Mother in the process of unpacking crates, and had the tire on the Ford not been worn from a recent cross-country jaunt (Paolo's mother lived in Seattle, and they'd traveled there from New York, then down to Texas, where divorce laws permitted Mother to quickly get rid of husband number three before signing up with number four). . . . All these events conspired to strand my mother quite literally at my father's feet on Highway 73 that night.

He said there was a General Electric moon shining the first time he saw her, so bright it was like a spotlight on her. She refused his help jacking up the car and proceeded to cuss like a sailor when she couldn't get the lug nuts loose. My mother claims that she had only recently learned to cuss, from Paolo. Daddy said her string of practiced invectives, which seemed unlikely given her fancy clothes (she had on a beige silk suit) and New York license plates, impressed him no end. He'd never heard a woman cuss like that before.

She changed the tire and must have made some note of his raw good looks. He was some part Indian—we never figured out which tribe—black-haired and sharp-featured. His jug-eared grin reminded her of Clark Gable's. Since she fancied herself a sort of Bohemian Scarlett O'Hara, the attraction was deep and sudden. I should also note that Mother was prone to conversion experiences of various kinds, and had entered a fervent Marxist stage. She toted *Das Kapital* around in her purse for years. Daddy was active in the Oil Chemical and Atomic Workers Union. Whenever they renegotiated a contract—every two years—he was known as an able picket-line brawler. He was, in short, a Texas working man, with a smattering of Indian blood and with personality traits that she had begun to consider heroic.

Out in Lubbock, Grandma was rolling a cobbler crust for Mother's homecoming dinner when the call came that she had been detained in Leechfield. Grandma had prayed for her to make up with Paolo. She'd started auctioning Mother off to various husbands when she was only fifteen. Like some prize cow, Mother liked to say, fattened for the highest bidder. With a paid-for Ford and a ship waiting for him in the Gulf, Paolo had what Grandma thought of as the Ability to Provide. Plus he had dragged Mother out of New York, where God knew what-all went on, and relocated her in Texas. Grandma subsequently viewed my father as some slick-talking hick who had buffaloed her only child into settling for a two-bedroom tract house when she deserved a big ranch. In fact, Paolo was the only husband of Mother's whose existence Grandma would acknowledge—other than Daddy, of course, and him she couldn't very well ignore. She felt that Paolo's story would teach me a lesson, the punch line of which was something like divorcing a salary man for somebody who punches a clock was bad manners. At least Grandma told me a few stories about Paolo. Pressing Mother for details of her past always led to eye-rolling and aspirin-taking and long afternoon naps.

To Paolo's credit, he didn't give Mother up as easily as the others had. He chased her—so the saying goes—like a duck would a june bug. He sent yellow roses to her hotel room every week, and Daddy finally took to setting the boxes of chocolate-covered cherries that kept arriving for her in the common parlor of his boarding house, where his roommates ate them by the fistful. Paolo finally got up enough courage or desperation to appear there for a final showdown. For some reason, I picture Daddy stretched out on a narrow bed in a string T-shirt and boxer shorts, his eyes narrowing like a snake's when Paolo, whom I imagine in the seersucker suit he wore for his wedding snapshot, ducked into the room with slanty ceilings. Mother was there to watch all this. At some point the talk got heated, and Paolo called Mother a strumpet, for which Daddy was said to have stomped a serious mudhole in Paolo's ass. It was the first time Mother saw Daddy fight. (In fact, there wasn't ever much fighting to it, at least that I ever saw. Daddy hit people, and then they fell down. End of fight.) After that, I picture Paolo more or less crawling down the stairs. He shipped out to Saudi Arabia, never to be seen again until his picture cropped up in a box some decades later and I asked Mom who the hell that was.

At my parents' wedding in the Leechfield Town Hall, Daddy concluded the ceremony by toasting Mother with the silver flask she'd bought him for a present. "Thank you for marrying poor old me," he said. He was used to carhops and cowgirls, and said Mother represented a new and higher order of creature altogether.

The truth seems to be that Mother married Daddy at least in part because she'd gotten scared. As much as she liked to brag about being an art student in Greenwich Village during the war—and believe me, in Leechfield she stood out—she had racked up a frightening number of husbands, so frightening that she did her best to keep them secret. And her economic decline had been steady: over fifteen years she'd gone from a country house in Connecticut to a trailer park in Leechfield. Somehow all her wildness just didn't wash in the anesthetized fifties. She'd lost some things along the way, and losing things scared her. Daddy was handsome enough and the proper blend of outlaw and citizen. And he didn't bow much to the mannerisms she'd picked up to impress her cold-blooded Yankee husbands. The only Marx he knew was Groucho, the only dance the Cajun two-step. The first night he slept with her, he took a washrag and a jug of wood alcohol to get rid of her makeup, saying he wanted to see what he was getting into.

Their early time sounded happy. With the G.I. Bill, they bought a small house in a line of identical small houses. It was more than Daddy had ever dreamed of owning. He was so proud that she had more going on north of her neck than her hairdo that he built bookshelves for her art books, hung her paintings all over the house, and promised someday to construct a studio so she wouldn't have to keep her easel propped in the dining room.

My daddy had grown up with three loud brothers and a sister in a logging camp in the piney section of East Texas called The Big Thicket. His family lived mostly without hard currency, buying coffee and sugar with credit vouchers at the Kirby Lumber Company Store. Other than that and such luxuries as calico for dresses, they grew and shot and caught what they needed.

That world was long gone before my birth, but I remember it. In fact, my father told me so many stories about his childhood that it seems in most ways more vivid to me than my own. His stories got told and retold before an audience of drinking men he played dominoes with on days off. They met at the American Legion or in the back room of Fisher's Bait Shop at times when their wives thought they were paying bills or down at the union hall. Somebody's pissed-off wife eventually christened them the Liars' Club, and it stuck. Certainly not much of the truth in any technical sense got told there.

Except for Christmas Eve morning, when they met in the Legion parking lot at dawn to exchange identical gift bottles of Jack Daniel's from the windows of their pickups, the men had no official meeting time and place. I never saw evidence of any planning. They never called each other on the phone. No one's wife or kids ever carried a message to meet at thus-and-such a place. They all just seemed to meander together, seemingly by instinct, to a given place and hour that had magically planted itself in their collective noggins. No women ever came along. I was the only child allowed, a fact frequently held up as proof that I was hopelessly spoiled. I would ask Daddy for money for a Coke or shuffleboard or to unlock the pool table, and it was only a matter of time before somebody piped over at us that he was spoiling me and that if he kept it up, I wasn't going to be worth a shit. Comments like that always rang a little too true to me. Sometimes

I'd even fake starting to give the coin back or shying away from the pool table. But Daddy would just wag his head at whoever spoke. "Leave her alone. She can do anything she's big enough to do, cain't you, Pokey?" And then I would say I guessed I could.

Of all the men in the Liars' Club, Daddy told the best stories. When he started one, the guys invariably fell quiet, studying their laps or their cards or the inner rims of their beer mugs like men in prayer. No matter how many tangents he took or how far the tale flew from its starting point before he reeled it back, he had this gift: he knew how to be believed. He mastered it the way he mastered bluffing in poker, which probably happened long before my appearance. His tough half-breed face would move between solemn blankness and sudden caricature. He kept stock expressions for stock characters. When his jaw jutted and stiffened and his eyes squinted, I expected to hear the faint brogue of his uncle Husky. A wide-eyed expression was the black man Ugh, who taught him cards and dice. His sister pursed her lips in steady disapproval. His mother wore an enormous bonnet like a big blue halo, so he'd always introduce her by fanning his hands behind his head, saying *Here comes Momma.*

My father comes into focus for me on a Liars' Club afternoon. He sits at a wobbly card table weighed down by a bottle. Even now the scene seems so real to me that I can't but write it in the present tense.

I am dangling my legs off the bar at the Legion and shelling unroasted peanuts from a burlap bag while Daddy slides the domino tiles around the table. They make a clicking sound. I haven't started going to school yet, so the day seems without beginning or end, stalled in the beer-smelling dark of the Legion.

Cooter has just asked Daddy if he had planned to run away from home. "They wasn't no planning to it," Daddy says, then lights a cigarette to stall, picking a few strands of tobacco off his tongue as if that gesture may take all the time in the world. "Poppa had give me a silver dollar and told me to get into town and buy some coffee. Had to cross the train tracks to get there. When that old train come around the turn, it had to slow up. Well, when it slowed up, I jumped, and that dollar come with me.

"Got a job threshing wheat up to Kansas. Slept at night with some other old boys in this fella's barn. Man by the name of Hamlet. Sorriest sonofabitch ever to tread shoe leather. Wouldn't bring you a drink from sunup to lunch. And married to the prettiest woman you ever seen. A butt like two bulldogs in a bag." This last makes everybody laugh.

I ask him how he got home, and he slides the story back on track. While I'm waiting for his answer, I split open a fresh peanut with my fingernail. The unroasted shell is soft as skin, the meat of the nut chewy and almost tasteless without salt. Daddy finishes his drink and moves a domino. "About didn't make it. Hopped the Double-E train from Kansas City to New Orleans. Cold?" He glares at each of us as if we might doubt the cold. "That wind come inching in those boxcar cracks like a straight razor. It'll cut your gizzard out, don't think it won't. They finally loaded some cattle on somewhere in Arkansas, and I cozied up to this old heifer. I'd of froze to death without her. Many's the time I think of that old cow. Tried milking her, but it come out froze solid. Like a Popsicle."

"It's getting high and deep in here," Shug says. He's the only black man I've ever seen in the Legion, and then only when the rest of the guys are there. He wears a forest-green porkpie hat with the joker from a deck of cards stuck on the side. He's famously intolerant of Daddy's horseshit, and so tends to up the credibility factor when around.

"I shit you not," Daddy says and sprinkles some salt in the triangular hole in his beer can. "You hop one of those bastards some January and ride her. You'll be pissing ice cubes. I guarangoddamntee you that." They shake their heads, and I can see Daddy considering his next move by pretending to study his dominoes. They're lined up like bricks in a wall, and after he chooses one, he makes a show of lining it up right on the tabletop, then marking down his score. "They unloaded one old boy stiff as a plank from down off the next car over. He was a old one. Didn't have no business riding trains that old. And when we tipped him down to haul him off—they was four or five of us lifting him—about a dozen of these round fuzzy things rolled out his pant leg. Big as your thumb, and white." He measures off the right length on his thumb.

"Those were the crown pearls, no doubt," Shug says.

Daddy stares seriously into the middle distance, as if the old man in question were standing there himself, waiting for his story to get told properly and witnessing the ignorance that Daddy had to suffer in the process. "Wasn't no such thing. If you shut up, I can tell your thickheaded self what they was."

"Let him tell it," Cooter says, then lowers his head into a cloud of cigar smoke. Cooter is bothered by the fact that Shug is colored, and takes any chance to scold him, which the other guys tend to ignore. Shug gives me Fig Newtons out of his glove compartment, and I feel evil seeing him scolded for no reason and not saying anything. But I know the rules and so lay low.

"One old boy had a big black skillet in his gear. So we built a fire on the edge of the freight yard. It was a kind of hobo camp already there, some other guys set up all around. Nobody bothered us. This old fella's stretched out behind us stiff as this bench I'm sitting on here."

"The dead one?" I ask, and the men shift around in their chairs, a signal for me to shut up, so I do.

"That's right. And you ain't never gonna guess what happens when they thaw." This is the turning point. Daddy cocks his head at everybody to savor it. The men don't even fake indifference. The domino tiles stop their endless clicking. The cigar smoke might even seem to quit winding around on itself for a minute. Nobody so much as takes a drink. "They pop like firecrackers and let off the biggest stink you ever smelled."

"They was farts?" Cooter finally screams, more high-pitched than is masculine, and at that the men start to laugh. Daddy's Adam's apple googles up and down, and Ben slaps the table, and Shug has to wipe his eyes after a minute.

When everybody settles down, Daddy passes the bottle around

again and jumps back to the story of his coming home without even a stab at a segue. "Ain't nothing else to tell. I just walked up through the razor grass to Daddy's old dirt yard. And there's the old man, sitting on the porch. Just exactly like I left him the year before. And he looks up at me serious as polio and says, 'You git the coffee?' "

To Mother, such stories showed that Daddy offered steadiness. He always returned to the logging camp at the end of whatever journey, and coming back was something she'd begun to need from a man, badly. He was a rock. Guys he worked with claimed you could set a watch by when he pulled into the parking lot or what time he clicked open his lunch box. When Mother described Daddy's childhood to us, she would sometimes fake horror at how savage it all sounded—boiling the bristles off a live hog and so forth. But really she admired this world, as she admired the scratchy misery of the blues she listened to on her Bessie Smith records.

Mother was also desperate to get pregnant when she met Daddy. She was thirty, and back then that was late. And Daddy was a fool for kids. During World War II, he wrote in hilarious detail to his sister's kids, Bob Earl and Patty Ann, whom he nicknamed Booger Red and Shadow, respectively. The letters were infrequent, but he made boot camp—and later the war—sound like giant camping trips. "Well Booger you ought to have heard the 50 cal. machine gun I fired at a plane today. Of corse it was radio operated thats a wonderful thing to send a plane up and no one in it. Tell my shadow to eat plenny of pinto beans so she can grow big enuff for the air force and stay out of the stinking army. Ha Ha." About the same time, he wrote his sister about wanting some kids. "I'm too old to start a famly now I gess but I had my day. I got a 48 hour pass to London and shore like them English girls." A card later postmarked Paris is more cryptic: "I way 176 pounds and am mean as hell."

The war letters were passed on to me by my aunt Iris, Daddy's sister, during one of my rare forays down south from grad school. I kept them in a cigar box I'd spray-painted gold for Father's Day once, and which he'd stuffed with old pay stubs from Gulf Oil and then rat-holed in the army footlocker we didn't open till after his memorial service.

I can still smell the odor that came out of the trunk when we'd crowbarred the padlock off and opened it. The smell had seeped into the letters and endures there—damp paper, and gun oil, and chalk from the edges of a puzzling cedar box, which we eventually figured out was a turkey call. (Its lid, held in place by a wooden peg at one end, gives a jagged gobble when you slide it back and forth across the chalked edges of the box.) He kept his Colt pistol wrapped in a flesh-colored chamois cloth. Though he'd preached to me about the dangers of loaded weapons when I first learned to shoot, I found a single bullet in the firing chamber, which to this day I don't believe he'd left there by accident. He was too careful for that. He put the bullet in there deliberately, for a reason I would today give a lot to know. Whose face was floating in your mind, Daddy, yours or some other's, when you snapped the chamber into place and after some thought, perhaps, put the safety on? Even if I'd had the wherewithal to ask this question before his death, he would have probably answered with a shrug, staring into a cloud of Camel smoke. Maybe he would have started a story about his first squirrel gun, or a lecture about how much to lead a mallard with a shotgun before you picked it off. Like most people, he lied best by omission, and what he didn't want you to know there was no point asking about.

The envelopes are smudged with gun oil that's turned the army-issue paper a transparent gray in spots. After the Normandy invasion, the envelopes are of uniform size, dated weekly with few exceptions. The story had it that my father's mother had written his commanding officer complaining that she hadn't heard from Daddy since he'd been shipped overseas. So Captain Pearse, a blue-eyed West Point grad who would eventually arrange to have my father offered a battlefield commission, ordered him to write her every Sunday. On the seal you can see the young man's mark, "Capt. P.," his matter-of-fact block print the opposite of Daddy's wobbly scrawl. Daddy's hands always shook, so maybe he was himself some form of Nervous and just hid it better than most.

The envelopes have no stamps, just the black cancellation mark of the army postal service, and the ones dated after 1944 have "Passed by the Base Censors" in one corner. The censors have razored out some words, leaving oblong slots in the pages where Daddy had tried dropping hints of his whereabouts to folks back home. The tone of the letters progresses from the early farm-boy bragging to a soldier's gravity: "I gess you will faint when I tell you I saw [blank] a few days ago and today I ran into some of his outfit and they said he'd [blank]. I sure hated to hear it. Plese tell his Daddy that I cut his name on a piss elum tree right where it happened near the [blank] River. Tell him it was sure a pretty place. I'll talk to him about it when I get home."

The trunk held sepia photos wrapped in cheesecloth from his childhood during the early part of this century. My favorite shows Aunt Iris with the four boys—Uncle A.D., Daddy (who also received no name, only initials—J.P.), Uncle Pug, and Uncle Tim. The boys range from just under six feet (Pug) to six four (A.D.). They are shirtless under their bib overalls; their matching close-cropped haircuts, which Daddy claimed you could rub the river water out of with three strokes of a flat palm, are dark and sleek as seals. With odd solemnity, they hold a single boat oar like a totem. And strung from the giant pecan tree behind them are half a dozen dead alligators, which they hunted for the hides. I remember Daddy's description of swamp gas circling their flat-bottomed boat. Baby Tim usually sat at the prow with a bull's-eye lantern that turned a gator's eyes an eerie reflecting red. In another picture, his mother—her face partly obscured by the huge bonnet—holds the halter of a mule my grandfather allegedly beat to death one day for its stubbornness in the field. My grandfather's picture resembles a younger, stouter version of what I had watched him calcify into before he finally died at eighty-six—a hard brown man in a Stetson, planted in a cane-bottomed rocker on a porch with three equally taciturn-looking bird dogs.

We found a clipping from *Life* on Normandy. Daddy had taken a pen to the spread, writing names underneath many of the men walking away from boats in the surf and holding their rifles up out of the spray. Others posed on tanks. Daddy had scribbled names under certain faces—Rogers, Kinney, Brown, Gustitus, and some faces he had inked out with a simple X.

The trunk also held just about every receipt from every bill he ever paid. He didn't trust banks and believed checking accounts and credit cards were big-company traps to make a man spend money he didn't have without even knowing it. If a Southwestern Gas representative ever had the gall to knock on our door to claim that Daddy owed three dollars for a 1947 gas bill, he would have met with one of the elastic-bound bundles of receipts from that year, then a rectangular piece of faded onionskin stamped PAID. It was a feat Daddy never got to perform, but on nights when he spread the receipts out chronologically, he made it clear to my sister and me that every day some suit-wearing, Republican sonofabitch (his term) weaseled a working man out of an extra three dollars for lack of a receipt. He would not be caught short.

These notorious Republicans were the bogeymen of my childhood. When I asked him to define one (I think it was during the Kennedy-Nixon debate), Daddy said a Republican was somebody who couldn't enjoy eating unless he knew somebody else was hungry, which I took to be gospel for longer than I care to admit. Maybe the only thing worse than being a Republican was being a scab.

Scabs were the cornerstones of one of Daddy's favorite lectures. For some reason, I remember him delivering it one particular morning when I was just old enough to drive and had picked him up from the night shift in his truck. I slid over so he could take the wheel. He brought into the cab the odors of stale coffee and of the cleaning solvent he used to get the oil off his hands. "Now you take me," he said. "Any kind of ciphering I could always do. Math or anything. I could have had that shift foreman's job right over there." He tilted his hard hat toward the white oil-storage tanks and the flaming towers by the roadside. "Twelve thousand dollars a year, straight salary. Mr. Briggs called me in. His secretary got me coffee like I like. And he had a desk near as wide as this highway, solid mahogany. 'Pete,' he tells me, 'if you'll stop worrying about crossing a picket line you'll do a helluva lot better by your family.' Well I thanked him just the same. Shook his hand. And a few days later I hear they give it to old Booger." Who old Booger was I had no idea, but this lecture had its own velocity, so there was no point in interrupting. "Pretty soon old Booger gets to feeling poorly. He's got the headache and the sore back. Pretty soon his belly's swelled out over the top of his britches. He's got the mulligrubs." Maybe Daddy thumped his cigarette butt out the triangular side window at this point to buy a minute of thought. "See, Pokey, there was more job there than there was man. And you don't believe me, his wife's a widow today.

"More money, my rosy red ass. That ignorant scab sonofabitch." When he said the word *scab* his knuckles would get white where he gripped the wheel. "Pokey, anybody cross a picket line—and not just here. I mean any picket line. I don't care if it's the drugstore or the carpenters or whoever . . ." What followed would be a grisly portrayal of people prying open children's mouths to steal the bread from them.

In the trunk's very bottom, under the stack of plastic-wrapped dress shirts we bought from Sears or Penney's each Christmas and never saw him even unwrap, we found a sock with a roll of bills adding up to some three thousand dollars—gambling money, I guess, his version of security.

CHAPTER 2

If Daddy's past was more intricate to me than my own present, Mother's was as blank as the West Texas desert she came from. She was born into the Dust Bowl, a vast flat landscape peppered with windmills and occasional cotton ranches. Instead of a kitty for a pet, she had a horny toad. She didn't see rain fall, she said, for the first decade of her life. The sky stayed rock-white and far away.

About all she later found to worship in Leechfield was the thunderstorms, which were frequent and heavy. The whole town sat at a semitropical latitude just spitting distance from the Gulf. It sat in a swamp, three feet below sea level at its highest point, and was crawled through by two rivers. Any hole you dug, no matter how shallow, magically filled up with brackish water. Even the wide ditches that ran in front of the houses, where I later learned that sidewalks ought to be, were not enough to keep the marsh from burbling up. Digging a basement in that part of the country was out of the question. So when a tornado warning was announced on the radio, everybody but Mother herded into doorways and bathrooms for fear of a touchdown. She tended to throw open the doors and windows. I can still hear the hard rain splatter on the broad banana leaves and the cape jasmine bush off the back porch, like a cow pissing on a flat rock, we liked to say.

Once, we saw a black funnel drop out of the low-bulging sky over the football field across the street. It tore the yellow goalpost up and wrenched it like a paper clip. We were forty yards away, watching through the screen. I leaned my head into Mother's denim hipbone and kept my ears stoppered with my fingers. But I could still hear the concrete posts torn out of the ground like some giant buttons getting popped off. Mother worshiped that kind of wild storm like nothing else.

I own just one picture from her childhood. She's alone on what looks like a wide whitewashed porch, wearing a stiff little wool coat and staring dead level at you from under Dutch-boy bangs that are blond and military-cut across her forehead. Her parents named her Charlie—not Charlotte or Charlene, but Charlie like a boy, a name that's required no end of explanation over the decades. It even got her a draft notice during World War II. At the time of the picture, she was two and had come down with pneumonia when a cold norther blew down. The doctor spent some hours trying to get her fever to fall with cold sponge baths and spoon-fed whiskey toddies, but he finally rolled his cuffs down and announced to my grandparents that the case was hopeless. If the child lived through the afternoon, he said, she would surely be gone by midnight. There was much hand-wringing on the part of my grandmother Moore. She had injured her female parts somehow during Mother's birth and couldn't bear any other children.

Nevertheless, about suppertime, Grandma got cheered by an idea. Like my mother after her, Grandma drew some parcel of relief from busy-ness. She recovered enough enthusiasm about the future to wash Mother's hair and hard-comb it dry, after which she summoned the town photographer. If Charlie Marie was going to die, she said, then they'd better hurry up and get a picture of her for a keepsake. My grandfather threatened to leave if my grandmother took that sick child outside just to get enough light for a photograph, but Grandma had her jaw set.

So it was that my mother's fevered two-year-old self was stuffed in a bright red coat and propped out on the open front porch on a freezing January afternoon. Mother said that she saw the whole sky through a gray curtain. She remembered the wind blowing full tilt at her from the west like a wide white hand of hard air slapping toward her face. There were no breaks or hills to interrupt the wind from its long slide off the northern Rockies. It hit her from across a thousand miles of flat-assed nothing. In the foreground you can see a spotted cat appear to rub its hind parts on Mother's shins. This gives the whole picture an aspect of haste. Mother doesn't smile. She said that she didn't feel like she was fixing to die or anything, only that a wooziness made her want to lie down but people kept standing her up.

What made this story endure in our family is that it ends in a miracle. When the preacher arrived the next morning, dressed in his freshly brushed black coat and ready to give comfort, Mother was sitting upright in bed rolling up rag dolls from old quilt scraps and still sucking whiskey off the rock candy her daddy had gone into town to buy her at the crack of dawn. Grandma liked to say later that it was the fresh air that healed her.

Our only visit to my grandmother's house in Lubbock is seared into memory for me by Mother's first serious threat to divorce Daddy. I don't remember what they fought about that morning, only that at some point she chucked a pot of oatmeal against the yellow kitchen tiles, grabbed her straw purse, and pulled us out to the car without even bothering to change us out of our pajamas. I do remember that before Lecia would agree to go into Stuckey's for breakfast, Mother had to buy us new dresses. (Even then, my sister had a sense of propriety I lacked: if I wet my underpants playing, back then, I just stepped out of them and kept running.)

Somewhere past Dallas that afternoon, we stopped again for a paper bag full of fifteen-cent burgers. Lecia and I had been playing Jewelry Store in the backseat, which involved my giving her real money for fake jewels. She kept a red fruitcake tin stuffed with buttons of every conceivable shape and material, including rhinestone and brass love knots. I had started the trip with a stack of dimes I'd collected in a glass cigar tube from Daddy, and a click-open plastic Barbie purse full of pennies. By Fort Worth, Lecia had taken nearly all the dimes by arguing that since they were littler, they were worth less. That was the kind of transaction that marked all our games. (Lecia went on to make an adult fortune selling whole-life insurance in Houston.)

Anyway, I was down to pennies, and she was down to trying to pawn off plain white plastic buttons as pearl when the afternoon sky first went dark.

Out in West Texas, the sky is bigger than other places. There are no hills or trees. The only building is an occasional filling station, and those are scarce. How the westward settlers decided to keep moving in the face of all that nothing, I can't imagine. The scenery is blank, and the sky total. Even today you can drive for hours with nothing but the hypnotic rise and slope of telephone lines to remind you that you're moving. So the sky getting dark was a major event, as if somebody had dropped a giant tarp over all that impossibly bright wideness. You could still see the water mirage lying in the middle of the blacktop road a ways ahead, but the sky it reflected had somehow gone all dirty brown. We looked up. Lecia pointed out a dark cloud racing toward us. It was strange. We'd seen tornadoes, but this was different. Instead of blue-black, this cloud was the color of an old penny, and it was wider, slower, not at all cone-shaped. It still seemed far off when handfuls of locusts began to spatter against the windshield like hail. You could hear the hum of wings as the cloud got closer. Then the world outside the car went black so fast it seemed the sun had been blown out. It didn't start slowly and build the way normal storms do. By the time Mother got us pulled over, I was crying, and the cloud had more or less enveloped the whole car in a deep crust, a sheet of locusts. They made an eerie roachlike clacking noise that multiplied about a million times in my head. Mother scrambled to close off the side vents, but some of them got inside anyway. That set her saying *Oh my God oh my God* and me screaming as I hunkered down in the black well of the backseat in the duck-and-cover posture we'd learned for the atom bomb. Lecia was quicker to the take than we were. She started smacking locusts with her flip-flop, calling each one a name: "Take that, you *sonofabitch,*" she'd say. Weird, but after that she was terrified of cockroaches like nobody else. Just the sight of one—and you had to shake them out of your shoes in the morning, down there—would send her climbing up the bookshelf and wailing. She could gut a coon or skin a snake without a wince, but flying roaches drove her nuts, which is odd because she seemed fearless that day, going after the locusts.

After a while all the flying around in there stopped. In fact, everything seemed to stop. The day itself stopped. Lecia elbowed me in the head to shut up my crying, so I did. Then for a long time there was just that clacking, humming sound.

They passed as fast as they had come. Lecia nudged me again, to look, and I lifted my head from my folded arms just in time to watch them peel away from the back windshield. You could see the cloud assemble and thicken before your very eyes. All over the inside of the curved back windshield, there were splats of locust goo with legs and antennae kind of spronged out, and a few hairy legs still flailing. Other than that, you could almost forget they were individual bugs at all and just look at the cloud. It rose up and seemed to shrink away, and blue sky appeared around it, and the humming receded. On either side of the road were bare fields, and it was that strip of naked road we followed to the outskirts of Lubbock and Grandma Moore's house.

Grandma never did sugarcoat her opinion of Daddy. In fact, any skills she had at sweet-talking or diplomacy were said to have died with my grandfather, decades earlier. She said something about Mother coming to her senses, then immediately set us all to work putting up an evil sweet relish she called chowchow. Open jars cooling on all the cupboards steamed up the whole farmhouse. I was a fairly lazy child, unaccustomed to chores, and it seemed Grandma always had peas to shuck or stinging cucumbers to pick or some big piece of furniture we had to buff real hard. So I tended to drag-ass and generally make a poor impression, whereas Lecia thrived on instruction.

My memory of that day drifts into focus again with all four of us in Grandma's bathroom, which seemed vast as a barn. The old woman was just out of the tub and dabbing drugstore powder all over herself with a big yellow puff. When I was little, she'd given me an enema once, and I could never look at her without fearing her bony strength. But naked, her body put me in mind of something real easy to hurt, like a turtle without a shell. Stripping down came more naturally to Mother. This was back when women's underwear was like armor: the bra cups were rocket cones, and the hose stayed shaped like somebody else's legs when you took them off. Mother wiggled out of her long-line girdle, which immediately shrank up with a dull snapping noise at her ankles. Why she wore that thing I don't know, because she hated a girdle in summer like nothing else and sure didn't need it. The diamond-shaped control panel left a mean imprint on her belly, where there was also a slanty scar from when I'd been born. (I had been a difficult birth, feet first, *like Caesar,* Mother liked to say.) She stepped into the steamy water with a grace she must have learned modeling for life study classes during art school in the forties, all flowing lines and violin curves.

I was sitting on the toilet waiting for my own bath and fiddling with one of Grandma's hair clamps. Grandma had cocked her hip out and leaned it against the bathroom sink while she crimped her lead-colored hair. She used these steel clamps with little teeth that made deep marks on my index finger as I played with them. Grandma had told Lecia to rinse out Mother's stockings in the sink, but Lecia was idly playing at fitting her arm inside one and peeling it off like a snakeskin. So Grandma kept cutting her a look as if to say, *Get on with it.* Every now and then, from my spot on the toilet, I'd lean out and try to snatch the other stocking away from Lecia, but she was way too fast.

"You can't keep raising these children like heathens, Charlie Marie. The little one can't even tie yet."

I don't remember making any defense of my shoe-tying disability. I just stood up from the toilet, pulling up my white underpants, which had little red apples printed all over them. Lecia had learned to tie at three. Grandma had even taught her how to tat lace by the time she was five. (Tatting is an insane activity that involves an eensy shuttle, thin silk thread, and maniacal patience. Belgian nuns are famous for tatting, it turns out.) Lecia had immediately generated half a dozen doilies, which Grandma had draped over worn spots on the sofa. In my hands, even the simple Jacob's ladder that any kid in Vacation Bible School could make went all tangled. No matter how many times I was shown, my brain refused to hold on to the pathways necessary to tying a shoe bow. I was thought not so much boneheaded as stubborn on this point.

Mother lay soaking in the tub with a mint-green washcloth over her face. Her mouth made a dark spot in the terry cloth as she breathed. I always associate my grandmother's house with Mother's silence and the old woman's endless bossy prattle. "Now this here is Crisco," she said, cold-creaming her face. "You should never let anybody sell you anything else. They squeeze a couple of eyedroppers of perfume in it, and Charlie Marie will buy a tablespoon for a dollar. She just wants to throw money away! Do y'all still have those clay banks I got you down in Laredo?" At some point, Mother said the water was like ice, and would I hand her a robe.

The next morning, we drove out to visit Mother's cousin Dotty, whose husband, Fermin, ran a cotton gin in Roundup, Texas. She had a sprawling white ranch house with so many bedrooms that none of us had to double up. Lecia and I had never been inside a house so fancy. There was a pool in the back and a storm cellar that a cleaning lady kept swept clean and stocked with jars of vegetables Dotty didn't have to deal with till she forked them up to eat. Her daughter, Tess, had a pink Princess phone by her bed and kept her toenails painted frost white. Dotty's son, Robert, wore a tie to his church school.

When you have relatives who farm, the first thing that always happens on a visit is a tour of the crop or the livestock or what-have-you. Other people trot out photo albums or new patio furniture or kids' trophies. With relatives who farm, it's almost impolite to ask about any of these things first. You get to them after lunch.

We took the farm road down through acres of cotton. The field was in full bloom. It almost made me dizzy the rows of plants rushing by. Each row ticked past as if marking time, and yet they all seemed to come together at one still point on the horizon. Dotty said it was a miracle that the locusts didn't bother them at all this year. The same way tornadoes cut narrow paths—so an outhouse would be left standing alongside a house blown to splinters—the locusts chewed up fields at random. They'd left this one alone.

Grandma told how her daddy had farmed her out to chop cotton that looked just like that by hand when she was still a teenager. Her sister Earle had to go to work in the fields too, but the three other girls stayed home and took singing lessons. They were pretty and expected to "make good marriages," which didn't mean they'd be happy, only that they wouldn't have to farm. The sepia portrait of all five sisters in Grandma's parlor photo shows five wispy blondes. Their seeming frailty made it nearly impossible to believe that the two youngest had been rented out to sharecroppers. They wore eyelet-lace necklines and had those loose-blown Victorian roses pinned to their slouchy Gibson girl hairdos. They were pale, translucent, and somebody had tinted the picture slightly so that their cheeks and the roses were a faint peach color.

In the middle of the cotton field, we stopped Dotty's Cadillac and climbed out of the air-conditioning. Up close, the plants were near black and spidery-looking. Each one had dozens of cotton bolls exploded in little clouds, each boll shot full of long skinny brown seeds. Grandma pulled one loose and expertly plucked out the seeds till she had a mass of pure fluff in her hand. She showed Lecia and me how to draw a thin thread out of it like spider silk by rolling the strand between thumb and forefinger and pulling just so.

Cotton was a mean crop, I recall her saying, like most money crops. It sucked a lot out of the ground and even more out of those who worked it. When I grew up and read Robert Caro's biography of Lyndon Johnson, much of the first volume was devoted to how hard life in that part of the country was on a woman in the Dust Bowl. Water was so scarce that the average thirty-year-old had a dowager's hump from toting buckets up to the house several times a day. Their faces wrinkled from too much sun, and their hands grew hard as boot leather. Every family buried a couple of kids, too, and that made them hard inside. Thinking of Grandma's picture in the gold oval frame above Mother's bed, I tried to imagine someone choosing those girly white hands of hers to do field work, but never quite fathomed it.

We stood in this field in our Sunday visiting clothes, Grandma dabbing at her temples with a hankie. About a stone's throw away, there stood a barn and tall silo aswarm with Mexican workers. At some point, Grandma announced that Dotty had sure made a good marriage, which judgment wasn't lost on Mother, I guess. She got all quiet. Then she took her sketch pad and a stub of charcoal from the backseat and wandered off to the barn. When I tried to follow, she squatted down and said to stay with Grandma. This caused Lecia to mouth that I was a baby, and subsequently I tossed a pebble at her kneecap, so Grandma clamped her bony hand on my shoulder and made me go sit in the hot car by myself.

On the way home, we pulled up to the barn to pick up Mother. The door to Dotty's Cadillac made a big impression on me: it must have weighed a hundred pounds, and also lit up like Broadway when I heaved it open. Mother was talking soft Spanish to two guys studying her sketch pad. One of them quickly tucked a pint bottle of clear liquid into his back pocket. You couldn't smell liquor on her when she got in, but she had that clipped, Yankee way of talking she always got when she'd had a few. She must have done ten thousand such sketches in my childhood, but for some reason, that drawing stays with me: a hasty sketch of the older man in a sombrero, done in bold scrawls with few shadings, his face withered up. She pulled a can of Aqua Net hair spray out of her bag and sprayed the sketch to fix it, then snapped shut the pad. It bothered me that nobody else asked to look at it.

We stayed in Roundup a few days. The only outward0 sign of trouble in Dotty's whole family during that time was that Robert had knocked up his high school girlfriend, who was Catholic and therefore needed marrying. The young wife lollygagged around the house in his football jersey, her belly so big she looked like a balloon from some parade. They were fifteen and slept in his room, on bunk beds. That sort of trouble happened often enough in those days. Robert was going to finish high school and eventually take over the cotton business.

He must have seen me as some sort of warm-up for being a daddy, because while Lecia was learning from Tess how to paint on eyeliner and tease her hair, he played tic-tac-toe with me on my magic slate. I remember he also drew me a Crayola picture of a train wreck he'd seen where people's legs and heads were scattered every which way among the cotton plants. The cotton was amazingly detailed given how rough the rest of the drawing was. When he tucked me into bed he told me such a vivid (and grotesquely inaccurate) version of Rumpelstiltskin (where the mean troll forced the lady to spin straw into gold herself) that I can still recall my nightmares about it. There was a carbuncular troll who had locusts spewing out of his mouth, and he was threatening to take away Mother's baby. I finally convinced Lecia to let me crawl into bed with her. But she made me sleep with my head down by her feet, stifled under the tucked-in covers. In the morning, Dotty lit into Robert for scaring me, and he lost interest in playing daddy.

I heard from him only a few other times. Two years later, he sent me a birthday card from China Beach, Vietnam. Mother said I must have made some kind of good impression on him, which was a first for me, so I sent him one of my school pictures. He sent back a picture of himself in jungle fatigues pointing what looked like a grenade launcher at a palm tree. The story is that three years later, home from the war in time for his twentieth birthday party, he stood up from the table saying he didn't know why he was alive and his buddies were dead. Then he went crying into the bedroom. His wife and son were slicing the white sheet cake when the shot came.

That was about the only story I ever heard implying that anybody in Mother's family was inherently Nervous. Oh, she had some outlaws everybody talked about. Her daddy had used his engineering degree to open a garage, which drove his banker daddy nuts. There was her great-uncle Earl who used to dress up like a matador when he got drunk, and her maternal grandfather, who'd been a bootlegger and who used to give her nickels to hear her cuss. I never heard anything more exotic than that. Most of the names block-printed in Grandma's huge family Bible, which sat in a heavy plastic wrapper on her coffee table, meant nothing to me.

The morning Mother decided to go back to Daddy, she and Grandma had a fight about whether her lipstick was too dark. Grandma had brought it up at breakfast and just clamped down on it like a Gila monster. Finally, Mother stuffed our new clothes in her dead father's Gladstone bag and piled us in the car in our pajamas again. Again the old woman had crimped her hair. Just before we pulled out, she poked her clamp-studded head in my window. Some curls had sprung loose from the clips, so she looked for all the world like the stone head of Medusa that Mother had shown us in her mythology book. The old lady called Leechfield a swamp, a suckhole, and the anus of the planet before Mother cranked up the engine. The too-sweet smell of Grandma's hyacinth perfume hung in the car till Mother lit a Salem.

We drove all night, Lecia curled on the backseat. I stretched out dozing on the flat shelf under the rear windshield's slope. The sheer stink of my hometown woke me before dawn. The oil refineries and chemical plants gave the whole place a rotten-egg smell. The right wind could bring you a whiff of the Gulf, but that was rare. Plus the place was in a swamp, so whatever industrial poisons got pumped into the sky just seemed to sink down and thicken in the heat. I later learned that Leechfield at that time was the manufacturing site for Agent Orange, which surprised me not one bit. That morning, when I woke up lying under the back slant of the windshield, the world smelled not unlike a wicked fart in a close room. I opened my eyes. In the fields of gator grass, you could see the ghostly outline of oil rigs bucking in slow motion. They always reminded me of rodeo riders, or of some huge servant creatures rising up and bowing down to nothing in particular. In the distance, giant towers rose from each refinery, with flames that turned every night's sky an odd, acid-green color. The first time I saw a glow-in-the-dark rosary, it reminded me of those five-story torches that circled the town at night. Then there were the white oil-storage tanks, miles of them, like the abandoned eggs of some terrible prehistoric insect.

In case you think I exaggerate Leechfield's overall nastiness, *Business Week* once voted it one of the ten ugliest towns on the planet. Mother was working as a stringer for the town paper when the story came out, and the mayor, whose only real job was to turn on the traffic light every morning, called a press conference. Mother brought Lecia and me along, and another reporter was there from *The Port Arthur News*. He was chewing Red Man tobacco, I remember, and spitting into a Folger's can he'd brought with him for that purpose. In the back of the firehouse, somebody had strung up one of those big flags made out of the royal-blue felt that you see only at Scout jamborees. It had the town motto on it in gold letters: Leechfield Will Grease The Planet! Mother took a Polaroid of the mayor standing in front of it holding up the copy of *Business Week* like he'd won it in a raffle. The big-jawed reporter from Port Arthur told Lecia and me that he felt like he was supposed to write up the winner of a shit-eating contest. After Mother got her picture, we all stood around the fire truck eating moon-shaped cookies dusted with powdered sugar that the mayor's wife had brought in some Tupperware. It was stuff like that that'd break your heart about Leechfield, what Daddy meant when he said the town was too ugly not to love.

The last stars were clicking out just as we pulled up in our yard. The old Impala's tires had left deep muddy grooves in the yard in front of our house when we'd backed out for Grandma's days earlier. Those were what we plunged back into coming home.

Daddy had come in from the graveyard shift and was shaving at the kitchen sink, his hard hat sitting in the drainboard. He always shaved without a mirror, using soap and cold water, something he'd learned in the war. It was a kind of modesty for him, not watching himself too much. He was standing shirtless at the kitchen sink with little speckles of blood all over his chin. Lecia and I came tearing in and threw ourselves around his skinny legs, but he made out like we hadn't been anywhere. Like his own daddy, he might well have asked us if we'd got the coffee.

Mother threatened divorce a lot of times, and Daddy's response to it was usually a kind of patient eye-rolling. He never spoke of divorce as an option. If I asked him worried questions about a particularly nasty fight, he'd just say I shouldn't talk bad about my mother, as if even suggesting they might split up insulted her somehow. In his world, only full-blown lunatics got divorced. Regular citizens in a bad marriage just hunkered down and stood it.

His uncle Lee Gleason, for instance, didn't speak to his wife for forty years before he died, but they didn't bother with divorce. According to Daddy, who broke horses for Uncle Lee in the summer of 1931, Uncle Lee and Annie stopped talking that very year, after they got into a fight about how much money she spent on sugar. Annie Gleason saddled up an old mule they kept to keep the horses calm and rode all the way into Anhuac, Texas, with her boots dragging in the dust. She bought a fifty-pound sack of sugar, turned the mule around, and rode straight back and into the barn where Daddy and Uncle Lee were just nailing the last square-head nail into a quarter horse's shoe. Still mounted on the mule, Annie slid a jackknife from her apron pocket and, staring straight at Uncle Lee, she raised it up and jammed it down into the burlap bag strapped across the mule's backside. The sugar poured out of the sack, Daddy said, like a liquid.

We're bass fishing with Cooter and Shug and Ben Bederman at the time I remember him telling it. We're in Ben's big fiberglass motorboat, which is way nicer than the little flat-bottomed rentals we're used to. We each have a floatable red Coca-Cola cushion to sit on. I don't know how old I am, but I haven't yet outgrown the concept of fishing with Daddy, which must have happened when I was about eleven. I don't even know yet that such concepts can be outgrown. All I know is that Cooter's cigar smoke stinks to heaven. I jerk the banana-yellow lure across the surface of the water so its tiny propellers whir and stop, whir and stop. What in God's name could a bass under water think that thing is, scooting along? I prefer a plastic worm sunk down in the bottom silt, but Ben has bossed me into this gadget.

"And so what'd Uncle Lee do?" Cooter asked. Sometimes I think the Liars' Club lets Cooter come along just because he always asks the next question. He's never caught a fish the others didn't make him throw back.

"Do?" Daddy cocked his head sideways. "Ain't nothing he could do. He just shakes his head and says, 'You silly sumbitch,' and that's the last they ever spoke. Them three words."

"Tell how they split up the house, Daddy."

"This goes on," Daddy says, "more than ten years." He roots around in the cooler for a beer. "First they leave notes around the house. Grocery lists, that sort of thing. But pretty soon they leave off with that too. Then something funny happens. It's like Lee knows what Annie wants before she even wants it. And vicey-versa. Say she needs some lard or some such thing. In walks Lee with just-bought lard. Or he wakes up hungry for biscuits, and she's got the jar lid pressed into the dough already."

Shug makes a mmh-mmh-mmh sound that says the wonders never cease.

"Not a goddamn peep between them," Daddy says. "Sleep in the same bed. Eat out the same pot. When I get back from Germany, I'm walking up the road, and he's just climbing outta his Jeep. 'Pete,' he says, 'you're the very duck I been waiting for.' And he tells me this plan he's worked out.

"Next morning we get up, and sure enough, they ain't talking. Old Annie hugged on my neck—she could flat hug you hard. Spoke to me like he wasn't even in the room. After a little while she gets the eggs and bacon cooked and a mess of grits. We set there and eat. And when she leaves for church, me and Lee we get the lumber saw and split that house as clean in half as a oyster. Top to bottom, roof down to the floor. I mean, when she pulls up in that old Jeep that night—they had some function or other that kept her all day—we're just hooking up the tractor to haul her half off."

"And she don't have nothing to say about all this?" Shug asks. He's helping me untangle one of my lure's three-pronged hooks from the green nylon line.

"Wouldn't have said shit with a mouthful of it. See those reeds over there, Pokey?" He gestures with his Schlitz can. "I'd try and put it over there." He frequently leaves off his own fishing to instruct me, and I am today feeling too big to be instructed, having already been instructed out of my plastic worm and into this miserable excuse for a lure by Mr. Bederman.

"Why didn't they just get a divorce?" Shug asked.

Daddy cuts his eyes back over at Shug like he's nuts, then shrugs. My lure plops in the reeds while I squint to recollect the divided house. The two halves sat on the same acre of ground, a scruffy bank of pines separating one half from sight of the other. Daddy and Uncle Lee had nailed raw planks over the sawed-open part. But the idea of the house split wide open like that, showing everything inside, gave me the hives.

Maybe that's what Mother and Daddy should have done. Still, I swore to myself in that very boat that if they ever split up for good, I would run away and live in the bathroom of the Esso station. I would buy a thirty-five-cent corn dog one day and tamales from the road stand the next. However much that added up to, I planned to make it shining shoes at the barbershop.

Mother kept a copy of a map I left her once when I was running away from home. It shows a dashed line between our house and the Gulf station. There's an X in the ladies' room with "me" marked above it.

What I didn't know until I finally did leave home at fifteen was that, if I had lit out, nobody would organize any posse to sniff me down. Hell, they just figured that wherever I was headed, it must be better than Leechfield. I was a seventh-generation Texan by way of Tennessee and before that Ireland. So I was descended from what the writer Harry Crews once called the great "If you git work, write" tradition. For generations my ancestors had been strapping skillets onto their oxen and walking west. It turned out to be impossible for me to "run away" in the sense other American teenagers did. Any movement at all was taken for progress in my family.

Sometimes, when my parents were raging at each other in the kitchen, Lecia and I would talk about finding a shack on the beach to live in. We'd sit cross-legged under the blue cotton quilt with a flashlight, doing parodies of their fights. "Reel Six, Tape Fifty-one. Let her roll," Lecia would say. She would clap her arms together like a gator jaw as if what we were listening to was only one more take in a long movie we were shooting. She had a way of shining the flashlight under her chin and sucking in her cheeks, so her eyes became hooded and her cheekbones got as sharp as Mother's. She also had a knack for Mother's sometime Yankee accent, which only came out under stress or chemical influence. Think of a young Katharine Hepburn somehow infected with the syntax and inflections of an evangelist: *I wish that whatever God there might be had struck my car with lightning before I crossed the bridge into this Goddamned East Texas Shithole.* Sometimes she'd just cry, and Lecia's imitation of that was cruelest: *There's no hope, there's no hope,* she'd say with a Gloria Swanson melodrama, her wrist flung back to her forehead like it had been stapled there.

I always did Daddy's part, which didn't require much in the way of thought, since he was either silent or his voice was too quiet to hear. The only thing he ever shouted clearly was *You kiss my ass!* He sometimes turned this invective into a line of advice aimed at whomever Mother found to rage about: *Tell them to kiss your ass,* he'd say. "They" could be the IRS or a pack of Bible-thumpers knocking on our door to convert us. *Tell them to kiss your ass* was what you could expect him to suggest. (To this day

I have some chute in my head from which "kiss my ass" tumbles. It's truly amazing the number of times it seems applicable.)

Sometimes we'd hear a crash or the sound of a body hitting the linoleum, and then we'd go streaking in there in our pajamas to see who'd thrown what or who'd passed out. If they were still halfway conscious, they'd scare us back to bed. "Git back to bed. This ain't nothing to do with you," Daddy would say, or Mother would point at us and say, "Don't talk to me like that in front of these kids!" Once I heard Daddy roar up out of sleep when Mother had apparently dumped a glass of vodka on him, after which she broke and ran for the back door. We got into the kitchen in time to see him dragging her back to the kitchen sink, where he systematically filled three glasses of water and emptied them on her head. That was one of the rare nights that ended with them laughing. In fact, it put them in such a good mood that they took us out to the drive-in to see *The Night of the Iguana* while they nuzzled in the front seat.

When I stepped out the front door into sunlight after a night of their fighting, the activities of the neighbors who looked up from their trash cans or lawn mowers always seemed impossibly innocent. How could people fill their days with those kinds of chores? Sometimes I felt our house divided like Lee and Annie's. Or I felt like the neighbors' stares had bored so many imaginary holes in our walls that the whole house was rotten as wormy wood. I never quite got over thinking that folks looked at us funny on mornings after Mother and Daddy had fought. Whether this was prescient or paranoid on my part, I don't know. If one of the ladies bumped into our grocery cart at the store, she might ask Mother over for coffee, almost as a reflex, before she'd had time to imagine such an ordeal. But a woman's face always showed palpable relief when Mother declined. And I noticed that when somebody's mom went knocking on doors for company, she never knocked on ours. The more devout families wouldn't even let their kids come into our yard.

This wasn't all Mother's fault, God knows. Daddy scared the

hell out of people. Some days he was just spring-loaded on having a fight. For instance, once when we were standing in line to pay the gas bill, he socked a young Coca-Cola driver for saying we shouldn't be in Vietnam.

And Lecia and I both behaved like savages at any opportunity. When she was only twelve, Lecia could beat the dogshit out of any neighbor boy up to the age of fifteen. For my part, I can remember standing behind the drainage ditch in our yard cussing Carol Sharp for bloodying my nose. I had blood sprayed down the front of my new yellow sunsuit, one that tied at the shoulders and had elastic around the legs. I couldn't have been more than six, but I was calling her an ignorant little bitch. Her momma stood on the porch step shaking her mop at me and saying there were snakes and lizards coming out of my mouth, to which I said I didn't give a shit. Following Daddy's advice for any sort of conflict, I was likely to yell at any of the neighbor ladies to kiss my rosy red ass, then dodge into our house before they could catch and spank me.

At dusk in the late summer in 1962, the mosquitos rose up from the bayous and drainage ditches. Kids fell ill with the sleeping sickness, as we called encephalitis. Marvalene Seesacque came out of a six-month coma that left her what we called half-a-bubble off plumb. Other kids weren't lucky enough even to wake up, and for the front page of the paper, Mother had taken a slew of funeral pictures with tiny coffins. A mosquito truck was dispatched from Leechfield Public Works to smoke down the bad swarms. It puttered down the streets every evening trailing a long cloud of DDT from a hose as big around as a dinner plate. Our last game of the day that summer often involved mounting our bikes and having a slow race behind the mosquito truck.

A slow race is the definitive Leechfield competition. You win it by coming in last. This might sound easy enough to do unless you're riding a two-wheeler, in which case slowing too far down makes you tump over. The trick was to pedal just fast enough to stay upright, but not fast enough to pull ahead of anybody. Add to this the wet white cloud of poison the mosquito truck pumped out to wrap around your sweaty body and send a sweet burn through your lungs, and you have just the kind of game we liked best—one where the winners got to vomit and faint. That was what I remember Tommy Sharp doing, vomiting in the ditch in front of the swimming pool. Shirley Carter set down the kickstand on her red Schwinn just in time to pass out cold as a wedge on the roadside, so that Lyle Petit's mother, who worked as a nurse, had to be called to blow into her face and get her going again. Not a winner, I was standing in the crowd of kids watching her blue face get pinker when my mother started calling me.

All the kids looked up. It was never Mother who called us. Mother rarely even came out in the front yard since Mr. Sharp had told her she was going to hell for drinking beer and breast-feeding me on the porch. "You could see evil in the crotch of a tree, you old fart," she was supposed to have said in reply. Since then, it was Daddy who hauled the garbage out front and did any calling home for supper. At the sound of her voice, the kids all startled a little the way a herd of antelope on one of those African documentaries will lift their heads from the water hole at the first scent of a lion.

I started running, vaulting the muddy ditches that ran in front of the identical houses. I'd just leapt over one of the squat towers of mud that crawdads left when I saw my grandmother's red Ford wagon parked in front of our house. Our car always arrived from even the shortest trip strewn with candy wrappers and soda bottles and a coffee can sloshing with pee. But when I peeked into the Ford's window, it looked like the old woman had driven clear across the state of Texas with nothing more than a box of pink tissues. Mother was holding the screen door open and shading her eyes as I climbed up onto the concrete porch. Her cheekbones winged out, and her eyes were the flawed green of cracked marbles. She told me that Grandma had cancer and had come to stay with us for a while, but that I shouldn't let on I knew.

Maybe it's wrong to blame the arrival of Grandma Moore for much of the worst hurt in my family, but she was such a ring-tailed bitch that I do. She sat like some dissipated empress in

Mother's huge art deco chair (mint-green vinyl with square black arms), which she turned to face right out of our front picture window like she was about to start issuing proclamations any minute.

All day, she doled out criticisms that set my mother to scurrying around with her face set so tight her mouth was a hyphen. The drapes were awful; let's make some new. When was the last time we'd cleaned our windows? (Never.) Had Mother put on weight? She seemed pudged up. I looked plumb like a wetback I was so dark. (Lecia had managed to come out blond like her people, but Grandma never got over my looking vaguely Indian like Daddy.) And I was *pore-looking,* a term she reserved for underfed farm animals and the hookworm-ridden Cajun kids we saw trying to catch crawfish on summer afternoons on the edge of Taylor's Bayou. (Marvalene Seesacque once described her incentive for crawdadding all day: "You don't catch, you don't eat.")

In a house where I often opened a can of tamales for breakfast and ate them cold (I remember sucking the cuminy tomato sauce off the paper each one was wrapped in) Grandma cut out a *Reader's Digest* story on the four major food groups and taped it to the refrigerator. Suddenly our family dinners involved dishes you saw on TV, like meatloaf—stuff you had to light the oven to make, which Mother normally didn't even bother doing for Thanksgiving.

Our family's habit of eating meals in the middle of my parents' bed also broke overnight. Mother had made the bed extra big by stitching two mattresses together and using coat hangers to hook up their frames. She'd said that she needed some spread-out space because of the humidity, a word Lecia and I misheard for a long time as *stupidity.* (Hence, our tendency to say, *It ain't the heat, it's the stupidity.)* It was the biggest bed I ever saw, and filled their whole bedroom wall-to-wall. She had to stitch up special sheets for it, and even the chest of drawers had to be put out in the hall. The only pieces of furniture that still fit next to the bed were a standing brass ashtray shaped like a Viking ship on Daddy's side and a tall black reading lamp next to a wobbly tower of hardback books on Mother's.

Anyway, the four of us tended to eat our family meals sitting cross-legged on the edges of that bed. We faced opposite walls, our backs together, looking like some four-headed totem, our plates balanced on the spot of quilt between our legs. Mother called it picnic-style, but since I've been grown, I recall it as just plain odd. I've often longed to take out an ad in a major metropolitan paper and ask whether anybody else's family ate back-to-back in the parents' bed, and what such a habit might signify.

With Grandma there, we used not just the table but table linens. Mother hired a black woman named Mae Brown to wash and iron the tablecloth and napkins when they got greased up. And we couldn't just come in out of the heat at midday and pull off our clothes anymore with Grandma there. We'd had this habit of stripping down to underwear or putting on pajamas in the house, no matter what the time. In the serious heat, we'd lie for hours half-naked on the wooden floor in front of the black blade-fan sucking chipped ice out of wadded-up dish towels. Now Grandma even tried to get us to keep shoes and socks on. Plus we had to take baths every night. One of these first baths ended with the old woman holding me in a rough towel on her lap while she scrubbed at my neck with fingernail-polish remover. (It had supposedly accumulated quite a crust.)

She undertook to supervise our religious training, which had until then consisted of sporadic visits to Christian Science Sunday school alternating with the exercises from a book Mother had on yoga postures. (I could sustain a full-lotus position at five.) Grandma bought Lecia and me each white leather Bibles that zipped shut. "If you read three chapters a day and five on Sunday, you can read the Holy Bible in one year," she said. I don't remember ever unzipping mine once after unwrapping it, for Grandma was prone to abandoning any project that came to seem too daunting, as making us into Christians must have seemed.

Much later, when Mother could be brought to talk about her

own childhood, she told stories about how peculiar her mother's habits had been. Grandma Moore didn't sound like such a religious fanatic back then. She just seemed like a fanatic in general. For instance, she had once sent away for a detective-training kit from a magazine. The plan was for her and Mother to spy on their neighbors—this, back when the Lubbock population still fit into three digits. According to Mother, this surveillance went on for weeks. Grandma would stirrup Mother up to the parson's curtained windows—and not because of any suspected adultery or flagrant sinning, but to find out whether his wife did her cakes from scratch or not. She kept the answers to these kinds of questions in an alphabetized log of prominent families. She would also zero in on some particular person who troubled her and keep track of all his comings and goings for weeks on end. She knew the procedure for taking fingerprints and kept Mother's on a recipe card, in case she was ever kidnapped. Grandma even began to collect little forensic envelopes of hair and dust that she found on people's furniture when she visited them. Mother said that for the better part of a year, they'd be taking tea at some lady's house, when her mother would suddenly sneak an envelope with something like a dustball in it into the pocket of her pinafore. Whatever became of this *evidence* Mother couldn't say. The whole detective-training deal got dropped as abruptly as it had been undertaken.

When Grandma came to our house, she brought with her that same kind of slightly deranged scrutiny. Before, our lives had been closed to outsiders. The noise of my parents' fights might leak out through the screens at night, and I might guess at the neighbors' scorn, but nobody really asked after our family, about Mother's being Nervous. We didn't go to church. No one came to visit. We probably seemed as blurry to the rest of the neighborhood as bad TV. Suddenly Grandma was staring at us with laser-blue eyes from behind her horn rims, saying *Can I make a suggestion?* or beginning every sentence with *Why don't you . . . ?*

Also, she was herself secretive. She bustled around as if she had some earnest agenda, but God knows what it was. She carried, for instance, an enormous black alligator doctor's bag, which held, along with the regular lady stuff in there—cosmetics and little peony-embroidered hankies—an honest-to-God hacksaw. It was the kind you see only in B movies, when criminals need it to saw through jail bars. Lest you think I fabricate, Lecia saw it, too. We even had a standing joke that we were keeping Grandma prisoner, and she was planning to bust out.

I had always thought that what I lacked in my family was some attentive, brownie-baking female to keep my hair curled and generally Donna-Reed over me. But my behavior got worse with Grandma's new order. I became a nail-biter. My tantrums escalated to the point where even Daddy didn't think they were funny anymore. I tore down the new drapes they'd hung across the dining room windows and clawed scratch marks down both of Lecia's cheeks. Beating me didn't seem to discourage me one whit. Though I was a world-famous crybaby, I refused to cry during spankings. I still can recall Daddy holding a small horse quirt, my calves striped with its imprint and stinging and my saying, "Go on and hit me then, if it makes you feel like a man to beat on a little girl like me." End of spanking.

Lecia was both better-tempered and better at kissing ass than I was, so she fared better. But the pressure must have gotten to her too. It was during Grandma's residency that my sister stuffed me struggling into the clothes hamper that pulled out from the bathroom wall, and left me screaming among the mildewed towels till Mae Brown came back from getting groceries. Also, she took to plastering down her bangs with so much hair spray that neither wind nor rain could move them. (I called her Helmethead.) And she lengthened all her skirts so her knees didn't show anymore. In pictures from then, she looks like a child trying to impersonate an adult and coming out some strange gargoyle neither adult nor child. Once she even had me climb up on her shoulders, then draped a brown corduroy painter's smock to hang from my shoulders to her knees. We staggered from house to house pretending we were some lady collecting for the American Cancer Society. I remember holding a coffee can out to various strangers as I listed side to side on her shoulders. We didn't clear a dime.

In fairness to Grandma, she was dying of cancer at fifty, which can't do much for your disposition. Still, I remember not one tender feeling for or from her. Her cheek was withered like a bad apple and smelled of hyacinth. I had to be physically forced to kiss this cheek, even though I was prone to throwing my arms around the neck of any vaguely friendly grown-up—vacuum-cleaner salesman, mechanic, checkout lady.

The worst part wasn't all the change she brought, but the silence that came with it. Nobody said anything about how we'd lived before. It felt as if the changes themselves had just swept over us like some great wave, flattening whatever we'd once been. I somehow knew that suggesting a dinner in the middle of the bed, or stripping down when I came in from playing, would have thrown such a pall of shame over the household that I couldn't even consider it. Clearly, we had, all this time, been doing everything all wrong.

CHAPTER 3

I had this succinct way of explaining the progression of my grandmother's cancer to neighbor ladies who asked: "First, they took off her toenail, then her toe, then her foot. Then they shot mustard gas through her leg till it was burnt black, and she screamed for six weeks nonstop. Then they took off her leg, and it was like a black stump laid up on a pillow. When we came to see her, she called Lecia by the wrong name. Then she came home, and it went to her brain, so she went crazy, and ants were crawling all over her arm. Then she died."

At the end of this report, Lecia and I would start scanning around whoever's kitchen it was for cookies or Kool-Aid. We knew with certain instinct that reporting on a dead grandma deserved some payoff. After a while, Lecia even learned to muster some tears, which could jack-up the ante as high as a Popsicle. (If I gave my big sister a paragraph here, she would correct my memory. To this day, she claims that she genuinely mourned for the old lady, who was a kindly soul, and that I was too little and mean-spirited then to remember things right. I contend that her happy memories are shaped more by convenience than reality: she also recalls tatting as fun, and Ronald Reagan, for whom she voted twice, as a good guy.) I couldn't have cried for Grandma under torture. But I knew my spiel and could nod earnestly to back up Lecia's snot-nosed snubbing. As in most public dealings with grown-ups, I blindly counted on people's pity to get me what I wanted.

For a long time Grandma's entire slow death from cancer stayed fenced inside that pat report. It's a clear case of language standing in for reality. Perhaps the neighbor ladies who heard me tell it back then were justly horrified by my lack of grief instead of being wowed—as I intended them to be—by how well I was bearing up. To them, I nod mea culpa for this lie. Believe me, I fooled no one worse than I fooled myself by blotting out the whole eighteen-month horror show.

Lecia kowtowed to the old lady because it kept the peace and bought her points with Mother. I just tried to slip around her, the reasons for which avoidance are vague. Whether she liked to wash me or to pull at my hair snarls with a fine-toothed comb, I could not for many decades figure. The central feeling that arises from memory of that time is a fear that starts low in my spine and creeps upward till it borders on low-level panic. Even now, part of me flinches at any mention of her. I would just as soon keep that wheelchair she occupied in my head empty of its ghost.

Maybe this aversion comes partly from a kid's normal intolerance for the infirm. Somebody dying sucks quite a bit of attention-voltage from grown-ups in a family, but believe me, for a kid it's like watching paint dry. Truly, I could not gin up much enthusiasm for it. Maybe some kids can; maybe there are Christian children reared with deep saintly streaks who read Scripture to their rotting grandparents in the early dusk. I did not. She lasted too long and made my mother cry too much.

Besides, we hadn't known her that well before she got sick. I had inherited her name, Mary. Except for our one trip to Lubbock, she had been little more than that name carefully executed in Venus pencil on a series of construction-paper cards. One of these was red and heart-shaped, pasted onto a lacy paper doily. It got saved in Daddy's gold cigar box, for some reason. The envelope has M. D. Anderson Hospital (which is now the Houston Medical

Center) for an address. The heart opens up to this odd message: "Dear Grandma, I hope you are getting better. There was a man in a car wreck who died three feet tall. Here is the man." Then there's a horizontal stick figure with X's for eyes next to a bubble-shaped car with what looks like a Band-Aid on it. I guess that was my studied approximation of death, at the time.

Still, no matter how bland a gaze you try to put on remembering an ugly illness, to protect yourself from the sheer tedium of it, if you spend any time at all speaking about it to some nodding psychiatrist, you will eventually stumble into a deep silence. And from that silence in your skull there will develop—almost chemically, like film paper doused in that magic solution—a snapshot of cold horror. So just when I'd started to believe that the terse chronology of Grandma's cancer that I'd prattled off all my life held all the truth, some windowshade in the experience flew up to show me what suffering really is. It's not the old man with arthritic fingers you glimpsed trying to open one of those little black, click-open purses for soda change at the Coke machine. It isn't even the toddler you once passed in a yard behind a chain-link fence, tethered to a clothesline like a dog in midday heat. Those are only rumors of suffering. Real suffering has a face and a smell. It lasts in its most intense form no matter what you drape over it. And it knows your name.

The doctors piped mustard gas through Grandma's leg to try to stop the spread of her melanoma, and the result was suffering of the caliber I mention. Today it's hard to imagine a treatment more medieval. When I grew up and read about the Great War, how clouds of mustard gas floated over trenches and seared the lungs of soldiers, I couldn't begin to fathom the doctors' reasoning in applying it to that old woman, whose fair-complected leg was charred by the treatment into something petrified-looking. But of course the leg was flesh and bone, from which the marrow cooked away. She did indeed, according to my mother, scream without break for weeks, not days, this despite morphine. Gangrene set in, and they had to amputate anyway.

The idea of Grandma losing her leg didn't bother me much at

first because it stayed in the realm of make-believe. Lecia and I fancied her having a wheelchair we could take for rides. We were big on Peter Pan at the time, so I tended to imagine her with a peg leg, like a pirate. Riding in the car to the hospital that first day, I even drew a picture of her with a wooden peg and a plumed hat with skull and crossbones à la Captain Hook. Lecia had the infinite good sense to fold this into quarters and rathole it in her back pocket before Mother got a glimpse of it.

But Mother was running on such psychic overdrive that it might not have even registered. As Nervous as she tended to be, she could always rally in times of crisis. Really, she was something to watch. I have seen her dismantle and reassemble a washing machine, stitch up a dress from a thirty-piece Vogue pattern in a day, ace a college calculus course after she'd gone back to school at forty, and lay brick. We used to say that if she really had her titty in a wringer, she could flat go to work wrestling it out. Grandma's sickness was such a time. All trace of Nervous just evaporated from my mother. Her chin tilted up to suggest a kind of determined ease. She slimmed down and moved only when absolutely necessary, yet she seemed never to rest. It's no wonder that she collapsed after the funeral, since she was running on fumes from the git-go.

There must have been rules back then about kids not being on cancer wards. But Mother had the idea that we would cheer Grandma up. Plus Daddy was working days, and she had run out of people to leave us with. I'd never been in a hospital before. And of course what you generally remember from that era is the smell of Pine Sol, that and all the impressive running around, people being wheeled in and out of places with tubes and bottles swaying over them.

The hospital gets vivid at the instant when Lecia pulled my elbow to turn me away from a guy horking up what looked like clean water into a little kidney-shaped silver pan. I turned from the sick man and entered the invisible cloud of odors that floated around Mother at that time: Shalimar and tobacco and peppermint Life Savers. For some reason, I recall it drifting just above my head, which moved at the level of her hipbone, so I could crane my head up and breathe deeply and draw some of her down into my lungs. She wore a long army-green silk dress and a brown alligator belt from Chanel. She had a long stride and led with her thigh like a fashion model. Her high heels hardly made any noise the way she set her foot down in them. Her head seemed far away from me. Her hair was short and thick and brushed straight back from her face and looked from my height like a lion's mane.

She pushed open some double doors. You could hear somebody crying *please please please* but in a whispery voice. We passed the room of a surprisingly young woman whose black hair was woven into a big tower. She lay back on a La-Z-Boy recliner, holding a red rubber enema bottle pressed against her jaw, and you could hear organ music from a radio ball game as you walked by. Then we were at Grandma's room, easing a big silent door open.

The really shocking thing about an amputation is how crude it looks. Really, you would think that they could tidy it up, and maybe by now they have. Anybody who has ever had to dismantle a deer with a hunting knife or even fried up a chicken or a rabbit knows how brutal it feels to hack through bone and cartilage. I guess in the operating room at that time they used a small circular saw, but it all amounts to the same thing. Somehow I had expected Grandma's lopped-off leg to seem more like a doll's, bloodless and neat. Maybe I expected a bandage on it.

They had taken the leg off above the knee, and Grandma's remaining thigh was propped on a hospital pillow. It looked very interrupted. There were still streaks of black running from the stump end up her thigh in what looked like narrowing rivers. Whether these were from the gas burns or the subsequent blood poisoning, I don't know. You could see how they'd tried to save enough flesh from the thigh to fold it over the cut bone. Somebody had tried to stitch it all down neatly so it might look as if it had grown that way. But you could tell from the stitching that the edges were randomly folded over in the ragged way you might try to close up a pork roast you were stuffing. The stitches were flat black and pinched at her very white skin. Plus they had slathered some kind of ointment all over the thigh, so the whole thing looked painfully shiny and wet. Even with the five bunches of flowers her sisters had sent, the room reeked of something like a black stinging horse liniment I had smelled on a ranch once. That was the burn medicine, I suppose.

I wanted to leave right away, just looking at that leg. But the door had hissed shut behind us, and Grandma's face was rolling our way already. (Here time telescopes and gets slow, for some reason. I almost have to hold my head very still to keep from backing away.) She was so thin and pale you could practically see straight through her. Her lips were bluish and her hair had gotten whiter, so that her eyes, when the lids flickered open, seemed paler, as if she'd seen something that scalded her inside. Lecia walked right over to the edge of the bed like it was no big deal. Grandma opened and closed her mouth a few times like a fish, not saying anything. They had taken out her dentures, which sat on a napkin on top of her bed table. There were also those little white strings of spit running between her lips, and she had some yellow crust in the corners. Mother said that somebody really might have washed her up and put her teeth in, but she didn't seem alarmed really. That put me off, because I could usually count on Mother to be at least as big a sissy as I was, and I was ready to bolt. Grandma's hand kind of patted the mattress by her, and Lecia grabbed it right off. That made Grandma suck in her breath real suddenly, so Lecia dropped the hand and took a step back. Then Mother stepped in and smoothed her white hair back gently and asked how she felt. Grandma just started patting the bed toward Lecia again. She fixed that empty stare on Lecia as if she had just descended to the bedside from the clouds. She sucked in her breath hard again and said, "Belinda! Where have you been? Thank God, Belinda." Then her voice got quiet again, and she went on and on about how she'd missed her and looked for her, and Lecia just played along like she was this person we'd never heard of.

But for some reason this Belinda stuff put a cold corkscrew through the center of where I stood. It was even worse than seeing that stump all Frankensteined-up with black stitches and black streaks running up her crepey white thigh.

Before we left, Mother threw a screaming cuss fit at the two doctors who'd done the mustard gas treatment. It was never fun when Mother raised hell in public, but in this instance, I almost welcomed it. After being shut down all day, zombielike, she seemed to descend back into her body. (Maybe, like the Greeks used to say, her *ate* suddenly filled her.) The doctors just stood with their coffee mugs, as if it didn't occur to them to walk away. I remember some hospital administrator, an enormous woman in a flowered dress that made her look a lot like a sofa, rushing out from behind her glass window to run interference for them. Mother was screaming that doctors were vultures feeding off people's pain, and at that point the woman put her hand on Mother's arm and offered to say a rosary for Grandma, to which Mother said, "Don't you go Hail-Marying over my mother!"

Then we were rushing away from the doctors and the sofa-lady, and the long hall that would have led us back to Grandma was getting longer and smaller behind us. The hospital doors hissed open, and the wet heat swamped over us. Mother needed a dish towel to hold the steering wheel.

She didn't cry that day, though we tried to make enough quiet in the car to permit crying. Oh, at first I had climbed in the backseat babbling about wanting a towel to sit on and being thirsty, but Lecia had a way of grabbing ahold of me with a look that shut down any of my whining in a heartbeat's time. It was a serious look coming off of her child's face. I still think of the expression as senatorial. Her brown eyes sloped down at the corners, and the bangs above them were hair-sprayed into a row of shiny blond spikes. She could always nail me with that look, make me stop mid-sentence.

For some reason, we went to the Houston Zoo, which trip Mother must have bribed us with in advance. No sane person would have chosen to spend the afternoon outdoors in that heat. There was a miniature train running through it for free back then, and we climbed on. But it was crammed with the kind of spilling, chewing, farting farm kids who made Mother nuts, so we got off at the gift shop.

She bought us Peter Pan hats with our names stitched on the sides in a loopy longhand. Then I played with the jeweler's little Ferris wheel. You could push a button to stop it turning when you liked something, and I kept stopping it at a gold bracelet dangling with animal charms. She bought one for all three of us without my even asking. I remember that when the jeweler latched hers, he used his index finger to stroke the inside of her wrist in a way that brought the fear sharply back to my solar plexus. Even this didn't make her say anything, though she was hell on any man touching her, and had once hit my uncle A.D. upside the head with her purse for pinching her butt.

Later, we ate burgers on round concrete picnic tables, which were oddly placed to get the full stink of the nearby monkey pits. Lecia mentioned what boneheads the doctors were as a way of taking Mother's side against the hospital. But Mother just cocked her head as if she had no idea what Lecia meant. She drank black coffee and stared into the middle distance. She had long since passed the mark where she might normally have started railing against the medical profession or claiming that our miserable swamp climate was unfit for anything but snakes and cockroaches. Toward the end of the meal, I couldn't sit in her silence anymore. It just weighed too much. I left the table to watch the monkeys. They were hurling what looked like their turds at each other. One little spider monkey broke away from the rest and stood at the edge of the pit with his bright red penis in his hand, screaming and jacking off furiously. Even that, Mother didn't seem to notice.

The big cat cages also stank in the heat. This was before zoos built natural habitats with boulders and waterfalls, and the cages back then were painfully small, the animals miserable. The Bengal tiger had flies creeping all over its eyelids, and he didn't even blink. There was a kid throwing peanuts at him, and Lecia somehow menaced the boy into stopping.

When I grew up and discovered the German poet Rilke, it was this zoo's sorry-looking cats that I thought back to. As a young poet, Rilke had been sent by the sculptor Rodin to study zoo animals, and he captured in a few lines the same frustrated power that I sensed that day in the dull-coated panther:

It seems there are
a thousand bars; and behind the bars, no world.

As he paces in cramped circles, over and over
the movement of his powerful soft strides
is like a ritual dance around a center
in which a mighty will stands paralyzed.

Looking back from this distance, I can also see Mother trapped in some way, stranded in her own silence. How small she seems in her silk dress, drinking stale coffee. I can see the panther pace back and forth behind the bars on the surface of her sunglasses, as if he were inside her peering out at us. Sometimes seeing her that way in memory, I want to offer her a glass of water, or suggest that she lie down in the shade of the willow behind her. Other times, I want to pull the glasses from her face, put my large capable hands on her square shoulders, and shake her till she begins to weep or scream or do whatever would break her loose from that island of quiet.

To get out of the heat, we went into a cavelike building, very cool and damp. At that time, I was fascinated with Dracula's silky evil and headed straight for the vampire bats, which were disappointingly tiny through the thick glass. They were hardly bigger than field mice and hanging upside-down from a stick. Their teeth were tiny, not at all like Bela Lugosi's on TV. One finally dropped down and wobbled near a petri dish of blood in the center of the display. He seemed so awkward trying to arrange his frail-looking wings that I kept thinking of a broken umbrella. Lecia moved from window to window, looking at owls and opossums and the other nocturnals—she wanted to be a vet back then, or a nurse. Mother sat on a stone bench under the red EXIT sign, smoking.

I got hypnotized waiting for the clumsy bat to drink the blood. I tapped the glass pointing it out, but he never did.

By dusk we were on the spaghetti freeways looking for Highway 73 home, and I kept cutting my eyes between my window, where the new glass skyscrapers going up just slid past, and the small rearview mirror, where Mother's eyes were still eerily blank. Nothing showed in those eyes but the road's white dashed lines, which seemed to be flying off the road and into the darkest part of her pupils, where they disappeared like knives.

After the amputation and that trip to Houston, we didn't see Mother much. She either came home from the hospital briefly in the mornings to change clothes before heading back, or she returned after we were in bed. I would wake to her weight tilting our mattress, her Shalimar settling over me when she leaned in to kiss me and pull up the chenille bedspread, which had a nubble like braille under my hands. A few times, she would sit on my side of the bed all night smoking, till the yellow light started in the windows. She had a way of waving away the smoke from my face and making a pleasant little wind in the process. I kept my eyes closed, knowing that if I roused she'd leave, and I wanted nothing more from her on those nights than to let me lie in the mist of that perfume I still wear and to imagine the shapes her Salem smoke made. Inside the great deep pit that I had already begun digging in my skull, I had buried the scariness of Grandma's hacked-off leg and Mother's psychic paralysis at the zoo. So I did not long to talk of those things or to hear her reassurances about them. (Children can be a lot like cats or dogs, sometimes, in how physical comfort soothes them.) I could feel through the bedspread the faint heat of her body as she sat a few inches from where I lay, and that heat was all I needed.

Except for these apparitions of Mother, we were left the rest of the summer in Daddy's steady if distracted care. At some point, the men of the Liars' Club arrived with their pickups and toolboxes to turn our garage into an extra bedroom for my parents, who had been sleeping on a pull-out sofa in the living room during Grandma's visit. I guess they wanted to make her a nicer place in which to die. That didn't register in me at the time. I had neatly blocked all glimmer of her very existence—alive or dead, sick or well—from my waking thoughts. Each morning, about the time that Lecia and I reached the bottom of our soggy Cheerios, somebody's work boots would stamp up the porch steps, and the screen would bang open, and Daddy would start getting down clean coffee mugs.

The men arrived early and worked steadily through the hottest part of every day. They had all taken their vacations then in order to help out. They worked for nothing but free coffee and beer. By mid-morning they had stripped off their shirts. They had broad backs and ropy arms. They suffered the fiercest sunburns that summer I ever remember seeing. Ben Bederman had a round hairless beer belly that pooched over his carpenter apron, and his back burned and peeled off in sheets, then burned again until it finally darkened to the color of cane syrup. The men pulled Lone Star beers all afternoon from the ice in two red Coleman coolers that Daddy packed to the brim every morning.

A few times a day, somebody's wife would show up with food. Say what you like about the misery of hard labor—I once had a summer job painting college dorms that I thought would kill me—but it can jack up your appetite to the point where eating takes on a kind of holiness. Whether there were white bags of barbecued crabs from Sabine Pass or tamales in corn husks from a roadside stand, the men would set down their tools and grin at the sheer good fortune of it. They always took time to admire the food before they started to eat—a form of modesty, I guess, or appreciation, as if wanting to be sure the meal wouldn't vanish like some mirage. Daddy would stop to soak his red bandana in a cooler's slush and study whatever was steaming out of the torn-open sack while he mopped himself off. "Lord God, look at that," he'd say, and he'd wink at whoever had brought it.

Ben's wife, Ruby, pulled in once with a washtub of sandy unshucked oysters that it took two of the men to heave out of the truck bed. She spent the better part of a morning opening them with a stubby knife. When she was done, there were two huge pickle jars of cleaned oysters sitting in the washtub's cold water. We ate them with hot sauce and black pepper and lemon. (Lecia says that I would eat them only in pairs, so none would feel lonely in my stomach.) The oysters had a way of seeming to wince when you squeezed the lemon on them. They started off cold in your mouth, but warmed right up and went down fast and left you that musty aftertaste of the sea. You washed that back with a sip of cold beer you'd salted a little. (Even at seven I had a taste for liquor.) And you followed that with a soda cracker.

Before that summer, I had many times heard long-winded Baptist preachers take ten minutes to pray over card tables of potato salad and fried chicken at church picnics, but the way those sweating, red-faced men sat around on stacked pallets of lumber gulping oysters taught me most of what I know about simple gladness. They were glad to get fed for their labor, glad they had the force to pound nails and draw breath. Of course, they bitched loudly about their aches and mocked each other's bitching. But unless I've completely idealized that fellowship, there was something redeeming that moved between those men. Even the roofing part of the job, which involved a vat of boiling tar and whole days on top of the new garage beyond the cool shade of our chinaberry, didn't wipe it out. At evening, they would pull off their work boots, then peel off their double layers of cotton socks and lay them to dry across the warm bricks. Daddy had a habit of tipping the beer coolers out right where they stood in the grass, so cool water rushed over their sweaty feet. At that time of day, with night coming in fast, and the men taking a minute to pass a pint of Tennessee whiskey between them or to light their smokes, there was a glamour between them that I sensed somehow was about to disappear. When they climbed into the cabs of their trucks, I sometimes had a terrible urge to rush after them and call them back.

With Mother, I always felt on the edge of something new, something never before seen or read about or bought, something that would change us. When you climbed in the car with her, you never knew where you'd end up. If an encyclopedia salesman happened to knock on the door, she might spend a month's salary on books you would pore over all day. With Daddy and his friends, I always knew what would happen and that left me feeling a sort of dreamy safety.

By August they were done, and my folks had a paneled bedroom with a separate tiled shower. And out in back of the house, there stood a detached garage big enough for two cars. It also held a separate work studio for Mother, my father's one nod to her desire to paint. The studio had a high ceiling and skylights, which were unheard-of in those days, and a black stove where she could build a fire on a rainy night. She wasted no time setting up her easel and starting to work in oils. The first thing she did was a portrait of Grandma wearing a plain blue dress. She worked from a Polaroid taken just before Grandma lost the leg.

Mother must have worked on it late at night after she came in from the hospital. God knows she had no other time. She'd even sacrificed her job at the paper to nurse Grandma. But the amber-colored sketch that first appeared on the white canvas turned into a facsimile of my grandmother inside of a week. I snuck the studio key off the nail in the kitchen to check its progress every few days. Truly, when I pulled the padlock off and the studio door swung open, I felt like a thief in church. I was entering a realm that had before only filled the bedtime stories, about artists of which Mother was fond: Van Gogh's lopped-off ear; Gauguin's native girls; the humpbacked Degas mad for love of his dancers; how Pollock once paid a fortune for a Picasso drawing, then erased it in order to see how it was made. The combination of turpentine fumes and damp wood smoke and the distant sting of vodka in the studio was unlike any other batch of smells before or since. The whole idea of erecting a person—from tinted oil and from whatever swirled inside my mother's skull—filled me with a slack-jawed wonder.

The portrait of Grandma wound up stiffer, more formal than her other work, which was wildly expressionistic. The arms bend at right angles. The shoulders square like a military man's, and the face is totally devoid of feeling. Maybe it was that blankness that I was trying to fix when I squirted orange paint onto a sable brush and dabbed at the mouth. Ultimately, though, I left an orange smudge in the middle of the painting's face. Maybe I was trying to blot her out somehow, or shut her up. If you'd asked me, I would have said I was trying to brighten her lipstick.

Mother wept when she saw it, wept and cursed the ignorant vandals who must have broken in. She never even asked whether one of us had done it. She got drunk wearing a Mexican serape and built a fire and cursed the Motherfucking Swamp and its occupants. *They do not,* she told us with terse judgment, *even deserve to call themselves members of the cordate phylum,* which Lecia had to explain meant that they didn't have spinal columns, and were, ergo, like worms, slugs, and leeches. The next morning, Mother drove to the hardware store and bought a heavy lock you couldn't get through with any bolt cutter. The new key stayed on the same kitchen nail, but after that, I was afraid of wrecking something else and so stayed out of the studio unescorted.

When Grandma came back to our house she had ossified into something elemental and really scary. She seemed way thinner than she had been in the hospital, though perhaps not as pale. She had been fitted with an artificial leg that she strapped on every morning. It wore a sturdy black shoe that never came off. At night, she detached the leg and stood it by her bed. Once, when I passed her door on my way to the toilet, I caught sight of it standing there with no person tacked on top of it, and it was casting a long shadow into the hall that nearly reached my bare feet, so I scrambled back under the quilt with Lecia, my heart thumping, not caring whether I wet the bed that night (I did). The honeysuckle that grew up our screens made spiky wall-shadows on nights like that. Sometimes I'd hear Grandma hop down the short hall into the bathroom, her cane whacking the door molding. Lecia says that I misremember one specific sight of her standing in our doorway with that stump bluntly hanging down under her nightie, her arms spread so she could hold herself up by the doorjamb, and her hair fanned out around her face like white fire. I can see it like yesterday's breakfast, but Lecia claims it never happened.

Grandma wore very pale pink nylon pajamas with a matching robe, and her wheelchair was spookily silent in the way somebody walking never was. With Daddy's 3-In-One oil and the same maniacal patience she had brought to tatting, she kept it tuned silent on purpose. She'd upend the chair by her bed and squirt oil in all the tiny hollow places so it was nothing but glide. Then she could materialize soundlessly around a corner. She had a habit of sneaking up on Lecia and me and shouting *Aha!* as if she'd discovered us shooting up heroin with a turkey baster or eviscerating some small animal. Once she found us playing gin rummy and let out her *Aha!*, then called Mother. Grandma even watched us the whole time she was yelling as if we were going to cover up the cards before Mother got there. "Charlie Marie! Come in here and whip these children. I swear to God . . ." Mother, who never excelled as a spanker, arrived and asked some bewildered questions. Grandma gave an evangelistic-sounding lecture on the evils of gambling (and liquor, oddly enough), this despite the fact that she'd been an avid cheater at church bingo (and was, since her surgery, consuming about a case of beer every day). After a while, Mother just gave in to Grandma's rantings and went through the motions of flailing at our legs with a flyswatter till we ran into our room and slammed the door. I remember crawling up in Lecia's lap and whining about how I hadn't done anything. Lecia reasoned that we'd probably gotten away with fifty things we should have been spanked for that day, anyway, so we should just call it even.

It was sometime in August that I started walking in my sleep. Actually I did things other than just walk: I'd go squat behind the living room drapes and go to the bathroom in a pile they sometimes didn't find till the next morning. Once I wandered outside, and Daddy had to come chasing after me.

That fall my school career didn't go much better. I got suspended from my second-grade class twice, first for biting a kid named Phyllis who wasn't, to my mind, getting her scissors out fast enough to comply with the teacher, then again for breaking my plastic ruler over the head of a boy named Sammy Joe Tyler, whom I adored. A pale blue knot rose through the blond stubble of his crew cut. Both times I got sent to the principal, a handsome ex–football coach named Frank Doleman who let Lecia and me call him Uncle Frank. (Lecia and I had impressed Uncle Frank by both learning to read pretty much without instruction before we were three. Mother took us each down to his office in turn, and we each dutifully read the front page of the day's paper out loud to him, so he could be sure it wasn't just some story we'd memorized.)

He let me stay in his office playing chess all afternoon with whoever wandered in. He loved pitting me against particularly lunkheaded fifth- and sixth-grade boys who'd been sent down for paddlings they never got. He'd try to use my whipping them at chess to make them nervous about how dumb they were. "Now this little bitty old second-grader here took you clean in six plays. Don't you reckon you need to be listening to Miss Vilimez instead of cutting up?" When Mrs. Hess led me solemnly down the hall to Frank Doleman's office, I would pretend to cry, but thought instead about Brer Rabbit as he was being thrown into the briar patch where he'd been born and raised, and screaming *Please don't throw me in that briar patch!* At the end of both days, Uncle Frank drove me home himself in his white convertible, the waves of kids parting as we passed and me flapping my hand at all of them like I was Jackie Kennedy.

It was also at this time that I came to be cut out of the herd of neighborhood kids by an older boy. Before that happened there was almost something sacred about that pack of kids we got folded into. No matter how strange our family was thought to be, we blended into the tribe when we all played together. For some reasons, I always remember us running barefoot down the football field together, banking and turning in a single unit like those public-TV airplane shots of zebras in Africa.

But obviously I had some kind of fear or hurt on me that an

evil boy could smell. He knew I could be drawn aside and scared or hurt a little extra. When he came for me, I went with him, and my going afterwards felt as if it had been long before plotted out by something large and invisible—God, I guess.

But before that boy singled me out, the sheer velocity of running across a wet field with other kids felt safe. There were dozens of us. We ranged in age from thirteen or fourteen for the big boys down to Babby Carter, who at two trailed behind the herd everywhere. I was seven and fit into the group about dead center, age-wise. I was small-boned and skinny, but more than able to make up for that with sheer meanness. Lecia still holds that I would have jumped a buzz saw. Daddy had instructed me in the virtue of what he called equalizers, which meant not only sticks, boards, and rocks, but having one hell of a long memory for mistreatment. So I wouldn't hesitate to sneak up blindside and bite a bigger kid who'd gotten the better of me a week before. To my knowledge, I never slouched off an ass-kicking, even the ones that made me double up and cry. It might take me a week or so, but I always came back. (To this day, I don't know whether to measure this as courage or cowardice, but it stuck. After I grew up, the only man ever to punch me found himself awakened two nights later from a dead sleep by a solid right to the jaw, after which I informed him that, should he ever wish to sleep again, he shouldn't hit me. My sister grew up with an almost insane physical bravery: once in the parking lot outside her insurance office, she brushed aside the .22 pistol of a gunman demanding her jewelry. "Fuck you," she said and opened her Mercedes while the guy ran off. The police investigator made a point of asking her what her husband did, and when she said she didn't have one, the cop said, "I bet I know why.")

In some ways, all the kids in my neighborhood were identical. Our fathers belonged to the same union. ("Oil Chemical and Atomic Workers, Local 1242" was how they answered the phone on Daddy's unit.) They punched the same clocks for almost exactly the same wage. (Our family had been considered rich because of Mother's part-time newspaper work.) Maybe one kid's daddy worked Gulf and another Texaco and another Atlantic Richfield, but it amounted to the same thing. Maybe one was a boilermaker and another controlled the flow of catalyst in a cracking unit. But they all worked turning crude oil into the various by-products you had to memorize by weight in seventh-grade science class—kerosene, gasoline, and so on. The men all worked shift work because that paid a little better, so all of us knew how to tiptoe on days when the old man was on graveyards. The union handed out cardboard signs that ladies tacked to their doors: SHHH! SHIFT WORKERS ASLEEP. Nobody but Mother had ever been to college. (She'd attended both Texas Tech and art school.)

When the football field was cut on weekends, we'd gather hay from behind the tractor and lay it out in lines that followed the same square floor plans our fathers had unrolled on blueprints when their GI loans were approved—two bedrooms, one bath, attached garage, every one. The cut brown clover and St. Augustine grass smelled wetter and greener than any field cuttings I ever encountered in my adult elsewheres.

It's that odor that carries me to a particular cool day when I lay down within the careful lines of my own grass house. I was sure that I could feel the curve of the earth under my spine. I watched the clouds scud behind the water tower. Then I rolled over on my stomach. There were wild pepper plants that had hot little seeds you could pop between your teeth. Clover squeaked when you pulled it out of the ground, and its root was white and pulpy sweet.

Once I got stung by a bee, and this older boy I mentioned doctored me with a plaster of spit and mud till I stopped my snubbing. So I believed he liked me, and I was thirsty for liking.

On the hot days, when running was forbidden—heatstroke was always bringing little kids down—we played a game some kid invented called Torture. This sounds worse than it was. A bigger kid would herd us into the skin-tightening heat of the most miserably close spot we could find—the spidery crawl space under the Carters' back porch, say, or Tommy Sharp's old pigeon cage, or some leftover refrigerator box waiting for the garbage truck.

There we'd squat into the hunched and beaten forms we thought made us look like concentration-camp inmates. This evil boy had a picture of Buchenwald survivors in his history book. All of us collectively studied it, memorized it. We did so not out of any tender feeling for the victims' pain or to ponder injustice, but so we could impersonate them playing Torture. We lined up shoulder to shoulder and thigh to thigh under the cold dull eye of this big boy's Nazi. He didn't twist arms or squish heads or inflict wounds. He was too smart for that. He just reigned over us while our parents called us home for lunch. We hunkered down without moving. I imagine all those bodies when crammed into a tight space generated temperatures well over a hundred and twenty degrees. Blinking or whimpering wasn't permitted. We melted into a single compliant shape. It was almost a form of meditation. The world slowed down, and your sense of your own body got almost unbearably distinct. Sweat rivered down my rib cage. I could feel every particle of grit in the fold of my neck. The Nazi boy would menace us not with overt cruelty but with an empty professional stare. There was no need to switch-whip us; we didn't dare move anyway. That was the whole game. We sat there together, radiant with misery. Eventually, of course, some adult arm would poke into where we were hiding and signal the arrival of somebody's mom come to pull us out and drag us home for lunch or supper.

And it was one of these times—an evening, oddly enough—when the arm felt around and didn't find me huddled in the corner, that all the other kids poured out and scattered to their separate homes for supper, so this big boy and I were left alone.

It was going dark when he got hold of me under God knows what pretext. He took me into somebody's garage. He unbuttoned my white shirt and told me I was getting breasts. Here's what he said: "You're getting pretty little titties now, aren't you." I don't recall any other thing being said. His grandparents had chipped in on braces for his snaggly teeth. They glinted in the half dark like a robot's grillwork. He pulled off my shorts and underwear and threw them in the corner in a ball, over where I knew there could be spiders. He pushed down his pants and put my hand on his thing, which was unlike any of the boys' jokes about hot dogs and garden hoses. It was hard as wood and felt big around as my arm. He wrapped both my hands around it, and showed me how to slide them up and down, and it felt like a wet bone encased in something. At some point, he tired of that. He got an empty concrete sack and laid it down on the floor, and me down on top of that, and pumped between my legs till he got where he was headed. I remember I kept my arms folded across my chest, because the thing he'd said about my breasts seemed such an obvious lie. It made me feel ashamed. I was seven and a good ten years from anything like breasts. My school record says I weighed about fifty pounds. Think of two good-sized Smithfield hams—that's roughly how big I was. Then think of a newly erect teenaged boy on top of that and pumping between my legs. It couldn't have taken very long.

(I picture him now reading this, and long to reach out of the page and grab ahold of his shirt front that we might together reminisce some. Hey, bucko. Probably you don't read, but you must have somebody who reads for you—your pretty wife or some old neighbor boy you still go fishing with. Where will you be when the news of this paragraph floats back to you? For some reason, I picture you changing your wife's tire. She'll mention that in some book I wrote, somebody from the neighborhood is accused of diddling me at seven. Maybe your head will click back a notch as this registers. Maybe you'll see your face's image spread across the silver hubcap as though it's been flattened by a ball-peen hammer. Probably you thought I forgot what you did, or you figured it was no big deal. I say this now across decades and thousands of miles solely to remind you of the long memory my daddy always said I had.)

When he was done with me it was full dark. I unballed my clothes and tried to brush off any insects. He helped me to pull them on and tied my Keds for me. He washed me off at the faucet that came out of the side of somebody's house. The water was warm from being in the pipe on a hot day, and my legs were still sticky after.

Our porch light was amber. The rest of the houses were dark. You could see the spotlights from the Little League park and hear the loudspeaker announcing somebody at bat. I wondered if this boy had planned to get ahold of me way in advance, if he'd picked the time when everybody would be at the game. Which was worse—if he'd only grabbed me at the opportune moment, or if he'd plotted and stalked me? I couldn't decide. I didn't want to be taken too easily, but I had been, of course. Even at seven I knew that. On the other hand, the idea that he'd consciously chosen to do this, then tracked me down like a rabbit, made me feel sick. He walked me home not saying anything, like he was doing a baby-sitting chore.

Then I was standing on my porch by myself. I could hear his tennis shoes slapping away down the street. I watched the square of his white T-shirt get smaller till it disappeared around the corner.

The honeysuckle was sickly sweet that night. I stood outside for a long time. I tried to arrange my face into nothing special having happened. There was a gray wasp nest in the corner of our porch. It had chambers like a honeycomb, each with the little worm of a baby wasp inside, sleeping. I thought sleeping that way would be good. After a while, Daddy pulled open the door and shoved the screen wide and asked me had I been at the game. "Come in, Pokey. Lemme fix you a plate," he said. I still fit under his armpit walking in. You could hear a roar from the park as somebody turned a double play or got a hit. I thought of the boy climbing the bleachers toward his admirers. I thought of all the jokes I'd heard about blow jobs and how a girl's vagina smelled like popcorn.

I looked at my father, who would have climbed straight up those bleachers and gutted this boy like a fish, and at my mother, who for some reason I imagined bursting into tears and locking herself in the bathroom over the whole thing. Grandma in her wheelchair would have said she wasn't surprised at all. Lecia was at the game, probably at the top of the bleachers combing down her bangs with a rattail comb and laughing when this boy came climbing toward her. He didn't even have to threaten me to keep quiet. I knew what I would be if I told.

CHAPTER 4

By mid-fall, the cancer had spread to Grandma's brain. This would have sent most people to bed, according to an oncologist pal of mine. But Grandma just bore down on us harder. If anything, whatever pain she was in or ideas she had about dying seemed to jack up her resolve.

She didn't take morphine or any other pain drugs. Instead, she drank beer nonstop but never seemed to get drunk. She stopped wearing her prosthetic leg, claiming it hurt her, so her stump poked out of her nightie at about eye level to a kid. That gave the impression—when she wheeled toward you—of some finger pointing you down. And it was around this time that her eyes seemed to get more bleached out behind her horn rims. Maybe she had cataracts, or maybe I just imagined the whole thing. But the blue part was lightening up daily, and sharp white spikes stabbed out from the black pupil into the iris. This was the time when you could order X-Ray Specs from the back of Superman comics, and when lasers were just starting to make the Walter Cronkite reports. In some weird conjunction of these two phenomena, I started believing that Grandma watched me through the wall when I slept. Sometimes I'd start up from a dead sleep thinking that two hot beams of white light were coming out of her eyes in the next room, fixed on me, trying to bore right through the wall between us. Nights, I wouldn't look out the door when she clunked around trying to get to the bathroom. I was scared that I'd see something like little headlights beaming her path down the dark hall. Actually, I wasn't so scared of seeing this as I was of her seeing me see it, which knowledge might make her angle those beams on me and melt me like wax.

Basically, I tried not to notice her at night at all. When I was about five, I had cooked up a technique that kept me from throwing up when I rode the Tilt-A-Whirl at the county fair. If I tightened my stomach muscles and squinched my eyes shut and grabbed the chrome front bar as hard as I could, then the ride's sick bucking around didn't reach me somehow. Oh, my hair still twisted every which way, and I could feel the lights move across my face, but it was like I could sink back into myself, away from all the diesel engine's heaving, and not wind up horking my corn dog all over Lecia's penny loafers. I got famous in our neighborhood for being the littlest kid to ride the scary rides. Anyway, that's what I tried to do in bed when I heard Grandma thumping around, just hunker down and harden up till everything I was fit into a small stone I held in place behind my stomach muscles.

Mother was her own kind of rock. She seemed distracted all the time, moving in some addled way through the rising sea of chores Grandma thought up. The only time she displayed much more than a low-level pulse was when Grandma talked her into spanking me about once a week, and then only if I really fought back.

Don't get me wrong. My mother's flailings at me didn't bring enough physical hurt or fear to qualify as child abuse. Her spankings were more pathetic than anything. She was way too scared of hurting anybody to hit with much of a sting. She must have been scared, too, of her own temper, or of feeling anything at all, because, as I said, she stayed pretty blank-eyed no matter what we did unless Grandma hollered her into action. At one point, Lecia and I emptied a box of Tide on the kitchen floor, then dragged in the garden hose till the whole house, carpet and all, was running with suds about a foot high. (We were imitating a floor wax commercial.) Grandma happened to be asleep during this, and Mother just sent us outside to play, then set about mopping the whole mess up without so much as a cuss word.

But some kind of serious fury must have been roiling around inside her. Sometimes, instead of spanking us, she would stand in the kitchen with her fists all white-knuckled and scream up at the light fixture that she wasn't whipping us, because she knew if she got started she'd kill us. This worked way better than any spanking could have. Your mother's threat of homicide—however unlikely she tries to make it sound—will flat dampen down your spirits.

Anyway, her whippings, when they did come, were almost a relief given the spooky alternative of her silence. And they didn't last very long if you stood still, as Lecia had the sense to do. Me, I never stopped trying to break loose for a second, which protracted the whole thing. (My spankings were a kind of family sporting event complete with rounds and what my sister still claims was a system of scoring more subtle and intricate than the mating signals of certain spiders.) Unless Mother managed to get me down in a corner, she would have to hold one of my wrists to keep me within flyswatter distance while she flailed in my direction. At best, she made contact about ten percent of the time. I dug my heels into the gray carpet and used my weight as you would in crack the whip. I became the pivot point in the spankings, a jerking, central force that she had to wheel around.

Locked together this way, the two of us would spin from room to room with Grandma at our perimeter in her wheelchair, scolding and bitching and calling down the wrath of God on that spoiled ungrateful child, all the time seesawing the big wheels of her chair to keep herself in position.

I hold a distinct image of Lecia's face, the distant sister as referee. She is standing in the doorway, grinning and shaking her head about how hard I am making things. (Being spanked is never near as bad as being laughed at during the spanking. Trust me. The presence of another kid ups the humiliation quotient exponentially.) Mother's arm makes a shadow on the wall rising and falling with the flyswatter, and with every turn I make, Lecia's smile slides off of me as if she's saying, *You don't have the sense to pour piss from a boot*—then I wheel around the room one more time before coming back to that weary grin of hers—*with the instructions on the heel.*

I almost felt a weird power over Mother during such a time. She had ahold of me, at least. And her grip felt like she would hang on no matter what I yanked her through.

By this time it was hurricane season. And just the way the weatherman on TV explained how hot and cold air fronts could smack up against each other over open water and make a wild-assed storm that turned around a still center of blue sky miles wide, so I felt almost calm during these whippings, as if all the misery in our house whirled around me somehow. Getting spanked at least brought some motion and force to the surface of the household. You could see us spinning around the room crazy instead of just walking through the day quiet and fretting about how miserable everybody felt and wondering where the ghost of that misery would pop up, and in what form.

In school when I stumbled on the famous Yeats poem about things falling apart, it was the spin of those spankings I thought back to, where the falcon breaks loose from its tether and from the guy who's supposed to be holding it:

> *Turning and turning in the widening gyre*
> *The falcon cannot hear the falconer;*
> *Things fall apart; the centre cannot hold;*
> *Mere anarchy is loosed upon the world,*
> *The blood-dimmed tide is loosed, and everywhere*
> *The ceremony of innocence is drowned;*
> *The best lack all conviction, while the worst*
> *Are full of passionate intensity.*

I always loved that last part, about the best lacking all conviction, which phrase made me think of Mother. And the worst being full of passionate intensity always put me in mind of Grandma, who was nothing if not intense.

Of course, at that time, Mother was still hanging on to the shreds of what she thought right, a grip she would lose entirely after Grandma died.

One morning, while Mother was plaiting my hair, the old woman got all pumped up about some project she had read about once in a magazine. She only took about two bites from a bowl of buttered grits before she hauled herself off to Kitty's Hobby Shop. She didn't even strap on her leg or bother with the wheelchair. Mother set her in the car seat, and she just drove off to town, then sat behind the steering wheel till Kitty came out to the parking lot and said could she help. We also heard later that she stopped by the hardware store for a three-foot length of industrial rubber tubing. Grandma came home with this stuff in paper bags and locked the door to her room for the better part of the day. When she finally rolled into the living room at dusk, she was waving a tasseled horse quirt over her head like Annie Oakley. She had braided long leather strips in brown and beige and tan around the rubber tubing, which instrument she wanted Mother to use for whipping us.

It was the only time I ever saw Mother defy her head-on, and Grandma was batshit about it: "These children are being ruined! You think you have trouble now, you just wait." Mother started crying but shook her head about using the quirt. She wouldn't meet Grandma's eyes, but she stood in one spot with her arms folded and shook her head no. She was studying her own feet the whole time.

Then the old woman went on to waggle her quirt tassels at Lecia and call her Belinda, just like she'd done in the hospital. "I hope Belinda does to you what all you've done to me," Grandma said, staring hard at Mother and waggling the horse quirt at Lecia the whole time. Again I got that dim stab of fear that this lady who bossed our mother's soul didn't even know our right names.

Lecia tried to make peace by saying that she wouldn't mind so much getting whipped with a horse quirt. It was no worse than

Daddy's belt or the limber chinaberry switches Mae Brown had been known to cut from the backyard. I said that I wasn't some old barnyard mule and didn't want to get whipped like one. Grandma pointed out to Mother how I thought I was in charge of my punishments. This seemed to her undeniable evidence that I needed my butt blistered. I aggravated her worse by saying that all the baths and whippings I'd got since Grandma came were "warping my character." That's a direct quote, according to Mother, who started to laugh and shake her head. Then she asked would I get her some orange baby aspirin because she felt like she had an ax in her forehead. (She became a terrible baby-aspirin junkie at this time, ate them like peanuts from an economy-sized jar with a depressing label on which two pink-cheeked Swedish-looking children trudged off to a red schoolhouse hand in hand.) She hung the quirt on the doorknob of her new bedroom and continued to conduct our whippings with either the flyswatter or a rolled-up *New Yorker*.

Daddy was never around after Grandma came home. It was some unspoken deal everybody had. Since she thought that he was low-rent and since she was herself dying, she sort of trumped him into staying away from his own house. He worked days and pulled a lot of double shifts. On days off, he fished till it turned squirrel season. Then he hunted.

One Saturday, he brought home dozens of squirrel tails for me to play with. The tails had bloody stub ends where they'd been lopped off, and I remember pinning them all together with clothespins and looping them around my neck, which grossed Lecia out. I think I fancied myself, in this squirrel-tail stole, some cross between Greta Garbo and Daniel Boone.

Lecia put herself in charge of cooking squirrel gumbo. She had a recipe for a black and garlicky roux that a Cajun neighbor lady had taught her. One whiff of that gumbo will make some gland draw up in the back of your throat and ache. Yankee gumbos are full of tomatoes and okra and all manner of pussyfied spices, but that game gumbo Lecia fixed—made with squirrel or duck or deer sausage—came together out of nothing quite so pretty. Instead it was mixed up from things you cannot live without—lard and flour and onion. It was a thin, black, elemental soup that opened your sinuses from the three kinds of pepper and left you tasting garlic and sassafras root for days after. Grandma said just the smell of the roux browning made her want to hork. She took Mother out for shrimp rémoulade at Al's Seafood. (Shrimp rémoulade, I might explain here, was my grandma's moral antidote to all those little split-up squirrel carcasses dismantled and frying in fat.) The shrimp are blanched pink, peeled and deveined, then hooked over the side of a sundae dish like the legs of so many young girls hanging over the edge of a swimming pool. The sundae dish may get piled up with shredded lettuce in the middle just for show. The rémoulade sauce is an extra-lemony kind of mayonnaise that has the muted luster of good pearls.

When the car backed out to take them to the restaurant, the headlights streaked across the kitchen wall behind Daddy. He sat in his string T-shirt at the table he'd built from sheet plywood and clear varnish. He held his spoon the way I later learned guys in jail are supposed to. He looped his arm around his plate so it was sort of guarding the bowl from somebody snatching at it. Positioned like this, he scooped the gumbo into his mouth in a steady motion that didn't stop till the bowl was clean. I still had the squirrel tails looped around my neck and said didn't it hurt his feelings that they wouldn't eat what he'd brought home. The idea made him laugh. "Shit, that's okay too, Pokey," he said with a lopsided grin. "Just more squirrel for me and you."

One Sunday, when Daddy was working days, I woke up late and found the old lady sitting in her wheelchair by herself in the kitchen. Breakfast dishes were scattered around, and she had a beer stuck between her thighs. I'd never been alone with her before and didn't fancy it. She lifted her head like she'd been dozed off; then she jumped a little when she saw me. "Don't shout!" I remember her saying. She gave me a walleyed stare. I told her I hadn't made a peep. She said that Lecia had asked Mother to drive her to church, which idea made me want to dip snuff. Lecia's religious ardors were at least as vague as mine. But her going to church had the desired effect on Grandma: she got a rapturous look telling me about it, as if that one piddling trip to the house of the Lord might hold Lecia a place in heaven. Then Grandma said she had something to show me in her room.

I was grateful, at least, that she had her leg on that morning. She'd even covered it up with these thick support hose, Supp-Hose, they were called. They were orange and heavier than sausage casings. Anyway, she wore those and had wedged the black shoe back on the plastic foot. (There's something overdressed about a shoe on a plastic foot, like it's beside the point.) Once we were in her room, she closed the door and posted herself, wheelchair and all, right in front of it.

Let me take a minute to tell you about the smell in that room. It stank of snake, specifically water moccasin.

If you are walking in waders through a marsh, say, on a warm winter morning, scanning the sky for mallards riding their jagged V overhead, you can smell a moccasin slithering alongside you long before you see it. It has an odor like something dead just before the rot sets in and the worms in its belly skin get it to jiggling around unnaturally. Often the smell of some rotting carcass—armadillo or nutria rat or bird—has stopped me in my tracks and gotten me to turn my eyes expecting to find on the ground the triangular, near-black head of a cottonmouth, which is related to both cobra and pit viper and the most vicious snake on this continent. I could never smell one swimming in a bayou, but on land it gives off a musk easily as strong as skunk. (I knew a drug dealer once who collected them in glass tanks all over his trailer. He had a harelip that somehow protected him from the stink, but the rest of us became, when dickering over pharmaceuticals with him, the noisiest and most adenoidal mouth breathers. We all sounded like Elmer Fudd, so a coke deal took on a cartoonlike quality: "You weally tink dis is uncut?" It was particularly hard to talk this way when you were tripping your brains out on LSD and had gone there only as a last resort to buy something to help you come down.) It's not just the smell of death, but the smell of something thriving on death, a smell you link up to maggots, or those bacteria that eat up corpses one cell at a time.

Anyway, we were wrapped in this smell when Grandma announced that she had been waiting for some "alone time"—that's what she called it—to show me this surprise. I could see she had something ratholed in the pocket of her blue cotton dress. Finally, she drew out what looked like a small brass book. It fit in the palm of her hand. There were two halves folded shut, like two tablets closed on each other. And she held her hands around it for a minute like she was praying. In my head there flashed the image of Moses as he appeared in the full-color picture in her Bible, hoisting two stone tablets joined with a leather thong.

After a while, she opened the small tablets on her lap, and they turned out to be dime-store brass frames around school pictures of two children, a boy and a girl. The pictures had a celery-green tint to them, like they'd been too long in the sun. "That's your sister and brother," she said. "That's Tex and Belinda."

Oddly enough, my first feeling at this news was relief. Here finally was this Belinda person that Grandma had been harping on. She was a real little girl, and blond like Lecia. She had a tight little Afro, and this was long before Angela Davis made that hairdo mean something. In fact, it was the age of the Toni Home Permanent, a kind of chemical skull-burn enacted on girl children all through the late fifties and early sixties. In our area, the perm solution was so strong that they rigged matchboxes over your ears with rubber bands and cotton wool to keep the drippings from blistering your ears slap off. I empathized with this Belinda person on that point. Tex was more abstract to me somehow for being male. He was bucktoothed, his dark hair slicked back. He wore a black string tie of the sort that cowboys favor.

She said they were a lot older than Lecia and me. They were going to high school now in another state. Here, in my memory, her voice trails off into a sort of fog, and my brain moves away from what she's saying into a state of pure puzzlement. What did these two kids have to do with me, anyway?

I'd never seen them before, and here Grandma was announcing

them as kin, not just cousins, but brother and sister. Even when she said that they were my half brother and half sister, I couldn't figure it out. Hell, other than Mother divorcing Paolo, which was a kind of family secret, I'd never known anybody who'd divorced, never even heard about anybody divorcing other than Elizabeth Taylor. The idea of having *half* a sister fascinated me. Which half was mine? I must have asked Grandma about this, because at some point she explained that they were Mother's Other Kids from her Other Husband. I asked was that Paolo, whom Daddy had whomped so good so long ago, and she said no. She always got weary thinking of how Mother had thrown Paolo over, so she took a second to look weary before saying that their daddy was another husband, Mother's first husband, Tex, who was news to me. The whole idea of a new husband and two kids added up to my not knowing squat about Mother's life before she came to Leechfield. Her history was almost a cipher as it stood. Oh, I knew she'd gone to art school in New York City during the war. But none of that story involved any other babies. She always made a big deal about how Lecia and I were her first babies, how she was thirty and that was old. I kept staring at the pictures in Grandma's lap till she snapped them closed and slid them back in her dress pocket.

While the fact of these two kids was trying to take shape in my head, Grandma did something that to this day my sister claims was so out of character for her it could not have happened. She grabbed my shoulder and breathed that death smell all over my face and said that should I fail to mind my mother—here Grandma brought her mouth right up to my face—if I continued to sass back and crud everything up—her eyes were almost pure white by now behind her smeary horn-rims—I would be Sent Away, just like they had been. They had never seen their mother again, not since they were babies.

It was then that I found out that the snake smell wasn't just from her bedpan or some old food getting nasty somewhere in the room. It came from her. In fact, it came from her open mouth, from deep inside her where the cancer was doubtless eating out whatever was human. If you had told me at that minute that writhing in her belly were dozens of newly hatched baby moccasins just busted loose from their eggs, I doubt I would have expressed surprise. She had also put Vicks VapoRub around her nostrils, maybe to shield her very self from her mouth's own death stink. That eucalyptus in the Vicks rode right on top of her cottonmouth breath in a way that made it worse.

(The closest I had ever come to that smell before Grandma's room was the closest I'd come to a snakebite. One evening when Daddy had rowed our rented boat into a patch of morning glories, he all of a sudden lifted the dripping oar from the bayou and took a swipe about three inches above my head, so the water from the oar fanned down over my face and bare arms. There was a quick plop in the water next to the boat. The cottonmouth had been draped off a branch right over me, he said. We watched it drag its S-shaped body through the brown water. I started shaking, not from cold.)

That day in Grandma's room, with no one in the house to rescue me, I started to tremble at that smell. I shoved past her chair and ran for the kitchen.

When Mother came home, Grandma made her spank me. She said she'd caught me going through her drawers trying to steal her ear bobs, which lie I didn't even bother arguing with. I just followed Lecia's advice for once and stood still, and sure enough, the whipping was over in a Yankee minute. But I could see a rigid set to Mother's jaw and feel something mechanical about the whapping of her hand on my rear end.

Sometime during that whipping, I began to get rid of Tex and Belinda's existence—an erasure that held for nineteen years. Some chasm in my skull opened up that morning and swallowed those children so totally that I never even mentioned them to Lecia, who served at that time as a live-in checkpoint for theories relating to Mother. (I later learned that she'd been shown the same pictures by Grandma. She had also promptly forgotten them. In this way, we entered amnesia together.) I knew, of course, that three husbands was a lot. Three husbands crossed the line between a small mistake and a nasty habit. (An often-divorced friend of mine once declared that when you're saying "I do" for the third or fourth time, you have to admit to yourself that they can't be entirely at fault.) So two extra kids who'd appeared from a pocket in Grandma's apron were unfathomable.

This doesn't completely explain my blanking out Tex and Belinda, though, because usually you could convince me of anything. That very year, Lecia had persuaded me—with zero evidence—that I was a robot assembled to serve her and to help with chores. She said I was in constant danger of being turned off if I didn't work out. I was not, therefore, exactly broke out in brains, particularly when it came to being convinced that I was inadequate, inhuman, or otherwise Not Right. I now know that I couldn't twig to the fact of those two spare kids because they were lost kids. And if they could be lost—two whole children, born of Mother's body just like us—so might we be. To believe that she'd lost those kids was to believe that on any day our mother could vanish from our lives, back into the void she came from, that we could become another secret she kept.

In short, when Grandma told me that I could be Sent Away for badness, that threat had the hard, dull sound of truth to it.

After Grandma's threat, I started to watch Mother even more closely for signs of Nervous. But until Hurricane Carla hit, I saw nothing, which is—I've since come to know—perhaps the surest sign of Nervous there is.

I watched her. She in turn watched the hurricane tracking reports every evening on the weather. We had a little portable TV that she had broken the antennae off of in some temper fit. It was rigged up with coat hangers for rabbit ears and produced a pale-blue and ash-white picture. The weatherman wore the shimmery full-body halo of indifferent reception. This was before satellite pictures where stop-action clouds swirled across the honest-to-God coastline. The weatherman, who also hosted an afternoon kids' show called *Cattleman Bill*, stood before a white greaseboard map of the Gulf drawing in Magic Marker. Little spirals were tropical storms. He drew fleets of arcing black arrows to indicate the general direction of the storm (which invariably blew at the east Texas coast either northwest from the Caribbean or northwest across the Florida Keys). When a spiral got big enough—once it took up a hundred miles of coastline and had winds of about a hundred and fifty miles per hour—it was a hurricane.

Then the game became guessing where where the storm would hit, or, in local parlance, "go in," as if it were some stray relative in search of lodging. Pull into any gas station and the grease monkey would invariably start the pump, then lean into your window to ask where you thought it was going in. Guessing the hurricane's point of entry was a town-wide sport every fall, easily as popular as high school football. Anybody who worked on the Gulf—a shrimper or a fellow tending some offshore oil rig—became an oracle overnight. When one of these guys hit the door of the American Legion, the bartender would crank down the TV or jukebox and draw a free cold beer while the patrons got all quiet and spun around on their stools or lifted their pool cues from the table. Most of the fishermen played it to the hilt. Their pronouncements took on the imagery of some voodoo chieftain: "Hit was a yellow rang around the moon last night," one Cajun shrimper said. "Dat storm's coming in right here at Sabine Pass." The offshore guys were tamer in their premonitions: old So-and-so out on the rig off of Morgan City, Louisiana, had a football knee start paining him like never before. No sooner did this sort of thing get said than fellows at the bar would leave their stools and head for the pay phone booth out in the parking lot. They'd line up to call their bookies so as to up or hedge their bets.

Leechfield had evacuated a few years before for Hurricane Audrey. That was the first storm I remember in the alphabetical lineup of girls' names. During Audrey, Mother made a big stink about the female gender taking the heat for all that destruction. "Hell, it's men who fight wars," I remember her saying. After Audrey came Betsy. She skirted us, but spilled over the levees and sandbags piled up around New Orleans so the whole town filled up like a saucer with seawater.

Hurricane Carla first arrived in my skull on a particular evening when Grandma was sitting in her wheelchair tatting with movements so tiny they looked like worry itself. Mother was stretched the length of the couch with a mug of coffee miraculously balanced on her breastbone. Lecia and I were squatting down at her feet inflicting our version of a pedicure on her. This involved coloring in her toenails with various shades of Crayola. (I favored purples and lavenders and royal blues. Lecia stuck with the more fashionable pinks.) They ran film clips of Audrey, with Cattleman Bill bragging that he had personally rowed a pirogue—a kind of Cajun kayak—up Main Street with a camera crew in the motorboat beside him. Mother said, *Oh horseshit.* She claimed that he'd left his wife and kids eating handout food in the high school gym while he "evacuated" up to Oklahoma City with his secretary. Cattleman Bill was, in Mother's estimation, nearly as big a sissy as Grandma, who was apparently so terrified of any kind of storm that she was always the first one down in the storm cellar out in West Texas when the wind started blowing. Grandma didn't even seem to hear about Carla. She just kept worrying that lace into being with that mean little shuttle.

When the storm did wheel in toward us, Grandma rallied some crazed kind of courage, so we weren't the first ones out of town. I don't suppose we were the last to leave, either. But the guys from the National Guard who were driving up and down the streets with bullhorns telling folks to evacuate had to stop at our house twice.

For two days before the storm came inland, folks had been getting ready. Weather reports got scarier. Windows were boarded up with sheets of plywood. Bags were packed. The supermarket had runs on batteries and candles and canned beans. Higher ground was just about anywhere else, and people were heading for it. Transistor radios repeated over and over that this was a Class Four hurricane. Nobody wanted to ride that out. A lot of families took time to root around in their attics to rescue special photographs and papers like marriage licenses from the tidal wave that Cattleman Bill was calling inevitable. I remember

Carol Sharp's mother wrapped her baby shoes up in tissue paper to take along.

We did none of these things. Daddy tended to shrug about a storm. "Shit, if it hits here, it'll take the house," he said. He didn't figure there was much point in scrabbling around, since a direct hit would wipe us out anyway. Which attitude didn't go far toward reassuring me. While other fathers were taking sick leave and folding up their lawn chairs and storing special furniture high in their attics, Daddy just kept plodding off to the plant and coming home long enough to refill his mess kit with food and plodding back. Eventually, he didn't bother coming home at all.

It's odd to me now how easily I let him leave our lives that fall at such an ugly time. Maybe he'd been slowly backpedaling out of the daddy business since Grandma came. Things just ran smoother without him around for the old woman to carp at. Maybe his absence was inevitable as we got older.

In fairness to Daddy, we at that point had plenty of time to evacuate, so it's not like the storm threatened our lives or anything, just our property, which didn't actually amount to much dollarwise. Plus the Gulf Oil Corporation kept those men who hadn't run off with their families working more or less nonstop, at double overtime, trying to get the plant battened down. Daddy would have felt like a fool turning that down. Still, I wonder why we loosened our grip on him so easy. Having Mother take care of us without him meant that—with the right amount of whining —we could talk her into buying nearly any toy, article of clothing, or treat. She saw us as grossly underprivileged. We were practically urchins, by her standards. So, in her care, we did things things that Daddy, with his forty-acres-and-a-mule sense of thrift, wouldn't have stood for: cutting up a sheet over a card table for a playhouse, say, or painting murals on the garage wall with oil paints. Daddy had an extravagance of heart. He pretty much indulged us in a way neighbors found shameful. But he drew a hard line at anything that seemed to waste money, which was where Mother started to overtake him in our hearts.

The first day that he didn't come home at all, Lecia and I called him a bunch of times. I always imagined our voices snailing through the telephone lines in an intricate pattern of stops and transfers trying to get to him. "Gulf Oil. Hep you?" was how the operator answered at the first ring. "Extension 691, please," we'd tell her. Lecia and I would stand nearly ear to ear in the kitchen, each one trying to squeeze the other off the receiver. Our forearms, on this day, got covered with little half-moon bruises where we'd pinched each other trying to hog the whole receiver. He would always talk as long as we wanted, but he wouldn't come home, no matter how we whined or begged. I remember his saying, "You take care of your momma," and my asking who was going take care of us. (Which I don't remember his answering.) Right before he hung up, Lecia suggested that he talk to Mother himself—maybe hoping he'd get the idea that she didn't quite have both oars in the water. At that point, he claimed somebody was calling him and just hung up.

By that afternoon, the town was emptying itself of people, and still we didn't leave. The news reports were getting real specific. They showed the tidal surges that wiped out the beach road. They showed the cars bumper to bumper heading upcountry over the Orange Bridge. People evacuated with their headlights on in daylight like it was all some town-wide funeral procession.

The next morning, the front page of the paper carried a shot of palm trees snapped off at Crystal Beach. School got closed, so Lecia and I sat around the house making puppets from paper bags and watching endless TV: *I Love Lucy*, *Leave It to Beaver*, all family sitcoms where the dads walked around in suit jackets and the women wore heels to vacuum all day.

Cattleman Bill himself had disappeared from that morning's news. In his place stood the stout and sweating sportscaster wearing his button-bulging suit and skinny tie. He told us that the front end of the storm would hit us by noon. "You are advised to seek shelter," he said. "Repeat. You are advised to seek shelter." He had that terrific sort of self-importance in making the announcement, like Barney Fife on *Andy Griffith* pretending he was some tough-guy detective instead of a small-town deputy in charge of the school crossing. About half an hour after this newscast, they set the tornado sirens blowing.

Some of the local church folks had been preaching the world's end in that storm. Carol Sharp gave me all the details in her front yard before her family evacuated. We were standing under the mimosa tree at the time. Its pink hairy blossoms were falling all around us in the wind, and her daddy and mother were roping down a tarp over the roof of their Chevy. Carol described how the Four Horseman of the Apocalypse would come riding down out of the clouds with their black capes flapping behind them, and how the burning pit would open up in the earth for sinners like me, and how Jesus would lead her and her family right up a golden stair to heaven. Some evangelist had put his hand on her forehead the day before, and that very instant a seed wart on her right thumb had up and vanished. I had personally done surgery on that wart, picking the seeds out of it with a straight pin not a week before, and sure enough, there was no trace of it that morning. Which gave me pause. But I was spiteful enough to tell her that I didn't much want to sign up with any god who sent tidal waves crashing down on trailer parks but took time for her old wart. (Despite my breathtaking gullibility, I was able to spew out such random hunks of elementary logic sometimes.)

Back home, the light in our windows was gradually turning a darker and darker shade of charcoal. Mother was hanging draperies over the big picture window, and through that window, I could see the Sharps' Chevy backing out of their driveway, tarp and all. *What if old Mr. Sharp's right about God and Jesus?* I must have said out loud. Or maybe I suggested we pray just in case—I don't remember. What's dead clear now is how Mother lifted her middle finger to the ceiling and said, *Oh, fuck that God!* Between that and the tornado sirens and the black sky that had slid over all our windows and Grandma stone deaf to that blasphemy because she was tatting those weensy stitches, I began to think we'd be washed out to sea for all our sins at any minute.

Lecia must have gotten scared too, because she started lobbying for us to get in the car and drive to Aunt Iris's house right away. Daddy's sister lived sixty miles north in the hills outside Kirbyville. "Let's just go," she kept saying. I remember she argued that the big traffic had already died down. She even tried to talk to Grandma, who was lost in her lace-making.

Daddy called about then, and Mother surprised us by picking up the phone herself. I remember that she had a dish towel in one hand, and she sounded pissed off that he was calling at all. She told him that the car was running outside, that we were walking out the door that very minute. In fact, she hadn't even hauled her daddy's Gladstone bag out of the closet yet. The TV was blaring *Dennis the Menace.* I was sitting on the floor with Lecia, cutting fringe on a paper-bag Indian costume, when Mother slammed down the receiver.

Now I know that she needed him there that day, and her fury was the closest she could get to an invitation. Daddy was lost to us in that fury. The line was severed, and in the mist that occupied my skull that morning, he floated away, getting smaller and smaller. I looked over to Lecia, who shrugged and went back to cutting her fringe with a sick precision. At that instant, I knew we should have evacuated long before. The slow psychic weight of doom settled over me.

Mother later explained to us that we would have gone at sunrise, but Grandma for some reason refused to leave. She got it in her head that there was only a little rain shower coming. It was as if her lifelong terror of storms had imploded somehow and left her believing that a Class Four hurricane moving directly across our house couldn't budge her. Even the nice young Guardsman in the camouflage suit who came to stand in our living room with his bullhorn at his side didn't rile her up. "We appreciate your stopping by," she said, trying to herd him out of the house by bumping the backs of his knees with her chair wheels. By this time, Mother sat at the dining table sobbing and wiping at her face with that dish towel. The soldier finally threatened to pick Grandma up physically and tote her to the car, to which she said okay, she'd go, but she had to take a bath first. He said that he reckoned they'd already stopped water service, but Lecia got the water running, and Grandma wheeled herself in there and shut the door.

It was when that door clicked shut that Lecia decided to call Daddy to come get us out of there. Right that minute. But the phone line had gone dead. I saw the shock of this fact on her face before she even handed me the receiver. (Lecia was nothing if not cool in a crisis. She learned to drive at twelve, at which age I once saw her convince a state trooper that she'd just left her license at home because she was running out to get her baby milk while he was still sleeping.) But her expression that morning with the black phone at her ear betrayed her age. Her eyes got shiny for a second. She was really only nine, after all, and what with the tornado sirens wailing the way our music teacher had warned they would only when the Russian missiles were launched from Cuba, and the phone line to Daddy snapped dead, Lecia looked ready to give up the grown-up act altogether.

She handed me the phone. She didn't want to be alone in knowing how alone we were, so she handed it to me, so I'd know too. And that flat silence right up against my ear brought it all home to me. You never notice how hooked up to everybody you feel when you hear that rush of air under the dial tone, as if all the world's circuits are just waiting to hear you—anyway, you never notice that till it goes away. Then it's like you listen, expecting that faraway sound, and instead you get only the numb quiet of your own skull not knowing what to think of next.

It was the National Guardsman who wound up getting us out. He came back about when the rain had started to blow sideways against all the windows with a sound like BB pellets. Grandma's bath had wound up taking too long. Mother let him force the bathroom door with a screwdriver, and there Grandma sat unmoved from her chair, all her attention honed to that shuttle of hers manufacturing lace while bathwater poured over the edges of the tub and onto the floor.

He did have to pick her up, finally. He swooped her up in his arms like she was a bride. Her good leg hung down normally enough, but her stump kept slipping down past his elbow and starting to dangle. Lecia and I had a giggle fit over this on the porch, because Grandma's legs kept splaying open in a way she would have found unladylike.

Outside, the wind had set the phone lines to swaying. It had already started to tear loose some shingles that were blowing up the street. Plus gusts somehow squirmed into the window cracks to make a high-pitched whistling that seemed to get louder by the second. Lecia and I ran for the car, a distance of ten yards, and got drenched to the skin. Getting in the car was like leaving the first big noise of the storm and sitting in a cold bubble. We could barely see the Guardsman through the water streaming off the windshield. He seemed somehow to be trying to move in a more gallant or stately way, what with Grandma's leg slipping down every other step and all. Anyway, he was slower than we had been, which made us laugh. But we stopped giggling pretty quick when Mother slid behind the wheel.

You could see by her eyes in the rearview that she wasn't crying anymore. That had come to be a bad sign, the not crying. Her mouth turned into a neat little hyphen.

I watched the Guardsman climb back in his jeep; then the gray and the rain sort of gobbled up everything but a big olive-drab smear that was moving out of our driveway behind us. I had this crazy urge to roll down my window and poke my head right out into the storm and holler to him to come back. But the wind would have eaten any words I yelled. So I watched the smear of his jeep get littler. Then it was gone, and there was just rain and sirens and Mother's cold gray eyes set smack in the middle of that silver oblong mirror.

The drive from Leechfield to Aunt Iris's house in Kirbyville would normally have taken an hour. That's in the best weather conditions. "Sixty minutes, door to door" was what Daddy always said climbing out of his truck cab or stepping up on their porch. (I once made the trip dead drunk on a summer morning in a souped-up Mustang in forty-five minutes, and I never got under eighty, slowed for a curve, or stopped for a light.) This particular day it took fifty-five minutes. Lecia timed it. That's in blinding rain, rain so heavy the wipers never really showed you the road. They just slapped over the blur and then slapped back to reveal more blur. Sure, we must have had wind at our backs. Still, I figure that Mother drove through the first onslaught of a hurricane with the gas pedal pressed flush to the floorboard, without a nickel's worth of hesitation. Maybe she knew that her mother was close to dying and just didn't care if we made it to high ground in one piece or not. We were late enough leaving town that there were no other vehicles on the road, which was good. Doubtless we would have hit them had they been there. Only shit-house luck kept us from sliding sideways off the narrow blacktop and into one of the umpteen jillion bayous we passed. For a good five miles out of town, you could hear the sirens getting littler, so the roar of the wind got bigger. That made it seem like we were heading into the storm instead of away from it.

When we hit Port Arthur, Texas, Mother started to sing under her breath. It was an old song she liked to play on our turntable when she was drinking. She had a scratchy recording of Peggy Lee or Della Reese, one of those whiskey-voiced lounge singers:

Oh the shark has zippy teeth, dear,
And he shows them pearly white.
Just a jack knife has his teeth, dear,
And he keeps them out of sight . . .

Nobody in my family can sing a note. The few times we went to church with neighbors, Lecia and I had the good sense to lip-synch the hymns so it wouldn't be too noticeable. My mother, too, had a bad voice—wavery and vague. She was a natural alto who'd probably been nagged into the higher ranges by overfeminine choir teachers. So she sang the wrong words in a ragged soprano under her breath that morning, whispery and high. The car seemed to pick up speed as she sang, and the fear that had been nuzzling around my solar plexus all morning started to get real definite when I saw, dead ahead of us, the gray steel girders of the Orange Bridge.

The Orange Bridge at that time was said to be the highest bridge in the country. Your ears popped when you drove over it. The engineers had built it that tall so that even tugs shoving oil platforms with full-sized derricks on them could pass under with room to spare. The Sabine River it ran over wasn't very wide, so the bridge had easily the sharpest incline of any I've ever crossed.

Not surprisingly, this was the scene of a suicide every year or so. Jilted suitors and bankrupt oilmen favored it. Those who jumped from the highest point of the bridge broke every bone in their bodies. I remember Mother reading this fact out loud from the paper one time, then saying that women tended to gas themselves or take sleeping pills—things that didn't mess them up on the outside so much. She liked to quote James Dean about leaving a beautiful corpse.

Anyway, it was this bridge that the car bumped onto with Mother singing the very scariest part of "Mack the Knife." She sang it very whispery, like a lullaby:

When the shark bites with his teeth, dear,
Scarlet billows start to spread. . . .

The car tipped way back when we mounted the bridge. It felt sort of like the long climb a roller coaster will start before its deep fall. Mother's singing immediately got drowned out by the steel webbing under the tires that made the whole car shimmy. At the same time—impossibly enough—we seemed to be going faster.

Lecia contends that at this point I started screaming, and that my screaming prompted Mother to wheel around and start grabbing at me, which caused what happened next. (Were Lecia writing this memoir, I would appear in one of only three guises: sobbing hysterically, wetting my pants in a deliberately inconvenient way, or biting somebody, usually her, with no provocation.)

I don't recall that Mother reached around to grab at me at all. And I flatly deny screaming. But despite my old trick of making my stomach into a rock, I did get carsick. The bile started rising in my throat the second we mounted the bridge, which involved the car flying over a metal rise that felt like a ski jump. We landed with a jolt and then fishtailed a little.

I knew right away that I was going to throw up. Still, I tried locking down my belly the way I had on the Tilt-A-Whirl. I squinched my eyes shut. I bore down on myself inside. But the rolling in my stomach wouldn't let me get ahold of it. I wouldn't have opened my window on a dare. And I sure didn't want to ask Mother to pull over mid-bridge. Lecia was in charge of all Mother-negotiations that day anyway, and she had opted for the same tooth-grinding silence we'd all fallen into. Even though she was normally devout about watching the speedometer and nagging Mother to slow down (or, conversely, Daddy to speed up), she kept her lip zipped that morning. Anyway, at the point when I felt the Cheerios start to rise in my throat, I just ducked my head, pulled the neck of my damp T-shirt over my nose and away from my body a little, and barfed down my shirt front. It was very warm sliding down my chest under the wet shirt, and it smelled like sour milk.

Mother responded to this not at all. Neither did Grandma, who had a nose like a bloodhound but had turned into some kind of mannequin. Really, she might have been carved from Ivory soap for all the color she had. Lecia would normally have seized the opportunity to whack me for being so gross. Maybe I even wanted whacking, at that point. Surely I wanted to break the bubble of quiet. But Lecia just tied her red bandana around her nose like a bank robber and shot me a sideways look. I knew then it was one of Mother's worst days, when my horking down my own shirt didn't warrant a word from anybody. Lecia watched Mother, who watched some bleary semblance of road.

Anyway, that's the last thing I remember before the crash—Lecia's bandana drawn over her nose.

Then for some reason I still don't understand, the car went into a three-hundred-and-sixty-degree spin. I don't know if this was accidental or deliberate on Mother's part. As I said before, Lecia holds that I was wailing and Mother was turning around to swat at me. I do remember seeing Mother turn the wheel sharply to the left, which forced the car into a spin. After a long time whirling around, I saw the railing on the other side of the bridge rush forward. Then for an instant, we were launched in the air. Our tires just left the bridge altogether. The car jumped the raised pedestrian walkway and flew toward the top rung of the railing. (People never walked over, of course, but workers hung platforms off it for painting and repairs). I saw the rail flying laterally at us. Then the car crunched to a stop. By this time I was screaming and crying.

Amazingly enough, the crash just crumpled the front fender and took out the right headlight. Nobody seemed that rattled about what happened but me. Mother didn't even get out to inspect the damage. Grandma just hunkered more deeply over her lace. Mother said, "Everybody all right!" but in a cheery voice, like a camp counselor after a long hike. She didn't even turn around when she said it. In the mirror her teeth were showing in a scary smile.

I was really howling by this time. The car got thrown in reverse, and we unpried ourselves from the rail. We bounced off the opposite walkway backward and headed down the slope, gaining speed.

Lecia slid over about this time and laced her fingers with mine, for which kindness I remain grateful. I can't have smelled very good. Plus I was blubbering. Big tusks of snot were hanging out of my nose. Anyway, she just took my big hand in her big hands. (We both have hands perfect only for fieldwork and volleyball.) I always felt safe when she did that. Usually it shut me up, too, but this time I whispered why was Mother trying to kill us and was she really going stark crazy. Lecia just said to pipe down, that we'd be at Auntie's house in twenty minutes and everything would be okay then.

But at Auntie's house, everything wasn't okay. We'd escaped

the storm, all right. Hurricane Carla couldn't reach us. Still, stepping down from that car, which was hissing and clicking from having been driven so hard, I didn't feel any relief. Somehow Aunt Iris's dirt yard under the tall pines wound up looking as dark to me as Leechfield had. I felt no grace. I had no urge to kiss the ground like some cartoon sailor delivered from shipwreck. The spotted bird dogs that circled my feet got only the most distracted pats before they whined their way back to the porch.

Auntie (pronounced Ain'tee) walked right to me through that pack of dogs, flapping her apron at them and saying to me how was the ride down, sugar? Then I heard my voice saying fine, which lie was beginning to come naturally to me. I was fine. The ride was fine. We were fine. My fear was too great for me to say more; it was so great, in fact, that I couldn't let myself collapse sobbing into Auntie's soft and calico-draped bosom. The only need I could state was the obvious one for a bath. The dogs had even shied away from me. They crouched low to the earth and sidestepped back to the porch, circling each other and whining. They had long spotted muzzles, and their yellowed eyes kept watching.

I cannot, however, describe Auntie's face from that day, or the welcoming faces of my cousins and uncle, who came out to greet us. I must have kept my gaze dog-level. Then even the dogs begin to get dimmer in memory, as if a heavy gauze is being wrapped around my eyes, and all I could see were the faint outlines of those beasts—sniffing and suspicious. I was turning the volume down. I was hardening up inside for another tough-bucking ride.

Grandma was put to bed in Auntie's back bedroom, and I got a bath. These things certainly registered as improvements over our sitting around in Leechfield, cut off from Daddy and waiting for a tidal wave to smash the house. But Mother's spooky silence held, and my father's father—himself seemingly older than Jesus—almost immediately took Grandma's place as an emblem of death.

My grandpa Karr was well up in his eighties and nowhere near dying. Still, everybody had been predicting his imminent death since I could remember. This and the suggestion of his Indian heritage gave him the kind of authority that I now think old people ought to have. But back then, I resented it. He didn't have to do any chores. He wouldn't even bother turning up his hearing aid half the time when you talked to him. He barely even said hello. Mostly he just sat in a cane-bottom rocker on the front porch while people brought him food or pipe tobacco, coffee or iced tea depending on the time of day. He had taken up this bad habit of sometimes climbing on top of things when left unwatched—the barn or a car roof, the shed, almost anything. Aunt Iris told us about it before she went off to work at the drugstore. He'd once even shinnied a fair ways up one of the tall pecan trees that stood in the yard. So Lecia and I were each given a dime by my cousin Bob Earl to watch him. The idea was that if he started climbing, we'd run and fetch our cousin, who was tending Black Angus cattle in the back field. Grandpa sat rocking and chewing on his pipe and sometimes singing a song about lost coon dogs that Mother couldn't stand because it was so backwoods country.

Somebody stole my old coon dogs
And I wish they'd bring 'em back.
They run the big ones over the fence
And the little ones through the crack.

I remember we felt torn between watching Grandpa, who looked like something set in concrete and unlikely to budge, but whom we had been paid to watch, and keeping track of Mother, who looked spring-loaded on serious trouble.

We finally made a compromise. Lecia would sit outside, with her back to the door screen, watching Grandpa. (I would give her my dime for this service.) I, in turn, would sit inside with my back against her back and the screen door watching Mother, who had the TV tuned to hurricane news. She had also built a fire in the front-room hearth, even though it was plenty hot already. She just sat poking at that fire, the sweat pouring down her face, which was lacquered red by the flames. She had pushed her thick hair back from her face with one of those black stretchy headbands. It fanned out all around her face in a sort of corona. She looked as scooped out and sunk in on herself—she was just squatting there poking at the fire with the cast-iron poker—as any human being I've ever seen before or since. She was hard for me to watch, so I watched TV instead—the white greaseboard map on Kirbyville Weather—and more footage of palm trees flattening out in wind.

I wanted to call Daddy. I even talked to the long-distance operator about this. But she said she couldn't put me through to Leechfield because all the circuits down that way were busy. I said did that mean there were too many calls on the trunk lines or that Daddy's phone out at the Gulf was broken. She said she didn't have time to talk about it and unplugged me.

I looked around at Lecia's plaid cowboy shirt pressed up against the screen grid. After a while, I decided I had to pee and went into Auntie's bathroom.

Coming out, I noticed Grandma's hand hanging down off the side of the bed in the back room. I tiptoed in. It was a small, musty-smelling room. Auntie kept a big white freezer packed with deer and squirrel and duck meat in there. The white iron bed, narrow and sagging, sat alongside the freezer. Grandma's glasses were also on the floor, so I knew she was asleep. I thought to put the glasses on the nighttable, then at the same time maybe snitch her sewing scissors so I could spend some time cutting newspaper snowflakes or making myself a cootie-catcher back in the living room. Grandma's eyes were mostly closed, sort of rolled up in her head so just white half-moons showed when I peered in.

When I squatted down to grab the glasses, I could see that she'd spilled something on the lenses, something pink and sticky-looking, so the little red ants we called sugar ants were crawling over the glasses. The previous spring I had liberated all the ants in Lecia's glass ant farm (I'd felt bad they were locked up), and had since been looking to snare some new ones for her. It had been a prizewinning science project. I was trying to figure out a way to shoo the ants off one arm of the glasses and trap them in a shoebox I found under the bed, when I noticed Grandma's hand.

It was curled partway open. The fingers almost touched the floor. And running in a track down the very white part of her arm was what I first thought to be a scratch or an eyebrow-pencil line. But the line was moving. I bent right next to her. Then I made out how she'd spilled that cough medicine or red soda pop on the inside of her arm, and the sugar ants were crawling up and down eating it off, and she didn't even feel it.

I don't know if I thought she was dead or what. All I knew was her state at that instant was way more than I'd bargained for. I backed out of the room and went back to the living room. I sat with my back flat against the screen so I could feel Lecia's vertebrae bumping against mine in a way I liked. I sat right there till Mother went in and found Grandma and started screaming.

CHAPTER 5

My daddy watched Hurricane Carla come up the Intercoastal Canal from the Gulf. He claimed to be high in a sort of crow's nest at the time, behind a thick glass wall that let him look out over half the county. The crow's nest was on a giant tower facing the refinery, beyond which lay the oil-storage tanks, and finally the canal, a glorified ditch that Houston oilmen had spent a fortune having dug so they could boat their oil from offshore rigs right to the refineries. Daddy later said the tower swayed back and forth in the gale. He and Ben Bederman swore they had to hold on to the countertops while the rolling chairs slid around. Through the observation window, they watched a gray wall of water twenty feet high move up the canal toward town. I can almost see my daddy cock his head and squint like it was some animal he was tracking in the distance. He even took a minute to point with his ropy arm when he was telling the story, like the tidal wave was coming right at us that minute. "It was like a whole building made out of water," he said. I later had cause to wonder how his view was so clear in the midst of the storm. But hearing him tell it, you would never doubt he'd somehow actually cowboyed his way through it all.

Remarkably enough, the hurricane didn't go in at Leechfield, this despite the fact that a tidal wave had been dead set on a course that would have squashed every remaining citizen flat as a roach. The odds on a direct hit had been high. But the storm took a weird turn, the kind of dodge people later likened to a fast quarterback barely scooting around some bullnecked lineman. The move was a forty-to-one fluke. Just before Carla came ashore at Leechfield, the storm stopped almost dead in place; then it made a sixty-degree turn. Only the edges swept over East Texas, the rest flying full force into Cameron, Louisiana, which hadn't battened down at all.

Cameron's preparations wouldn't have mattered much, though, since a good hunk of the Gulf of Mexico essentially lifted itself up and then toppled over right on the low-lying town. People shinnied up trees, trying to get away from the rising water. Civil Defense did what they could at the last minute, and some families managed to outrun the flood in their cars when the radio announced where the storm was heading in. But a lot of people didn't happen to have their radios turned on. Casualties were high. The TV ran footage of guys in hip waders sloshing through their own living rooms, feeling around underwater for pieces of furniture that hadn't washed away.

The storm also flooded the bayous and brought all manner of critters from both salt and fresh water right into buildings and houses. When the water went down, one guy I read about in the paper found an eight-foot nurse shark flopping on his kitchen tiles. Whole bunches of people opened dresser drawers to find cottonmouths nesting next to their balled-up socks. There were also nutria-rat bites, kids mostly, toddlers who got cornered in their own yards. The rats were as big as raccoons and had front teeth shaped like chisels with bright orange enamel on them, which made the attacks particularly scary to think about. Neighbors came back to town bringing stories about cousins or friends of friends who'd been bitten, then gone through the agonizing rabies shots in the belly. I was a vulture for this kind of story.

Grandma died during all this, of course. It turned out that she hadn't been fully dead at Auntie's, just in a coma. I've been told that she actually came out of that coma and spent a few days bedridden back at our house in Leechfield before she died. I don't remember it that way. Apparently I just blanked out her last visit along with a lot of other things. She died, and I wasn't sorry.

The afternoon it happened, Frank Doleman came to the door of my second-grade class with Lecia in tow. Mrs. Hess told me to get my lunch box and galoshes. Out in the hall, Lecia was snubbing into a brown paper towel that covered half her face so I couldn't see if she was ginning out real tears or just making snotty sounds in her head. Uncle Frank kneeled down eye-level to tell me that Grandma had "passed away." I remember this phrase seemed an unnaturally polite way of putting it, like something you'd hear on *Bonanza*. All the local terms for dying started more or less coursing through my head right then. *She bought the farm, bit the big one, cashed in her chips,* and my favorite: *she opened herself up a worm farm.* (I had the smug pleasure once of using this term up north and having a puzzled young banker-to-be then ask me if these worm farmers in Texas sold worms for fishing, or what.)

I sat in the back of Uncle Frank's white convertible going home with Lecia blubbering nonstop in the front bucket seat and him putting his hammy hand on her shoulder every now and then, telling her it was okay, to just cry it out. What was running through my head, though, was that song the Munchkins sing when Dorothy's house lands on the witch with the stripy socks: "Ding dong, the witch is dead." I knew better than to hum it out loud, of course, particularly with Lecia making such a good show, but that's what I thought.

Daddy was squatting on the porch in his blue overalls and hard hat, smoking, when we pulled up. He'd obviously been called right out of the field. He was dirty and smelled like crude oil when he hugged Lecia and me, one under each arm. Our principal didn't pause, though, before shaking his hand, didn't even dig out his hankie to wipe the oil off his palm after he shook. He was partial to white starched shirts, but knew when to set that aside.

While Uncle Frank backed out, Daddy and Lecia and I stood together a minute at the head of the driveway waving bye-bye. I remember leaning across the front of his blue work shirt to tell Lecia that was some good crying she did, to which she lowered the paper towel so I could finally see her face. It was like a coarse brown curtain dropping to show a mask entirely different than the grinning one I'd expected. Her eyes and nose were red and her mouth was twisted up and slobbery. All of a sudden, I knew she wasn't faking it, the grief I mean. It cut something out of me to see her hurt. And it put some psychic yardage between us that I was so far from sad and she was so deep in it.

It must have pissed Lecia off too, somehow, that gap between her misery and my relief. Later that evening, Daddy was frying up a chicken, and she chased me down over something mean I'd said about Grandma. She was fast even then (in junior high, she would run anchor on the four-forty relay), so I didn't make it a half turn around the yard before she caught me by the back collar and yanked me down from behind. The collar choked off my windpipe, and the fall knocked the breath out of me. Before I knew what hit me, she had me down on my back in the spiky St. Augustine grass.

She sat on my chest with her full weight. Her knees dug into the ball sockets of both my shoulders. She said take it back. I sucked up enough wind to say I wouldn't. I tried bucking my pelvis up to throw her off. Then I tried flinging my legs up to wrap around her shoulders, but she had me nailed. Still I wouldn't take it back. All I had to fight back with was my stubbornness (which I'd built up by being a smart mouth and getting my ass whipped a lot). I never actually won a stand-up fight, with Lecia or anybody. Hence my tendency to sneak up blindside somebody weeks after the fact. But I could sure as hell provoke one and then drag it out by not giving in. I took a warped sort of pride in this, though I can see now it's a pitiful thing to be proud of —being able to take an ass-stomping.

I don't know how long she had me pinned. Her knees dug

twin bruises in my shoulders. I found them when putting on my pajamas that night, the size and shape of big serving spoons. She kept me there a while. The sky was going pink. I could hear Daddy's spatula on the skillet scraping chicken drippings for cream gravy. Finally, she got tired of my not giving in and decided to spit in my eye. She hawked up a huge boogery gollop from way back in her throat, pausing every now and then to tell me she was fixing to huck it at me. It had bulk and geometry. It was hanging in a giant tear right over my face, swinging side to side like a pendulum, when Daddy came slamming out the screen to haul her off me.

That night in bed I could hear her crying into her pillow, but when I put my hand on her shoulder, she just shrugged me off.

Mother was on her way to bury Grandma during all this. Thank God, because Lecia and me fighting always made Mother sit down crying. She had always longed so fiercely for a sister that she couldn't understand why we whaled on each other.

Anyway, while Lecia was trying to spit in my eye, Mother was driving across the Texas desert in Grandma's old Impala, heading from the hospital in Houston to Lubbock and the funeral. She says that she wore her black Chanel suit with Grandma's beige-and-ivory cameo, which her great-grandmother had brought from Ireland. She also wore pearl earrings, and a white pillbox hat of the type Jackie Kennedy had on when her husband was shot. (It is a sad commentary on the women of my family that we can recite whole wardrobe assemblages from the most minor event in detail, but often forget almost everything else. In fact, the more important the occasion—funeral, wedding, divorce court—the more detailed the wardrobe memory and the dimmer the hope of dredging up anything that happened.) She took the trip solo because she didn't want to upset us. Or so she told us on the phone. "There's no need for y'all riding all the way out there just to get upset" was how she put it. That sudden surge of maternal feeling seems odd to me now. I mean, we'd already seen all manner of nastiness and butchery, including Grandma's lopped-off leg at

M. D. Anderson Hospital. Plus we'd watched Grandma achieve whole new levels of Nervous as the cancer ate out her brain. It just didn't make sense.

For years Lecia had me convinced that Mother left us behind because she was hauling Grandma's body in the backseat of the Impala. Lecia fed me this lie pretty soon after we got off the phone with Mother that night, and I swallowed it like a bigmouthed bass. I needed an excuse for being left behind, I guess. The truth—that we were murder on her nerves, which were already shot—must have been too much for me. In bed one morning I asked Lecia why didn't Mother just put Grandma in the trunk. Lecia propped up on her elbow and said that wasn't very nice for your dead mother. Following that same line of logic, I figured out for myself that she wouldn't let anybody truss the old lady on top of the car like a deer, just so we'd all get to ride out too. So for years, I pictured Mother driving the five hundred miles across Texas with Grandma's corpse stretched out on the backseat. (I guess it wasn't till I read William Faulkner's *As I Lay Dying*, where the kids are dragging their dead mother across Mississippi, and the stink gets so bad and the flies and maggots get at her, that I began to figure that some ambulance had probably carted the body back. Mother had small tolerance for odors.)

The trip must have been grisly. The newly dead do, after all, rent a lot of skull space from us. So I still imagine Mother alone in that car with some ghost of her dead mother sitting beside. Mother was driving at night as Grandma would have, for the cool and the lack of traffic night provided. It's a fourteen-hour drive, and the sky can get awful black in that time, like a big black bowl somebody set over you. One pair of headlights can put you in a trance with the white road dashes coming up in them at exact intervals. And as John Milton says, "The mind is its own place, and in itself / Can make a heav'n of hell, a hell of heav'n. I myself am Hell."

I sometimes want to beam myself back to the old Impala so Mother won't have to make that drive alone. I always picture myself being incredibly useful—pouring coffee from the thermos or finding something of a soothing and classical nature on the radio—never whining or asking to pee as I surely would have. Maybe I would roll down all the windows just to shoo the mean ghost of my grandmother out.

Mother had left us at home because she was hurt. For her, being hurt meant drawing into herself. (Old joke: What's the loneliest place in Louisiana? Bayou Self.) And that's where I have to leave her, alone on the dark highway with the cacti rearing up and falling back down as she passes.

Grandma's death gave me my first serious case of insomnia. When I lay in bed next to Lecia's solid, sleeping form, that picture of Grandma's pale arm with the ants would rear up behind my closed eyes. With it came a low humming in my head—a sound like a crazy cello player sawing the same note over and over, or like a zillion bees coming up out of the ground. In fact, that humming was the sound our car tires had made on the Orange Bridge when Mother either did or didn't try to crash through the guardrail and fly us screaming down to the river. If I kept my eyes open, the humming stopped. If they fell closed, even for a second, that humming would swamp over every good thought I'd ever had. Nights, I lay awake with my eyes burning. What I was protecting myself against on these vigils was, in fact, my own skull, which must be the textbook definition of early-onset Nervous if ever there was one.

That small psychic crisis kicked off a metaphysical one. Why was everybody so fired up about nature all the time, and God? These kids sitting around me with their heads crooked earnestly over their giant drawing papers seemed to have forgotten that the ocean had decided for no good reason to dislodge itself on top of hundreds of people across the river in Louisiana. Our bodies could have been the ones people saw on TV newsreels after school. Families on these film clips went from one child-sized body bag to another—the bags having been lined up in rows across some movie-theater parking lot. The sheriff would unzip the bag's top a little bit, and the daddy would peer in, then shake his head no. Then he'd step back while the sheriff rezipped before going on to the next bag. This happened over and over till the sheriff finally unzipped the face the family was looking for—little Junior or baby Jackie, blue-skinned and bloated, tongue black and sticking out.

The cameras didn't show those faces, of course. But Daddy had seen plenty guys dead in war. I remember he rubbed the sleeve of his faded chambray shirt and said that a human face could go just as blue as that. He also said it wasn't the coldness of a dead man's skin that gave you the willies, but how the skin went hard all over, so touching him was like touching wood or concrete.

During this talk, we were sitting in bed eating dinner, a habit we'd gone right back to after Grandma died. Only we'd added the drone of TV news. Its blue-white light was our family hearth. "I shit you not," Daddy said as he tore off a hunk of biscuit. "You touch a dead man sometime." He took a swallow of buttermilk. "Hard as that table. Got no more to do with being alive than that table does."

That description didn't scare me so much as the news footage of some daddy folding in on himself once he'd recognized a kid's face. The mothers cried too, of course, and bitterly. But they seemed better equipped for it. They held each other while they cried, or fell to their knees, or screamed up at the sky. But you could tell by the moans and bellows those grown men let out that their grief had absolutely nowhere to go. I watched from the middle of my parents' bed, a steaming plate of beans and biscuits balanced on my patch of covers, while one grown man after another buckled in the middle like everything inside him was going soft all at once, and I knew that the dead child's face would stay on each daddy's eyeballs forever. I stopped trusting the world partly from seeing how those meaty-faced men bellowed under the shadowy bills of their tractor caps or cowboy hats.

The rest of the second grade seemed immune to all this misery. Or they took our escape from the storm as a testament to our moral superiority. It was a sign from God that prayers had been answered, something to be pious about.

I asked Carol Sharp at recess didn't she think that the people over in Cameron had said any prayers before the storm came in. And she said that maybe God thought Leechfield Baptists somehow better Christians than folks over in Louisiana. They were probably Catholic anyway, she said. We were riding in the middle of the merry-go-round during this discussion. It was standard playground stuff, industrial steel painted fire-engine red. You had to brace yourself on these metal sawhorses to keep from flying off once the kids shoving it around got it up to speed. Once we were whirling pretty good, I tried to pry Carol's fingers loose from her sawhorse, but she hollered to Shirley Carter to help. They both tickled me deep in my armpits till my own fingers came loose, and I went flying, the whole playground going blurry under me as I flew. I skittered across the asphalt and ground to a stop on bloody knees, my plaid skirt hiked around my waist so my underpants showed. I was screaming to Carol Sharp that her Jesus was a mewling dipshit (a phrase I'd picked up from one of Mother's less-than-Christian tirades) when Mrs. Hess picked me up by the waist and carried me wrangling and cussing back to her room.

I was given a box of crayons and plopped at a desk that faced a bulletin board of crayon drawings. Mrs. Hess instructed me to make something pretty by the end of recess. The pictures tacked over me pissed me off worse—a spotted butterfly settling in the middle of a daisy, a sailboat bobbing on neatly sloping blue waves, a smiling yellow sun.

I wore my black crayon down to the nub during that recess period, making a sky full of funnel clouds. Over and over I sharpened the point on the back of the box, then quickly made it dull again doing the narrowing spirals. It was a big piece of paper and shiny with black crayon before I was through. On a green hill in the background, I drew grave mounds in brown and topped them off with white crosses, each penciled with "R.I.P."

That truth—that death came in a big blind swipe—was gradually taking form in my head, picking up force and gaining motion like its own kind of storm. It was drawing me away from the other kids in a way I didn't even notice. They still saw the world as some playground smiled over by God. I couldn't, and their innocence rankled me to the point of fury. When Baptist girls standing next to me on the choir risers got all misty-eyed singing about the purple mountains' majesty, I would often elbow or jostle them out of nothing but spite. If they turned my way in outrage, I'd make a wide-eyed apology. I couldn't help myself. Sundays, when Carol Sharp came home from Bible school—her black hair pinched and shining in twin plastic barrettes, her petticoat sticking her pink skirt out sideways—and announced, while I was digging for worms in the flower box, how God had made me from dirt, I said I wasn't dirt, and I wasn't God's Barbie doll either. And why would God set Death loose among us like some wind-up robot destroyer if he loved us so much. Carol was ready for this. "There are some mysteries in life the Lord doesn't want us to understand," which serene declaration caused me to turn our garden hose on her full force. Something in me had died when Grandma had, and while I didn't miss her one iota, I keenly felt the loss of my own trust in the world's order.

Leechfield itself would make you think that way—the landscape, I mean. You needed to watch out for the natural world down there, to defend yourself against it. One fall morning I was crossing a meadow to a sugarcane field with a friend's family when the bird dogs that had been running alongside the men with rifles turned and went into a hard point right at one little girl's feet. Somebody's daddy told us all to freeze still, which we did. He took aim with his Winchester where this four-year-old was standing in her red Keds, scared enough to wet her pants. When he fired, a rattlesnake flew thirty feet up in the still air. It landed with a plop in the weeds, where the dogs fell on it. You might well start toting a rifle or shotgun around after that, for reasons that had nothing to do with other human beings. It's nature itself, revered in other climates, that's Leechfield's best advertisement for firearms. The woods held every species of poisonous snake, spider, and rabid biting creature available in that latitude.

Even at the beach, there were signs warning you to stay out of the eelgrass because of the alligators. The Gulf itself was warm as dishwater, and brown. There were stingrays and sea snakes under its surface. Shark attacks were not unheard-of, though nobody had been completely toted off by one in decades. The undertow could drag your ass to Cuba before you even knew you'd been sucked down.

And it was on this wretched strip of shore at McFadden Beach that we took a family day trip once Mother came back.

We'd no idea she was coming home that day. She had just walked in the back door one morning without so much as a howdy. Daddy said, Hello, Joe, can I get you some coffee? She just waggled her head in a loose way, like one of those dogs you see on a dashboard with a long spring for a neck. Lecia and I must have flung ourselves on her right off, because I remember Daddy telling us not to bird-dog her the minute she hit the door.

She sat down on a kitchen stool, and we plopped down on the linoleum at her feet. She was in her stocking feet, which was no surprise since she always said that driving would ruin a good pair of heels like nothing else. Anyway, there were little runs in the stockings, narrow black ladders starting up over her toes. I got to fiddling with one of these right off. I pulled it a little bit so the run got longer and skittered up her shin. Then I pulled a little more to make it creep up over her knee where it got wide. I said did that tickle, and she just patted my hand in an idle way. She still hadn't said word one. She was massaging her temples with her eyes closed.

Lecia started rubbing Mother's feet, which were as twisted up as any dancer's, knotty and callused from decades of high heels. (Lecia became an adult devotee of such heels. Once at a party in Boston, a loafer-wearing debutante suggested jokingly to her that if God had wanted women to wear heels, He wouldn't have designed our feet as He did. Lecia replied that if God hadn't intended us to wear heels, She wouldn't have made our legs look so great in them.) Lecia's rubbing put me in mind of somebody from the Bible. Then Daddy came over and started digging his thumbs deep into Mother's shoulder muscles. This made her head flop back. She must have felt like Gulliver being swarmed on by the little people. And, looking up from the floor, I thought she was way taller than I'd remembered. (Silence can make somebody bigger, I've come to believe. Grief can, too. A big sad silence emanating from someone can cause you to invest that person with all manner of gravitas.) There were pouches under her eyes that hadn't been there before, and streaks dried in her rouge from where she'd been crying on the drive home. But her lipstick was fresh and shiny and the color of a dark plum. She'd touched it up in the car, and that's the last thought I had before my memory fuzzed over.

The next day we went to the beach to cheer Mother up—a good plan, in theory. The only reports of Lubbock we'd been able to drag out of her were that the funeral had been sparsely attended, the trip out and back long. She'd spent the whole week alone or in the company of her mother's witchy sisters.

But really our family didn't excel at outings of any kind. Put us in close quarters—inside the un-air-conditioned Ford, say, in our bathing suits, with our legs sweat-stuck to the vinyl—and things got ugly. Toward the end of this particular drive, Lecia and I leaned like vampires over the backseat repeating "Mama-Daddy-Mama-Daddy" in unison, in a fast auctioneer's prattle, until Daddy's huge arm came swinging at us about neck level. We ducked down, and the car went surging over a sand dune. Then we slid down to McFadden Beach and the Gulf.

It was dusk. We always went then to miss the crowd, although the state of the shore would have kept most sane people away at any hour. There'd been some kind of hurricane back-tide or oil spill, so you could smell whole schools of dead fish stinking on the beach as soon as you got out of the car. You parked right on the sand, facing the waves. Daddy started unloading stuff out of the trunk.

Lecia and I raced down to the water, assuming Mother would be behind us. Having been reared in the desert, Mother could spend the better part of daylight sitting near the tide cross-legged, dribbling wet sand through her fingers to build up the squiggly turrets of a castle. She couldn't swim worth a damn but adored floating in an inner tube. She could lie back and doze for hours while the swells bobbed her up and down. But that day, she didn't even get her ankles wet. We got down to the water in our suits and started leaping over the shorebreak right off. Finally we spotted her back by the eelgrass dunes, walking away from the car. The sun was low on my right. I had to shade my eyes to make her out. She moved into a patch of pale sun and then out again. She turned into a shadow.

Then that shadow was climbing the weathered steps of a beer joint called the Breeze Inn. It was a little screened-in shack, really, high on spindly stilts. More than one storm had blown it over, but they kept propping it back up. Inside was a bar for the shrimpers and for fellows needing a bump of something to help them get through their family picnics. There was also a pinball machine, usually played by sunburnt kids looking pissed off and waiting for their daddies to finish the last swallow and come back to swimming or cooking hot dogs. I studied Mother while she walked up the steps of the Breeze Inn in her black bathing suit. She wore an old white shirt of Daddy's for a coverup. Like a lot of women with great legs, she had a way of tiptoeing along an invisible line, especially on stairs. It made her butt kind of prissy, and I remember that bothered me somehow, too. She was carrying a sketch pad the size of a small card table, like she was planning to draw the fishermen, but I knew with a cold certainty while I stood ankle-deep in that lukewarm water that she was climbing up there to get drunk.

Maybe that pissed me off, because all of a sudden, I wheeled around to Lecia and whooshed as much of the Gulf at her as I could move with two cupped hands. She tried to cover her face so her bangs wouldn't get wet, but she was pretty well soaked. She was giving me the finger for having done this when Daddy stepped out from behind the trunk of the car.

But instead of just letting her hand relax, so he wouldn't see her shooting the bird, she hid the whole hand behind her head, still frozen in the fuck-you position. She stood there like that for way longer than it might have taken her to relax her hand.

I can still see Daddy coming down the beach toward us. He

had his black swim trunks on, and black basketball Keds. He'd put on a red Lone Star baseball cap and was slipping into his blue work shirt while he came toward us. He had the easy glide of men who labor for an hourly wage, a walk that wastes no effort and refuses to rush. His barrel chest and legs were pale. There was a wide blood-colored scar up one shin where one of Lee Gleason's quarter horses had thrown Daddy, then dragged him around the corral till six inches of white shinbone was visible on that leg. On the same leg, just above the knee, there was a knot of iron-blue shrapnel bulging under the skin left over from the war. Still, he didn't limp one bit coming toward us. He had an amused squint on his face. Maybe he even knew that Lecia was hiding that fuck-you finger in back of her neck, and that tickled him.

He stood on the packed sand and called to us. "Y'all come on out from there. I want you to look at something." We followed him up the beach.

We passed what looked like the whole roof off a good-sized shed. There were also stinking loads of dead fish, a whole school of mullet all facing one direction and blank-eyed, looking like they'd leapt up all at once and the wave that had carried them had just evaporated before they came down. Daddy also took a minute to flip over a baby stingray with his shoe so we could see its face. It had wide-spaced eyes and a little slit of a mouth like something you'd cut out of pie dough.

About hollering distance from our car, we could see a dozen men spread out over the beach in a seining party. Basically, it's a poor man's fishing, seining, a good way to scoop fish out of the water with neither bait nor boat nor patience. All you need is eight or ten partners and a long net about four or five feet high. First, the seiners wade out to sea together in a pack. If you were watching and couldn't make out that somebody was carrying the rolled-up net, you might think it was a mass suicide or some weird form of baptism, because people tend to wade out in their clothes. They wear canvas shoes so their feet don't get cut, and blue jeans or light khakis so nothing can sting their legs. You catch the best stuff by heading a good ways out, past the little sandbars that keep the shorebreak choppy. Daddy always said you have to go as far offshore as you can without getting dragged off by the Gulf Stream heading for the Florida Keys. The water's liable to get neck-deep on somebody short, and guys seining hold their beer cans up out of the waves while they walk out. (These cans get chucked into the surf when empty, of course, with no *mea culpa* to the environment.) Once the men figure the water's verging on deep enough, they fan out from each other, unrolling the net while they do it, passing it hand to hand, till it's pretty straight. All told, it might be thirty or forty yards long. Then everybody just walks back to the beach real slow, each fellow hanging on to his hunk of net, which strains out whatever swims in its path. By the time they get back to the beach, the net's loaded with creatures and takes some work to get laid out flat on the sand. Then you walk along the net picking out whatever's fit to eat.

They must have been done with the seining for a while on that particular evening because by the time we got up level with them, I spotted a washtub of seawater cooking over a big fire back by their trucks. You could smell the crab-boil spices—onion and garlic and probably whole ropes of Mexican peppers. Down by the water, two of the guys carrying white bait buckets were stooping to untangle soft-shell crabs and shrimp. One of these, a crew-cut guy in camouflage pants, straightened up from the beach holding a little shark two or three feet long in his hands. He told somebody named Bucky to run get the Polaroid. This set somebody (Bucky presumably) loping back to the car. Then the shark-holding guy (who was wearing pink rubber gloves of the type grandmas use to wash dishes) asked Daddy if his girls wanted to see the hammerhead, and Daddy said sure.

I'd never seen a shark up close before, and what struck me was how chinless it was, its mouth drawn low down where its neck should have been. This gave it a deep, snaggle-toothed frown and kept it from looking very smart. Plus its whole body was one big muscle. It couldn't have weighed more than fifteen or twenty pounds, but the guy was having to fight to hold it, yelling over to Bucky to hurry. The shark, meanwhile, was thrashing from side to side in the air. Finally, Daddy helped the man pin the thing on the sand with his foot so Lecia and I could feel how rough its skin was. I rubbed it the wrong way (exactly, Daddy pointed out to me, as he had told me not to do) and it chafed the skin off my fingers like sandpaper. In the black-and-white picture from Bucky's Polaroid camera, Lecia is looking solemnly at the shark, which is blurred into a kind of swinging bludgeon in the fellow's gloved hands, and Daddy is grinning a little bit too hard, and I am studying my bloody fingers like they're some code I'm about to crack. What was on my mind was Mother vanishing up those steps to drink, taking herself Away. There's no picture of that worry, of course. I can only guess it from the crease in my forehead.

Farther down the beach, we hit a kelp bed full of dead men-of-war, which was what Daddy had wanted us to see. There were more of these tangled up in the brown ribbons of kelp than I'd ever seen in one place before. The storm had blown them in, and Daddy wanted us to look out for them. If you've never seen a man-of-war, it's something right out of science fiction. The head's a translucent globe about the size of a softball and full of air, so it floats on top of the water, clear in places, but full of sunset-type colors in others—royal blue and red-violet, the colors bleeding into each other. A bunch of men-of-war bobbing on a wave looks at a slant like water flowers—lily or lotus, even. The colors are that strong. You can poke the head with a finger and feel it give like a bubble-gum bubble. But the tentacles dangling down under the surface hold serious poison. They're fuchsia and grow yards long. They sway around where you can't see them just looking for a leg to wrap onto, or so Daddy told us that afternoon. We knew jellyfish better. They had short hard tentacles that stayed in one place. We'd both been stung by jellyfish, and it was about like a honeybee sting. Plus you could just pick one up by the head and pitch it away if it brushed against you. Daddy said that a man-of-war could wrap around you like an octopus, suck itself tight to your leg so no amount of pulling could unwrap it.

He said if we saw one of those bubbles on a wave, to clear out of the water, even if it looked like it was ten yards away. The tentacles could reach that far. They had little suckers that ran down each tentacle and could sting you through each one of those, a thousand times all at once, worse than a nest of hornets. The creature could kill a grown man if he had a weak heart or something. Daddy wasn't one for idle warnings, so we backed away from the kelp pretty quick.

Maybe by the time he had vanished up the steps of the Breeze Inn to keep Mother company Lecia had forgotten to be scared. We were horsing around in the water. If we had a cent's worth of caution in us that day, we spent it trying to stay lined up with the car, since even a light undertow could pull you sideways a mile down the beach before you knew it. Lecia was a ways out by this time, hip deep at least. I remember she dove into a brown wave just before it crested so the white soles of her feet disappeared in it. *Like the tailfin of a mermaid,* I remember thinking. After the wave broke, she bobbed up on the backside of it, behind the white water, her blond hair all slicked back like a seal's.

Maybe I hung on the sand because I remembered Daddy's warning. I do recall kicking around the shorebreak and wondering very specifically what Mother was drinking and how much. I yelled to Lecia did the Breeze Inn just serve beer. This was a big question, since Mother didn't even drink beer, not on her worst hungover morning. Lecia ignored me and twisted around to dive into the next swell. (The terrible thing about children—I'd like to mention here—is that they're so childish.) When Lecia surfaced again, I yelled again. This time I waved my hands to show how dire I was feeling about my question. I couldn't remember if the Breeze Inn sold mixers, in which case I wondered did Mother have her purse with her. A purse might hold a fifth of vodka. I could picture the giant sketch pad but no purse. Was that right? I hopped up and down and pointed back to the bar. Lecia drew her face down into a grimace that mocked my expression. She flapped her arms like a chicken. She turned and dove again. It was then that I started scanning around for something to chuck at her, nothing too hurtful really, a pebble or a light hunk of driftwood.

I spied a huge cabbage-head jellyfish on the sand. It was a dull white color. It looked like a free-floating brain knocked out of somebody's skull. I found a pole to pick it up, stabbing up under the hard white tentacles till it was pretty deep on the stick with its inner goop squooshing out. This was the perfect weapon to chase Lecia with, jellyfish being somehow like roaches in their ability to make her squeal. I stood in the shorebreak and brandished it like a head on a pole, holding it angled away from myself so none of the poison would get on me. She'd backed up into a big piece of chop. The white top of the wave slapped over her head and got her hair in her face. She must have had hair spray in it, because it stayed glued together in a kind of slab, and she started rubbing at her eyes with a fury. She was still rubbing with one hand when she started squealing.

At first I thought she was screaming to mock me. It was such a high-pitched squeal, like a little shoat hog might make. Then she danced up and down in the water, pumping her knees too high. I kept wielding the jellyfish on the pole at her. If anything, I was happy because I was really scaring her with it. I waded out a little closer to her. I wanted her to stop making fun of me so I could find out what kind of liquor license they had at the Breeze Inn. But of course she kept squealing. The slab of hair over her eyes shielded her face. But when she began swatting and slapping at her leg below the water, I backed up pretty quick. Maybe a braver child would have rushed to help her. I was not a braver child, though. I backed up slow, afraid if I took my eyes off her she might vanish below the surface in the jaws of some sea creature. After a while, I dropped the pole and ran as fast as I could to the bar.

It was a hard run in deep sand from the waterline to the steps of the Breeze Inn. My feet sank and couldn't get traction, like the run in a bad dream.

Mother and Daddy ran back with me all the way down to the beach, but once they got there, they seemed way too calm. I mean, neither of them lit a cigarette or anything, but it took a long time before either of them really did much.

The guy in the camouflage pants had dragged Lecia out of the water while I was fetching my parents. He was kneeling beside her with his pink grandma gloves on when we came up. Lecia sat on the sand with her legs straight out in front of her like some drugstore doll. She had stopped squealing. In fact, she had a glassy look, as if the leg with the man-of-war fastened to it belonged to some other girl. She wasn't even crying, though every now and then she sucked in air through her teeth like she hurt. The camouflaged guy with the pink gloves was trying to peel the tentacles off her, but it was clumsy work. Mother was looking at Daddy and saying what should they do. She said this over and over, and Daddy didn't appear to be listening.

I sat down hard on the sand next to Lecia. I was getting that tight, buckled-down feeling in my stomach like I'd had during the hurricane. I wrapped my arms around my knees, bowed my head, and prayed to a god I didn't trust a prayer that probably went like this: *Please let Lecia not die. Make Daddy think of something fast. Don't let them chop off her leg either.* . . . But all of a sudden, there was that humming noise again, running underneath the prayer like an electrical current in my head. I opened my eyes fast so it went away.

Daddy finally scouted around for a sharp shell and cut the head off the man-of-war and then popped it like an old balloon. But he saw quick that that didn't do any good. The tentacles stayed wrapped around Lecia's leg, which had started to swell up. Up near her hip joint the tentacles came together where the bubblehead had been. They fanned out down her leg all the way to the ankle. Where the guy with gloves had picked off a length, I could see tiny circle marks left behind where it had suctioned onto the flesh. The flesh was pulpy where these had been attached. There were perfectly circular blisters rising up. This wasn't supposed to happen with Daddy around, I thought. I recalled a story of Daddy's in which he'd stood drunk on this very beach with Jimmy Bent, the most badass Cajun in four counties. Jimmy had been drunk too, on Tennessee whiskey. It was a seining party. Girls in capri pants had been sitting along an old log they used for a bench. The girls were eating shellfish from the kettle of crab boil when Jimmy started shooting at Daddy's feet with a Colt .45, saying, "It take a strong man to dance in the sand." And Daddy saying back, "I'm a strong man, Jimmy," dancing, till one of their seining buddies got up behind Mr. Bent and cracked him on the skull with a stick. That story came back to me as proof of my daddy's omnipotence. People weren't supposed to get hurt with him around.

The next instant I can see, they've somehow gotten all the tentacles off, and there are bright red welts around Lecia's leg in a swirly pattern, like she's been switch-whipped with willow branches. Mother has dug a trench in the sand for the leg, and she is packing wet sand on it, trying to get the swelling down the way you would with a poultice or mustard plaster. The leg doesn't look much like a leg anymore. The skin is too tight and inflamed. It looks to me a little like the gray blood sausage Cajuns make called boudain. There are more people standing around—all the men from the seining party and a family, and the light is fading fast behind all their heads. The sky has gone gray, and the colors from everybody's clothes seem muted, like somebody has sprinkled us all with lime. Somebody gives Lecia a slug of Coca-Cola, and she spits it right back out. She's going pale all over, to match the leg.

In the next slide, dark finally comes. Daddy is talking off to the side with some lawman about what hospital to take Lecia to—High Island or Port Arthur: which is closer, which better. Somebody's had the idea of turning everybody's car headlights on us, so lights shoot at us from all kinds of crazy angles. I am kneeling right next to Lecia, holding her hand, but I don't want to look at her face. The last time I checked it out, it was the color of the moon that's starting up. Mother is washing that face with a little damp Wash'n Dri cloth she got out of a foil packet in her purse, and I can smell the antiseptic from that under the sea smell and the musty smell of vodka they've given Lecia mixed up with

Coke to help with the pain. Instead of looking at Lecia, I am paying big attention to the Gulf, which has moved farther away, breaking in long, electric-white lines in the dark.

Mother starts talking. She says the light in the breaking waves is caused by phosphorus. She is telling Lecia this like Lecia's listening. Mother's voice is very whispery and makes me want to go to sleep. There are, in salt water, she says, microscopic sea animals that get excited by the turmoil of water and so give off light when waves break. One night the three of us took off all our clothes—a phosphorus night like this—and went skinny-dipping. Daddy picked our clothes off the sand and laughed at us from his truck. "You crazy, woman," he yelled to Mother, but there was joy in it. Then the waves ate his voice, and I dove in and watched my whole body light up.

Probably I was falling asleep on somebody's lap, because that's what I see us doing. Mother and I are flying underwater like light-green phantoms. It reminds me of the Matisse painting that she'd razored out of one of her art books and taped up over the bathtub. In it the women dance nude in a circle. And we are like those huge women, fluid and pale, Mother and I. Ahead of us in the green water, I can see Lecia's pale white feet like the neon tailfin of a mermaid slipping away just out of reach.

I was sure in my sleep that Lecia was fixing to die, which is why, I guess, I slept so deeply. I had wished her dead a thousand times, even prayed for it, no less fiercely than I'd prayed for Grandma to die. Now God, who had done me the kindness of killing Grandma, was taking payment for that kindness by killing Lecia too, poisoning her in the leg with a man-of-war, all because I had chased her with a jellyfish, all because she had mocked me when I was scared. I was a child—three feet tall, flat broke, unemployed, barely literate, yet already accountable somehow for two deaths.

I don't remember the hospital at all. Lecia and Mother rode there in the highway patrol car, I guess, with Daddy and me following behind. I slept next to Daddy while he drove home. The car slipped off the shoulder at one point, so I jerked awake and saw all that blackness rushing by the window with the stars getting long and streaking away behind me. Then he said to lay down, that Lecia was in the backseat. He told me the old lie that everything was fine and just to lay down. And that's what I did.

The next morning I counted more than a hundred water blisters on Lecia's leg where the man-of-war had wrapped around it. She'd been ordered to stay in bed but seemed perfectly happy to lie there with her puffy leg propped on a pillow. I was so grateful she hadn't died that all day I played servant to her empress. I brought her chicken pie for lunch on Mother's bone china and spent my own money buying her peppermint swirls at the drugstore. I broke out the *Encyclopaedia Britannica* and read aloud to her about squids the length of battleships and massive shark attacks on shipwrecked sailors during World War II.

By the next day, she was charging neighbor kids a nickel to see her blisters, a dime to touch one, and a quarter to pop one with a straight pin we'd dunked in alcohol. Sometime during those transactions, she got mad at me and eventually got out of bed to stuff me once more into the dirty clothes hamper that pulled out from the bathroom wall. I heaved my body against the hamper to open it a slot, but the heavy lid fell back closed and mashed my fingers before I could get out. I wished her dead again, Lecia. I sat in the dark among the sandy towels and damp bathing suits for nearly an hour before she finally let me out. It seems Daddy had gone back to work, and Mother had gone to bed for the foreseeable future. There was no one else around.

CHAPTER 6

"I'll tell you just exactly how my daddy died," Daddy says. "He hung hisself." This is easily the biggest lie Daddy ever told—that I heard, anyway. His daddy is alive and well and sitting on his porch in Kirbyville with his bird dogs. I gawk at Daddy's audacity, while the men in the room shift around at his seriousness. They take this death as gospel. They twist around on their folding chairs like they would rather corkscrew holes in the floor and drop out of sight than hear about somebody's daddy hanging hisself. Daddy unfolds the blade of his pocketknife—dragging out their squirming for them—and cuts a circle from a log of pepperoni. He lifts it to his mouth on the blade edge, then chews. "This is kind of tough, ain't it?"

It's Christmas Eve morning in the back room of Fisher's Bait Shop. Daddy hasn't taken me to the Liars' Club in months, and this is their most special day. I am squirting Cheez Whiz in curlicues on saltines for all the men in hopes that Daddy will notice me helping and invite me back. I miss going places with him. I miss shooting pool and drinking free Cokes and hearing stories with lots of swear words. I've been sitting around all month watching cobwebs grow between my mother's fingers while she lays in bed reading and wishing herself dead. She doesn't say that, of course, but it's not hard to figure, even for somebody as dense as Lecia says I am half the time. Just being out of the house with Daddy like this at Fisher's lights me up enough for somebody to read by me.

The men meet here every year to swap and start consuming gift bottles of Jack Daniel's. This year's is white with a molded pheasant flying out of the brush. Four of these open bottles sit on the card-table corners. In the middle, there's a little battery-operated monkey Ben bought for his granddaughter. It holds two cymbals. When you turn it on, it bangs them together until you smack the top of its head. Then it bares its teeth and hisses at you. Daddy thinks this is funnier than fart jokes.

When he figures the men have gotten shifty enough to change the subject out from under him, he starts back talking. "I knowed they was something wrong with him the day I got back from the war. He was standing in the ditch in front of the house. Cutting grass with a sickle. I seen him a long ways off. Coming down the hill from the train, I was. Walking. And he seen me. But he just keeps swinging that sickle. That grass was about titty-high on him. In them days, the mosquitos would get up and breed in ditch grass like that. Just about eat you alive. Hell, I seen them kill a bull. Crawl up his nose and down his lungs and draw all his breath out."

"They didn't have no mosquito trucks back then," Shug says. "The sleeping sickness'd get started, and they wasn't hardly no ways to stop it."

"Not out in that country," Daddy says. "Maybe up in town."

Cooter clears his throat, and Ben scratches on the monkey's neck like he's a live kitty or something. Me, I just lay low and feel tickled to be in on how the story's a lie. I wait for Daddy to reel the other fellows in.

"I got up level with him on the road and said hey. He didn't say nothing. Just kept swinging that sickle. One side to the other, like a clock a-working. So I said hey again. 'Howdy-doo,' he said." Daddy squints into the middle distance like he's sizing the old man up, getting sized up in return. "He just looked at me. Serious as a heart attack. After a minute he says, 'I know we kinfolk. But I don't know how.' "

"He'd done got simple," Cooter says.

"That's exactly right," Daddy says. Cooter nods at the other men, and they nod back. "He didn't have no more idea who I was than he would her." He points a thumb at me, and I straighten up. I'm sitting on an upended bait bucket, lining up saltines with curlicues of Cheez Whiz into an army on a plate I've got balanced on my lap. I'm killing time till Ben turns that monkey on again. It's Christmas, and I want that monkey so bad I can taste it. It stares at me like a long-lost cousin.

"Did he ever figure it out?" Ben asks.

"He'd have times he come to," Daddy says. "His mind was broke down most days. Poor old thing. Couldn't see no further than here to that minnow tank." Over in the tank the minnows shiver in their black bodies like a whole school of commas facing us through the glass. Daddy laughs like he's remembering something. "That didn't keep him from driving that Jeep, though. 'Tom,' Beaver Bishop'd say to him. Beaver was near as old as Poppa. Been sheriff of Jasper County since I could remember." Daddy squirrels his mouth around into its Beaver Bishop shape, kind of pudgy-cheeked, like he had a jaw full of chew. " 'Tom, I don't want to catch you climbing up in that Jeep. You too old to be out on them roads.' Poppa would just shake his head. 'Beaver, them's my roads out there,' he'd say. Hell, that's what he thought. Him and those other men had cut them roads with the Indians and colored guys and every other kind of fellow. Chinamen, even. Back when the trees was so thick a cat couldn't sneak through. Beaver would go along with him a little bit. 'Tom, you know that, and I know that, but the state of Texas has a different idea.' "

"They can scare you out on them roads," Cooter says. "I got behind me an old fellow the other day going to Central Mall—" Ben fires him a look that would melt rubber, so Cooter puts a lid on it.

"Mr. Bishop took Poppa's license. You think that bothered

Poppa?" He gazes from man to man, as if they question him. "Hell, that little square of paper didn't mean him nothing. Not if he took it in his mind to get somewheres. Beaver finally had to come out one Sunday and have his boy take the tires off the Jeep. 'Miz Karr,' he said. 'You need to go to the store or something, we'll come up here and get you. But I can't cut that old man loose on them roads.' "

"How long he stay that ways?" Shug asks. He tips the bottle of whiskey into his paper cup. Everybody else does the same. Usually, Daddy likes questions, unless they're meant to hurry him, the way Shug's is now. Daddy takes a cracker from my army of saltines and I get to work on a new one to fill in the spot. He uses the chewing time for them to stop their bottles shifting around. If the Liars' Club men start a silence contest, Daddy will always hold the last silence in the deck.

"I guess it wagged on a year or so," he finally says. "Sometimes he knowed me. Sometimes not.

"That whole time he got so he'd climb up on things. Get up on the barn or shed. Whatever he could lean a ladder to. Said he wanted to get closer to the Lord. And he was a fool to sleepwalk. I'd hear him bumping around in the middle of the night. 'Pete!' Momma'd call me. 'Pete, there he goes again. You go catch him.' " The high voice he uses for his Momma voice doesn't sound like he's mocking her, like some fellows do when they talk like women. It sounds real. It has that determined, old-lady tremble to it. "He'd run just as straight up Highway 60 in his drawers, fast as he could go. And me flapping behind him in mine. First thing he'd do when he got up was to put his hat on. It was a tan-colored Stetson with a short brim. Many's the night I followed that hat bobbing up the road in front of me." Daddy can see he's losing them, so he puts the story into high gear. "Had it on the day he died."

"Now that's something," Cooter says, "to hang yourself wearing a hat." Cooter thinks he's found some kind of secret in the story.

"That's not the point, Cooter," Shug says. They sull up at each other a second—Cooter and Shug—like there might be words between them. Ben sees the mean looks they swap. He slaps the table hard with the flat of his palm so whiskey sloshes and the monkey tips over. "Goddammit. It's Christmas," Ben says. He sets the monkey back up straight, but doesn't turn it on. Everybody settles back into listening.

"I was sleeping out on the porch when I heard something up on the roof. A coon or something, I figured at first. So I drift back off. Pretty soon I heard the old lady get up. 'Pete, he's climbing again.' Sure enough, we go outside, and there he was on the peak of that roof. Looking up the branches of a old long-needled pine like he's got something treed in it. He looks down over the gutters at me with that old hat on his head and says, 'You tell him to git down first.' " Daddy jerks his thumb up at the top of that invisible pine tree.

"Who'd he think was up there?" Cooter says.

"Ain't no way to tell. Just somebody he thought up, I reckon. The old lady had gone in the house to get some honeycomb. She could coax him down with that pretty good. Most times. I got the ladder and started up. I just got high enough to make out the buttons on the back of his drawers and the sweat-stains around the band of that hat—they was a moon out—when Poppa started talking again." Daddy stares up at the light fixture where the moths flicker around. His face twists into a mask of his daddy's face. It's Cherokee Irish and mean as a snake: " 'Haul your goddamn feathered ass off my land. Boy, go git my gun.' And them's the last words he spoke. He stomped on a rotted beam and fell straight through the roof. So skinny he didn't even make a hole big enough for his head. Else he twisted going down. It caught him up under the jaws. And there he hung. Time I got up to him, he was gone. Just staring up the tree branches with his tongue all poked out. That silly-assed hat setting on his head." Daddy taps a Camel on the tabletop for punctuation. Tap tap tap. Those taps are his way of saying The End.

"That's sure a awful way to go," Ben says.

"Ain't no good way," Shug says. "Sorry you had to be there,

Pete. With you momma and all." Shug knows better than to look at Daddy when he's saying something this nice. There are shrugs all around, like saying something nice is water you have to rise out of and let slip off your shoulders.

What's rolling around in my head at this time is all the dying and near dying I've run into lately. I can picture Grandma the way I found her all slack-jawed in the bed, then Lecia glassy-eyed on the sand. For a minute, I even think about Mother propped up in her bed night and day next to a tower of books that only seems to get taller and more wobbly. Then it's her face slack-jawed I see in place of Grandma's, her arm hanging down that the ants are running on. I've plumb forgot where I am for an instant, which is how a good lie should take you. At the same time, I'm more where I was inside myself than before Daddy started talking, which is how lies can tell you the truth. I am eye-level to the card table, sitting on an upended bait bucket, safe in my daddy's shadow, and yet in my head I'm finding my mother stretched out dead.

Before I know it, out of my mouth comes a question I know is wrong even before I hear my own voice saying it. I ask Daddy what he thinks happens when you die.

This makes Shug shoot me a look. Ben gets sensitive about being Baptist. Daddy tends to tease about it. He even made up a little song that he sings in a whiny voice like he's playing the violin all squeaky: *Jesus, lover of my soul. / Pass me down the sugar bowl. . . .* When Daddy sings this, it pisses Ben off, but then Ben feels it isn't Baptist to get pissed off at somebody so clearly heathen. Instead, he'll suddenly remember he's got a haircut appointment, or needs to quick pick up a carton of milk. That remembering marks the end of the Liars' Club for the day. So we don't want to get Daddy going on heaven. That's why Shug is looking at me all long-faced.

Maybe that's why Ben finally flips the switch on the monkey's back, to change the subject. That monkey starts banging the cymbals, twitching his head side to side like he's saying No, No, No, No. Or like he wants to be sure we're all watching.

Which we are, except for Daddy. Daddy's flipped the top off his Zippo lighter, and he's lipping his Camel and studying that blue flame. "I know what happens when you die," he finally says when the cigarette's lit. "Done seen what happens. You lay down in a box, and they throw some dirt on you." That said, he reaches a muscled arm across the table and slaps that monkey on the head, so the animal bares its metal teeth and hisses at him. And Daddy bares his dentures and hisses back, blowing a long highway of smoke in the process. That's where the memory freezes, that instant with Daddy and that monkey gazing down either side of that smoky road at each other like it's somewhere they both have to get to.

Daddy never fessed up to the lie that I know. It stayed built between him and the other men like a fence he'd put up to keep them from knowing him better.

That winter Mother wouldn't have let a word about Grandma's dying ever pass her lips. She wouldn't get out of bed, seemingly hypnotized with whatever book she propped on her middle reading.

Sometime after New Year's, two bad things jump-started my parents into an evil stretch—drinking and fighting. Mother blames Daddy for this, and I suspect if Daddy had ever talked about such things, he could have argued that it all started with Mother. It's one of those chicken-and-egg problems. Daddy might have said Mother's drinking and mulligrubbing drove him out of the house. Mother said that Daddy just bailed out during Grandma's cancer and after the funeral, which absence set her to drinking. I don't know who or what to blame.

Nor can I figure what exactly led to Mother's near-fatal attack of Nervous. Maybe drinking caused Mother to go crazy, or maybe the craziness was just sort of standing in line to happen and the drinking actually staved it off a while. All I know is that first Mother was drinking, then she and Daddy were fighting worse than ever, and finally they were hauling her away in leather four-point restraints.

Drinking was not a totally new hobby in our house. Daddy

always drank, and with few ill effects that I can see. By *always,* I mean he drank every day. He kept a six-pack in the fridge. Plus there was a fifth of whiskey ratholed under the seat of his truck. You knew he was heading for a drink when he made the mysterious pronouncement that he was going out to check on his truck, the idea being—or so I thought for years—that it might be scared out in the garage by itself or lonely for him. That was just maintenance drinking, as I see it now, as opposed to drinking so's you'd notice. He could also sip at shots of Jack Daniel's pretty steady when he was shooting pool or throwing dice or playing cards, which activities he pursued whenever we needed school shoes or such. But drinking didn't change him much back then. Every now and then he'd come home lurching around like a train conductor, and I remember a few times dancing around the kitchen in my nightgown with my bare feet on his steel-toed boots, both of us sliding around in the yummy cloud of whiskey he was breathing. That was it, really. He never missed a day of work in forty-two years at the plant; never cried—on the morning after—that he felt some ax wedged in his forehead; never drew his belt from his pant loops to strap on us or got weepy over cowboy songs the way some guys down at the Legion did.

Mother was another story. She had set down the drink when Grandma came home to die, out of necessity, I guess. Then she picked it up the night she got back from the funeral while we were all rubbing on her. She'd said could I fetch her some Gallo wine and 7-UP from under the china cabinet (a combination she likened to sparkling burgundy), and I said sure. Then I walked as slowly and miserably as any mule through any cotton row in order to assemble that drink.

The wineglass had a dusty yellow scum on it. That's how long it had stood empty. I made a big show of scrubbing it off with a Brillo pad, then polishing the glass dry with a dish towel. If I thought anything at all, it was probably *This won't hold much wine, not sparkled with 7-UP.* Mother had always been a binge drunk, not touching a thimbleful for weeks or months when she'd gotten her gullet full. But once she took that first drink, she was off.

That night she got home, she kept it down to that eensy glass of wine, after which she tumbled naked into her oversized bed and slept for twelve hours.

But at some point after New Year's that wine made her hanker for alcohol of the high-test variety. Then, she dialed up the liquor store to order her vodka by the case, and she reached down the biggest jelly glass she could find in the cupboard. There was no need for ice or a measuring shot glass or even vermouth or those weird baby onions people who play at Gibsons make such a fuss about. The vodka was sloshed out in five-fingered units. Oddly enough, she hated the taste so much that she literally had to hold her nose to swallow the first one, like a kid taking medicine. But after that one, she downed them the way people in hell must down ice water.

The big game for me once she'd started drinking was to gauge which way her mood was running that I might steer her away from the related type of trouble. Hiding her car keys would keep her off the roads and, ergo, out of a wreck, for instance. Or I'd tie up the phone by having a running chat with the busy signal (seven-year-olds don't yet have any phone life to speak of), so she couldn't dial up any teachers or neighbors she was liable to bad-mouth. If I could thwart her first urges to call So-and-So or head down the highway to Yonder-a-place, eventually she'd get onto something else or just give up and pass out.

Lecia didn't have the stomach for watching her that close, I think. She put herself in charge of counting Mother's drinks. She kept a long-running tally of both the number of drinks poured and the approximate number of ounces consumed, which was no small feat if Daddy happened to be drinking too. And she did all the ciphering in her head, minus pen and paper, itself impressive. Having exact numbers always reassured Lecia no end. (When she got older and studied calculus, she even worked out a formula that factored into account the percentage of alcohol in various liquors—wine's only about fourteen percent alcohol, for example—as well as how much time had elapsed from the first drink, whether Mother had eaten, and how much she weighed. She'd then compare the outcome to that from another drinking bout in a way that sounded like this: "At Thanksgiving she was doing at least four ounces of eighty-six-proof alcohol per hour for four hours, and she weighed ten pounds less but was nowhere near this wild. Of course she'd eaten a lot. . . .") The numbers seemed beside the point to me. You just never knew what would happen once Mother uncorked that bottle. The difference between two drinks and ten might not even show. So while my technical-minded sister counted, I myself zeroed in on the lines of Mother's face and the timbre of her voice in hopes of divining the degree of Nervous she might get to.

One big tip-off to her mood came from what record she plopped on the turntable. If she was feeling high-minded, for example, she'd play opera.

Opera was a good sign, because she never really cruised for a plate-smashing fight with Daddy while listening to *Aïda* or *Carmen*. It made her remember New York, though, which had been the holy land of her youth and from which she felt exiled. (When I read about Napoleon defeated and shipped off to that squatty volcanic island, how he lay pouting for days in his bath about his lost empire, it put me in mind of Mother in Leechfield conjuring New York.) No sooner did the needle scratch down on an overture than she was back there. Going back usually brought her some relief. Her eyes would fog over, and her voice would go smoky. Then she took on that Yankee accent.

For some reason, I remember a particular night with *La Traviata* playing. The turntable was balanced in the window over the sink. Mother had on an old black turtleneck with little flecks of cadmium-yellow oil paint on the sleeves. She sat at the plywood bar in the kitchen, where Lecia and I were just finishing up crockery bowls of vanilla mellorine—a low-rent form of ice cream. Mother had tried to doctor the rubbery taste off the stuff with a chocolate topping she made from Baker's chocolate and butter and real vanilla.

The memory gets sharp when I pick up that Mexican vanilla bean she kept in a sort of glass test tube. I thought, *Everybody else's mom uses oleo. Oleo and that fake vanilla high school boys drink fast for a buzz.* I hold that cool-feeling tube in my hand and study the bean. I'm trying to guess where Mother got such a thing. In the background, she's telling Lecia about going to see Maria Callas at the Metropolitan Opera. The turntable plays "Parigi mi cara." The vanilla bean in the tube is reddish black and wrinkled up like the snaky root of something, or a bird's long claw. When I look past it, I see Mother's face wearing that thousand-yard stare out the back door. Her jaw is jutting out and held tight to keep her East Coast lockjaw accent going.

The back door she's staring through opens on a wet black night. You can smell banana from the tree she planted outside last summer (a plantain tree, really), and the thick sweet of honeysuckle. The cape jasmine bush has, for no reason at all, burst out these white waxy blooms. It's winter and the bush shouldn't be blooming at all.

Mother says the smell reminds her of the gardenia corsage she wore on her wrist that night she went to see Callas. She pulled up to the big fountain in a taxi behind a long black car with silver bud vases on the insides, next to the windows.

At this point, I pipe up that I've never seen a fountain, other than the water-drinking kind in school. And this whaps Mother loose from the memory for a second. She looks at me full in the face and asks is my childhood that deprived. Then Lecia says that I'm full of shit, that I've seen the fountain at the bank (the one high school kids are always putting soap bubbles in), and the other fountain at the Houston museum, not to mention umpteen-zillion fountains in books on Florentine architecture that Mother has dragged me through. Lecia says I'm just interrupting to hear myself talk and should shut up. And I say it's Lecia who's interrupting.

Mother finally sighs her stop-bickering sigh. For a minute she looks out the screen door at that big rectangle of semitropical night. We get quiet and watch her watching. Then the music surges a little, like a wave rising up, and she fades away from us, back into her Manhattan taxi outside the Metropolitan again.

She reminds us about the limo up ahead of her, and says that out of that limo comes a white satin high heel and the drapy tail end of a white sequined evening gown slipping under the hem of a coat that looked to her like sheared beaver dyed the color of cream. Then on top of that shoe and gown pours none other than Marlene Dietrich. (If Daddy had been present, he would have reminded us at length at this point that Dietrich had kissed him full on the mouth during a USO show. Hence my middle name: Marlene.) For a minute her eyes lock on Mother's through the glass before the autograph hounds swooped around. Mother said that the wind had blown Dietrich's white chiffon scarf over her mouth like a mask in that second, so at first all Mother could see was her red lipstick through the chiffon and her eyes peering out from above the scarf. "She had the loneliest eyes," Mother said.

Then she gets the idea of showing me how to charcoal my eyes like Dietrich did. She strikes a big kitchen match off the rough underside of the table. She picks up my ice cream bowl and holds it up high and lets the match burn for a minute on the bottom, so there's a gray smoke smudge on the crockery. Then she digs around in her pocketbook for the jar of Vaseline she always carries. She dabs a tiny sable brush in the Vaseline and swooshes it around in the soot on the bowl's bottom.

She takes my chin in her left hand. She tells me to tilt my head back and make my eyes sleepy. Then she starts tickling at my eyelid with that brush. She goes on to say that I have the prettiest eyelashes in the universe. This matters to Mother because she's only got lashes if she takes time to paste on false ones. "When I was pregnant with you, I didn't care what sex you were, or if you had all your fingers and toes. I prayed to God you'd have long eyelashes." She draws on her Salem for a minute, and we hang there in the smoke and the Shalimar and the vodka smell, waiting for her to exhale. She waves the smoke away from my face before she sets back to work on me, this time brushing at the hollow place above my eyeball in an arc. "My mother said God would send me a blue-headed baby with water on the brain for saying that kind of prayer. And I said, 'Then that baby will have pretty eyelashes,' and you did." This is also the first time she's said word one about Grandma since she came back. I try to cut my eyes over to Lecia to figure out what such a mention could mean.

But Lecia has Mother's compact in one hand and her mascara wand in the other. And I can see she's worrying the mascara onto her lashes. Lecia is easily as broke out in eyelashes as I am, but Mother said mine were prettiest. It's my face Mother's holding. (In fights Lecia and I have as grown-ups, she'll scream at me, "You were always so fucking cute!" And I'll scream back, "You were always so fucking competent!" Which sums up our respective jobs in the family.) Mother steers my chin away from trying to sneak a look at Lecia, then it's just Mother and me again. I can feel her breath in light puffs on my nose. She rears back and looks at me, then starts to smudge at what she's done with her thumb pad above my eyeball. She's painted oil portraits of us before. We've sat in our Sunday clothes on the raised model's platform in her studio, watching her step out from behind the easel and study us all cool-eyed, but this is different. This is up close. Her hands feel like kid gloves and she is working right on my face, like she's using all her attention to paint me right into being. (I am Marlene Dietrich. I am the cathedral wall on which the painter Giotto outlines an angel.)

The memory turns to smoke right there. It floats out the door over the cape jasmine. But there were a lot of nights that winter when Lecia and I sat watching Mother drink and hearing her grieve for New York.

She always told us about famous people, though she was all we wanted to hear about. Instead, she described the Ink Spots swaying over a silver microphone in some Harlem nightclub, and how Bing Crosby once smoked marijuana on somebody's penthouse terrace under a big, buttoned-up moon.

She liked to repeat a story about seeing Einstein lecture at Bell Labs (where she'd done some mechanical drawing in the war years—a detail it took us years to unearth). She swore that during the question period afterward, Einstein had to have some engineer in the auditorium explain an elementary law of mechanics to him. When the guy was shocked that the great physicist didn't know such a simple thing, Einstein said, "I never bother to remember anything I can look up." She loved that idea—a genius who couldn't open a can of tuna fish but could order the entire universe in the caverns of his own skull. She also said that he bowed his head between questions like he was praying, then raised it up to give answers like those mechanical swamis wearing turbans that guessed your future for a quarter at Coney Island. At the crowded reception after the lecture, she claimed that nobody even tried to talk to him. He sat in a straight chair in the corner by himself looking like somebody's daffy uncle.

The opera also tended to get Mother hauling out art books. I can still see them stacked on the plywood next to her Flintstone jelly jar of vodka, the gold names in square letters on the big leather spines: Picasso, Matisse, Van Gogh, Toulouse-Lautrec, Cézanne. (The pictures themselves were being seared into my head with all the intensity of childhood. When I stumbled on the actual paintings years later in museums, I often lapsed into that feeling you get when stepping inside your old grade school, of being tiny again in a huge and uncontrollable world—and yet the low-slung water fountains tell you that you're a giant now. Van Gogh's *Bedroom at Arles,* when I stood before it at eighteen, seemed ridiculously small, yet intensely familiar.)

Opera had a big downside, though. It could lead Mother straight into the worst sort of crying jag. Some Italian soprano would start caterwauling how she lived for art, or some tubercular female would rasp out (in Italian, of course) *Come to Paris and be my breath* to her old boyfriend, and Mother would go weepy. Her face would settle into a series of faint lines you normally didn't see on her. Then she would bawl like a sick cat, hanging her head in her hands, blowing her nose on toilet paper, and saying that we didn't understand, and that it wasn't our fault she was crying. Like we cared whose fault it was instead of just wanting it stopped.

Lecia didn't exactly figure out how to stop it. She did learn how to lower the volume on it, though. She would lead Mother to bed when she got too slobbering and miserable. I don't know how my sister knew to do this, but she moved with such certainty that Mother would often pad along behind her to that oceanic bed, where she'd collapse. Lecia would then rustle around in the pajama drawer, ignoring all the silky rivers of lingerie that I would have chosen in favor of some heavy flannel men's pajamas that felt like sleep itself. Then she'd get a pitcher of ice and a big glass for Mother's morning thirst, and a jar of orange baby aspirin for the headache.

Those were the opera nights. The jazz nights were a little worse, and worst of all were the nights when Daddy was home, and Mother put on the blues.

My birthday was such a night. Esther Phillips was moaning out "Misery" from the turntable: "Put no headstone on my grave. / All my life I been a slave. . . ." Those lyrics should have tipped me off to all that was coming. But Mother was baking me a lasagna, which smell I loved better than breath itself. I was also caught up playing with an old pair of army binoculars Daddy had given me that morning.

I stepped through the back screen door and held them up to my eyes. Through our fence slats, I could make out Mickey Heinz sitting on his fat knees next door, running his dump truck through the dirt. I could never see Mickey without a wince. I had once gotten him to smoke a cigarette made out of Nestlé's Quik we'd rolled up in tissue paper. It burnt his tongue. In fact, he'd blistered it so bad that he'd run to show it to his mother, not considering how she and all his people belonged to one of those no-drinking, no-smoking, no-dancing churches. Mrs. Heinz whipped his butt bad with a hairbrush. We listened to the whole thing squatting right underneath the Heinzes' bathroom window—the whap-whap of that plastic brush on Mickey's blubbery little ass, him howling like a banshee.

That January morning, I watched Mickey through my birthday binoculars. I was halfway thinking maybe I'd trot over to his yard and get him to hide his eyes for hide-and-seek, then just go home and watch him look for me till he started snubbing. I had almost talked myself into doing this when I heard Daddy's truck lunge into the garage.

I turned my glasses to the garage door and made out his big silver hard hat bobbing toward me. (Mercury's helmet always put me in mind of that hard hat, for some reason—minus the wings, of course.) "How's the birthday, Pokey?" he said. Then his hard hat left my field of vision. A second later his work boot scuffed the concrete step beside me. I lowered the glasses and looked up and said fine.

Except for the late-night visits he always made to double-tuck the covers under my chin, I hadn't seen him much that January. The union's contract with Gulf Oil had run out, and he'd been out on strike all month, along with everybody else in the county. When he wasn't walking the picket line, he went shrimping or duck hunting—anything to put food on the table. Nights, he hung out at the union hall waiting for any news about the talks to trickle back. Like Mother, he'd become the sort of stranger I longed for a glimpse of without ever expecting to see up close.

But that morning he'd given me the binoculars and a new Archie comic all wrapped up before he headed off to the line. The sweetness of it had drawn tears from some deep sour place way behind my eyes. "Shit, don't cry, Pokey," he said with a wry grin. He'd finally promised to come home for supper and cake that evening if I'd stop crying so's to break his heart.

Anyway, I'd been waiting on the back step the better part of the afternoon, holding back a floodgate of talk for him. When his shadow finally fell on me, I started to prattle about how I'd gone to Beaumont with Mother and Lecia that morning to buy my birthday dress.

It was a black crepe dress—the first black dress I'd owned. Just sitting in it made me feel like a movie star, I'd told him. We'd had hell finding a kid's dress in black. But Mother had driven us all over the county. (Finding that dress, in fact, was about the first event other than an occasional meal that she'd gotten up for since coming back from the funeral.) We'd at last settled on an

A-line dress that had a big white clown collar hanging all loose and drapy, with three bona fide rhinestone buttons down the front. The dress had been "cut on the bias," according to the saleslady. Lecia took one look and said where's the funeral, but I was already prissing in front of the three-part mirror. When I spun around, both dress and collar fanned out sideways in fluttery ripples. Mother thought I looked like the ballet dancer in my Japanese music box. She rolled her eyes and said, "What the hell," when she handed the saleslady her charge plate. Not ten minutes later, she'd also bought Lecia a chemistry set from the toy department. On the way home, we'd stopped for shrimp rémoulade at Al's Seafood, where Mother made quick work of two vodka martinis, to celebrate.

Daddy said the dress looked pretty while he wiped his feet. But he wasn't even looking my way. He was being double-careful to worry all the mud off his boots and onto the black welcome mat. Then he slipped into the house.

Suddenly it dawned on me that I wasn't supposed to tell Daddy we'd charged stuff on Mother's plates—the shrimp and the chemistry set and all, not to mention my dress, which cost sixty-three dollars. Nobody said it was secret. But he wasn't drawing any pay, a fact he harped on more or less constantly. The image of him thumping the morning paper and talking about how Gulf Oil was trying to chicken-shit the working man out of a decent meal came to me. Not two days before he'd taken a box of canned goods and our outgrown clothes to the union hall. Kids in the big Catholic families were going hungry, he'd said. It didn't take a rocket scientist to figure out that what we'd done that day—Mother, Lecia, and I—crossed some unspoken line between good times and bad behavior. I also knew that the black dress I had on crossed another line between an outfit and a get-up. I felt like a witch in church. And I kept feeling that way till the black dress was dangling on its hanger, and I was back in blue jeans.

Later, I was on the rug undressing Barbie for the umpteenth time when my parents' mad voices floated back to me. Lecia was next to me, trying to pin her Barbie's straw-colored hair into a

French twist with a bobby pin. I couldn't make out the words but the gist was plain. Mother roared and slammed kitchen cupboards. The screen banging closed finally signaled Daddy's walking out. By this time, Daddy had adopted that mean dog Nipper, and he came out from under the house, yipping and lunging against his chain. Daddy's boots scuffed down the steps. The screen banged again, and I heard what I quickly figured out was the glass lasagna casserole shattering on the patio after him. "It's her birthday, you sonofabitch," Mother yelled. Lecia just wound that French twist into a tight coil and said, "Tape Ten, Reel One Thousand: Happy Goddamn Birthday."

Out in the kitchen, Mother stood at the sink, holding both wrists under running water. You could see a big splotch of red under her sharp cheekbone, like somebody had dabbed mad on her face with a paintbrush. "You want some aspirin?" she said to me, and I said no, thanks. Outside, Nipper was going yip yip yip. Mother tossed a handful of baby aspirin in her mouth, then dipped her head under the faucet to wash them down. She took the German chocolate cake down from the top of the fridge. "We can have this cake for supper," she said. Lecia came in, bringing a warm space up close behind me. I told Mother that she could take the dress back, it was no big deal. "No I can't," she said. Then she started planting candles in the muddy top of the cake. The house still smelled of lasagna and of the fresh coconut she'd split and carved and grated for the cake. "Forget about the dress, for Christ's sake," she said.

I went outside, where Mickey was still visible in slices through the fence slats. He was sitting in the dirt like a plaster lawn figurine. He'd heard it all, of course. You could count on Mickey to run tattling to the whole neighborhood that Mother had called Daddy an SOB. I took a minute to wish his kneeling figure harm before picking my way around the glass and splattered lasagna.

In the garage, I could at first see the ruby end of Daddy's cigarette and nothing else. After a second, my eyes adjusted. Then I could make out his white T-shirt and the glint of the bottle he lifted to his lips. "Daddy?" I said.

"Just go in the house," he said. The cigarette brightened for a moment as he drew on it. "It don't make a shit," he said. Then a minute later, "I'm sorry."

"It's okay." Outside the locusts started whirring in their husks. That was the only sound till I heard somewhere in the high trees outside what I took for a bat screech. "That a bat?"

"Go in the house, Pokey," he said. Then he said, almost like an afterthought, "Why don't you go on in and ask your mother if she wants to head over to Bridge City for some barbecue crabs."

Back in the house, the shattered lasagna dish sat in a dustpan on the sink's edge. Mother was touching the last match to the last candle when I came in. The black fan sweeping past us made the candles fade and brighten on her face. Lecia's face next to hers was as blank as a shovel. She said, go on and make a wish, you little turd. I squinted my eyes as hard as I could and wished silently to go and live some other where forever, with a brand-new family like on *Leave It to Beaver*. Then I sucked up as much air as I could get and blew the whole house dark.

I don't remember our family driving across the Orange Bridge to get to the Bridge City café that evening. Nor do I remember eating the barbecued crabs, which is a shame, since I love those crabs for their sweet grease and liquid-smoke taste. I don't remember how much Mother drank in that bayou café, where you could walk to the end of the dock after dinner and toss your leftover hush puppies to hungry alligators.

My memory comes back into focus when we're drawing close to the Orange Bridge on the way home. From my spot in the backseat, I can see a sliver of Daddy's hatchet-shaped profile—his hawk-beak nose and square jaw. Some headlights glide over him and then spill onto me. I want to see Mother's face, to see which way her mood is drifting after all the wine. But I'm staring at the back of her head in its short, wild tangle of auburn curls.

All at once, the car rears back the way a horse does underneath you if it shies away from a small, skittery animal on the road, and we're climbing up the bridge. The steel webbing of the road sets the tires humming. That matches up just right with that humming in my head left over from the hurricane day. The night streams over the car and fans away like black water. I can almost feel a long wake of dark dragged out behind us. Sometime during this ride, the car has filled up with that musky snake smell from Grandma's old room, a smell I hadn't even noticed had been gone from our lives till it flooded back. Lecia rolls down the window, maybe to get the stink out. Her hair is spronging loose from its French twist. The wind's about to suck me out that window and over the bridge rail. The rushing sound marries with the tires humming till a big rocket fills the small car space and makes me feel little.

I muster all my courage to look out my window at the long drop down. It makes my stomach lurch. The steel girders jerk by my window in a fast staccato. In the distance, I can see two flaming refinery towers. They make a weird Oz-like glow that bleeds up the whole bottom part of the sky. It's a chemical-green light the color of bread mold, rising up the night sky like a bad water stain climbing wallpaper. Out beyond the river there are marshes and bayous. A black barge moves slow under the bridge.

Mother is shouting, shouting she wished herself dead before she'd ever married Daddy. She wished she'd been struck by lightning on this very bridge before she crossed over into that goddamn bog. Leechfield is the asshole of the universe, the great Nowhere. And Daddy is a great Nothing. I feel over for Lecia's hand, and it's a cold fist knotted shut. I set it down the way you'd put down a glass of water you don't want to spill.

Then out of all the darkness I see Mother's white hands rising from her lap like they were powered and lit from inside. Like all the light in the world has been poured out to shape those hands. She's reaching over for the steering wheel, locking onto it with her knuckles tight. The car jumps to the side and skips up onto the sidewalk. She's trying to take us over the edge. There's no doubt this time. I mash my eyes closed, and Lecia heaves herself over on top of me. Both of us topple down in the backseat well, so I can't see anything, but I can feel the car swerve while Mother and Daddy wrestle for the wheel.

Then there's a loud noise in the front seat like a branch cracking, after which the car goes steady again. I can almost feel the tires click back in between the yellow lines. The rearview mirror got knocked long-ways when they were wrestling, I guess. So when Lecia and I crane up from the backseat, our two scared faces float in it. We look like sea creatures coming up from the fathoms.

Amazingly enough, the car is off the bridge and back on the road, safe. Mother's lying slack-jawed against her window where Daddy has socked her to get control of it. He's never hit her before, and the punch came from a very short distance, but she's down for the count.

When she wakes up, we'll be pulling into our driveway. She'll rake her fingernails all the way down Daddy's cheek, drawing deep blood so he looks for days like some leopard's paw has gone at him. The kids playing night tag in the Heinzes' yard will stop their game to gather at our property line and watch us spill out of the car, Mother still trying to claw Daddy, Daddy holding her wrists in his iron hands. At some point, Joe Dillard will sidle over to ask me what they're fighting about, and his brother will crack that they're fighting over a bottle. That's the last thing I remember anybody saying, Junior Dillard in his wise-assed voice saying, "Probably fighting over a bottle." Then Mother breaks loose from Daddy to stamp her foot at the group of kids, and they scatter like buckshot into their own dark yards. And that's it, that's what I remember about my birthday.

CHAPTER 7

Grandma wound up leaving Mother a big pile of money, which didn't do us a lick of good, though Lord knows we needed it. Daddy's strike had dragged on till mid-March, pulling us way down in our bill-paying. He managed to keep up with the mortgage and utilities okay, but the grocery and drug bills and other sundries got out from under him. When he picked up his check at the paymaster's window on Fridays, he cashed it right there. Then he'd drive to Leechfield Pharmacy and go straight up to the pill counter in back to tell Mr. Juarez—kids called him Bugsy, after the cartoon bunny—that he'd come to pay at his bill. I can still see Daddy winking while he said it, *at.* He'd squint down at his billfold and lick his thumb and make a show of picking out a single crisp five-dollar bill and squaring it up on the counter between them. But that little "at" held back a whole tide of shame. It implied the bill weighed more than Daddy, superseded him in a way. In Jasper County, where he'd been raised, buying on credit was a sure sign of a man overreaching what he was. Even car loans were unheard-of, and folks were known to set down whole laundry sacks stuffed with one-dollar bills when it came time to pick up a new Jeep or tractor.

Bugsy knew these things. They mattered to him. He was a

kind guy, prone to giving me comic books for free because it tickled him that I read so well. He always acted like he hated to take Daddy's money when it slid his way. "Heck, Pete. Put that back. We weren't a-waiting on this," he'd say, and Daddy would slide the bill closer and tell him to go on and take it. Then Bugsy would shrug out an okay. He'd ring some zeros up on the cash register and slip the bill into the right stack. He kept his accounts in a green book under the counter. He'd haul that out, find Daddy's name with his thick nicotine-stained finger, and note down the payment. Before we left, Bugsy usually led me to the back office, where he'd draw out his pocket knife to cut the binding cord on the new stack of funny books invariably standing in the corner. I'd sit on his desk and read out loud an entire issue of *Superman* or *Archie,* which skill caused him to smile into his coffee mug. Daddy would shake his head at this and say that I didn't need egging on because I had already gotten too big for my britches as it was.

That was the dance we went through with Bugsy on payday. The movements of it were both so exact and so fiercely casual that I never for a minute doubted that this whole money thing was, in fact, not casual at all, but serious as a stone. All the rest of the week, nobody talked about it. That silence slid over our house like a cold iron. But woe be it to you if you didn't finish your bowl of black-eyed peas, or if you failed to shut the icebox door flush so that it leaked cold and thereby ran up the electric. Daddy would come up behind you and shove that door all the way to or scoop the last peas into his own mouth with your very spoon. After doing so, he'd stare at you from the side of his face as if holding down a wealth of pissed-off over your evil wastefulness.

Evenings he wasn't working, he sat in bed to study his receipts and bills. He liked to spread out the old ones stamped PAID along the left side of the bedcovers. The new statements still in their envelopes ran along the right. He'd worked out a whole ritual to handle those bills. When one hit the mailbox, he slit it open, then marked down what he owed over the front address window where his name showed through. That way he sort of nodded at the debt right off, like he was saying *I know, I know.* Plus, he then didn't have to reopen and unfold every bill in order to worry over it. With all those envelopes staggered out in front of him, he drew hard on bottle after bottle of Lone Star beer and ciphered what he owed down the long margins of *The Leechfield Gazette,* all the time not saying boo about one dime of it.

I knew full well that people had way bigger problems than those Daddy had. Lots of guys didn't have jobs and houses at all. Or they had kids fall slobbering sick with leukemia, not to mention the umpteen-zillion people who were born in the Kalahari Desert or the streets of Calcutta blind or missing limbs or half-rotted-up as lepers. But Daddy's nightly cipherings were the most concentrated form of worry I've ever witnessed up close. That long line of numbers, done in his slanty, spidery scrawl, was not unlike the prayer that the penitent says over and over so that either the hope of that prayer or the full misery of what it's supposed to stave off will finally sink in.

Meanwhile, Mother was either laid up next to him slugging vodka from an aluminum green tumbler and reading, say, Leo Tolstoy (*Anna Karenina* was her favorite book) or else crying along with some Bessie Smith record. There was no more commerce between them than if a brick wall had run the length of that giant bed. Lecia and I tended to sprawl at the foot of it nights faking that we were doing the homework we both usually finished at school. We stayed there to keep an eye on all their worry, fearing it might somehow rise up above what they could handle and spill over us.

The mood in our house was tenser than when Grandma came to rot in the back bedroom. We'd gone back to our version of "normal." But our family habits seemed odder than ever, warped somehow by the judgment that Grandma's death implied and by Mother's sick, unspoken grief about it.

That spring Mother started walking around the house again buck naked. Daddy wore nothing but boxers, and Lecia and I alternately went flapping through the house either bare-assed when Daddy wasn't home, or wearing some combo of pajama tops and underpants (we called them *undersancies*) when he was. Don't get me wrong. We hadn't turned "naturist," though Mother did once shock the Leechfield PTA Mothers' Circle by claiming to have played volleyball on some nude beach in New Jersey. (That was the last time my school formally invited her anywhere; after that she occasionally gate-crashed the Christmas play, but otherwise was a vapor trail at school functions.) Lecia and I did earn nickels selling peeks at Mother's nudist cartoons from her *New Yorker* anthology. (We saved the art books for kids who could cough up as much as a quarter for a long stare at a Bosch painting with lots of skinny demons and some large-breasted matron being poked with sticks.)

Our staying undressed came from insomnia. As a family, we just couldn't sleep. From this state of constant, miserable exhaustion, we took up the hazy idea that sleep might come more often—it only arrived in spurts—if we were dressed for it, or, rather, undressed. Our bare bodies were walking invitations to any nap that might claim one of us. You could stagger into the living room most mornings and find one of our bodies sprawled asleep on the floorboards alongside the couch. Or you could come out at two A.M. and find Mother at the stove with her apron strings tied in a neat bow above her round butt as she worked on a Western omelet, while in the living room Lecia sat cross-legged in underpants slapping down cards for solitaire in front of the TV test pattern. We never came together in those hours, just wandered all over the house in various stages of neckedness.

In fact, the only time Mother got out of bed for any length of time that spring was to seal our windows off from the neighbors' view. One Sunday when I was hanging naked from the sturdy cast-iron rod over my window—Lecia and I were having a chin-up contest—I saw the Dillards' royal blue truck wheel slowly past carrying the whole gaggle of Dillards. They stared openmouthed at my hairless, dangling form. It startled me so I just hung there in full view a second, my nipples getting hard against the cold glass, before I got the wherewithal to drop from view. Then I crouched under the window ledge thinking how danged unfair it was: nobody on the block *ever* got up and out that early but us. Mrs. Dillard and Fay were in the truck cab with their black mantillas on like they were heading to six A.M. mass. Even Junior and Joe had been stuck into white shirts with clip-on bow ties. They squatted on the flatbed's built-in toolbox. Their two blond heads were slicked flat with Butch Rose Wax. I could hear their laughing over the truck's rumbling muffler.

When Mother heard Lecia tease me about it in the kitchen, she decided to get out of bed. She threw the bedcovers off her legs, a gesture we'd all but deleted from our memory banks, and said it was a lot of horseshit caring if people saw you naked because we were all naked under our clothes anyway, but goddamn if she'd listen to me caterwaul about those boneheaded Dillards anymore. She was gonna seal over the windows so God Herself (she made a point of the female pronoun) couldn't see in.

Her method for this was wacky. First, she took a cheese grater and made crayon shavings in all different colors. She sprinkled these between sheets of wax paper and ironed the paper together till the crayon melted. With sable brushes and Elmer's glue, Lecia and I set to work pasting these squares of paper and color over all extant windows, an effect Mother likened to stained glass.

It was Mother's first enthusiasm in a long time, and we pounced on it. Lecia started racing with herself right off. She timed the process to see how fast she could paste over a whole window, then tried to beat that time.

Not long after we blanked out the windows, I came home from school and found the front door open and the screen ajar. That was weird, not only given our fierce need for privacy, but on account of all the roaches and june bugs, lizards and mosquitoes down there. The semitropical climate could also send a spotty green-black mildew climbing your whitewashed walls if the full damp of the outdoors somehow got inside. You couldn't stop it entirely, but nobody left the door wide to it.

In my head, I go back to that open door. My penny loafers outside it are the color of oxblood and scuffed and run down on the inside from how pigeon-toed I am. I can almost feel the thump of my plaid book satchel on my right hip.

It was hot that day, the air thick as gauze. I bounded up the front steps after school having just gotten 100 on my spelling test. That grade barely beat out my class rival for the best grade, Peggy Fontenot, who'd lost two points for misspelling "said." I'd personally graded her paper, and my heart leapt up like a roe when I saw it spelled "sed." I had the winning test in my hand with the gold star that said my grade was highest. I raced up the concrete steps, even stopping short at the open screen before I slammed inside hollering I was home. I slung my book satchel over the sofa back and called again for Mother.

The silence that came back was even heavier than the air outside. It lay across the coarse rugs like swamp gas. Maybe that quiet somehow kick-started my fretting. Maybe then I paused to consider the oddness of that open door. I ran into the kitchen with the test still in hand looking to show it to Mother. There was only the black fan sweeping a dull little wind over a cup of cold coffee. No other sign. Back in the living room, I found the last page of the letter from Grandma's lawyer folded into about a dozen accordion pleats the way a kid would make a paper fan. Mother must have sat on the horsehair sofa using that fan to push a breeze across her face before dropping it there. I smoothed it out.

The oddest details from that letter have stayed with me, while other things—such as the exact amount of Mother's inheritance—have been sucked up into the void. Maybe the number was too large for my small skull to hold, being in the hundreds of thousands. (The figure also varies with Mother's telling, from "only $100,000" to "over half a million" depending on the point she's trying to make with the story. To this day, if pressed to give us the exact number, she presents a kind of walleyed expression with a loose-shouldered shrug that suggests such sums of money must be taken in stride, give or take a hundred thousand.) The stationery was thick and butter-colored. The page number was "6 of 6." The lawyer promised to wire $36,000—

about four times what Daddy could make in a year before overtime—from the sale of Grandma's Lubbock house and farm to the Leechfield Bank, to thus-and-such an account number. We'd all expected that money. What this letter went on to describe that I didn't expect was the money from a new oil lease.

Apparently, Grandma hung on to the mineral rights for her land, keeping them in her name more from habit than any real hope of drilling oil there. Enough Dust Bowl crackers and dirt farmers out that way had sold their farms at fifty cents per acre one week only to watch a gusher spout all over the buyer's Cadillac the next for a faint dream of oil money to lie embedded in every West Texan's brainpan. You just did not sell mineral rights outright, ever. You held them. Even I knew that. You leased them for huge sums. (To my knowledge we still hold drilling rights on that land, though every inch of it has long since been proven bone-dry to the earth's core.) Anyway, it turned out that loads of would-be drillers had hounded Grandma for two decades to start poking holes in her stretch of desert. We never quite figured out her reasons for snubbing their offers. In one letter I found later, the old woman had explained to Mother that she was in the cotton business, not the petroleum business. Maybe she'd worried about getting bilked by some silver-tongued oil-company fellow, which bilking wouldn't befit her status as a prudent Methodist widow-lady and lifetime member of the Eastern Star. Somewhere in her effects, however, Mother's lawyer had found a letter from a Dallas oil baron. With Mother's permission, the lawyer would "execute an oil lease" for this guy. That was the exact phrase. I also recall moving my index finger along a string of five zeros, but I'm damned if I can conjure the exact amount the letter laid out. There was a lot of other stuff, of course, but I just remember my index finger stumping from one zero to the next. I counted till it hit me that we were in the hundred-thousand-dollar range, just one zero shy of the million mark, that magic number that sent dollar signs flying through movie montages. *Here,* I doubtless thought, *is the spotted pony I've run out looking for every Christmas morning. Here's a garnet birthstone ring from the baby Ferris wheel in*

Gibson's Jewelry. And since I lacked for charity, I also probably had an idea like the following: *Maybe I can get to Disneyland and that lard-ass Peggy Fontenot can go screw.*

I ran through the house again then, calling out for Mother. What I found in her bathroom knocked the wind slap out of me. The big rectangular mirror over the sink had been scribbled up with lipstick of an orangey-red color. Somebody—Mother no doubt—had taken a tube of Mango Fandango or Kiss-Me Peach and scribbled that mirror almost solid, so the silver reflecting part came through only in streaks. In the sink there was a stub end of greasy lipstick. On the floor the empty gold tube lay like a spent shell casing on the fuzzy oval of yellow rug. I shied around it as I would a scorpion. A thin filter of fear came to slide between me and the world. Objects in the house started to get larger and more fluid. A standing lamp reared up at me as I came on it.

In Mother's bedroom, on the dresser mirror, I found the same lipstick scribbles done in hibiscus. The metal O of the tube had sawed through the silver surface. Other mirrors in other rooms held other lipstick colors—blue reds and mauves and pale titty-colored pinks, and that scary lipstick the color of muddy blood that Mother hardly ever wore because it made her look as pale and black-lipped as a silent-film star.

I went from mirror to scrawled-up mirror till I found the shattered one in our bathroom, which I imagined she'd gotten to last. A round smashed place in the center was about the diameter of her fist. Her face must have been floating in that exact spot when she broke it. The broken place itself was like a cyclone with whirled shatterings in the center and longer spikes radiating out. She must have watched the planes of her own angular face come apart like a cubist portrait. I backed away from the brokenness of it, giving the sink and the smatterings of glass on the floor wide berth.

I slammed outside and ran down the back steps, praying to God that the black spume of chimney smoke from the tin spout on the garage roof meant that I'd find Mother in her studio painting. If her car was missing, I knew I'd never see her again. I had no trouble picturing that car careening around a curve and then slamming into some concrete embankment. I could also see Mother slumped over the wheel with a picturesque trickle of blood coming from one ear. Surely she wanted to be stopped in her tracks that day. I prayed to find that car sitting in the garage, and I did; its headlights looked heavy-lidded and sleepy, like the car was some bored reptile squatting down over its own four tires.

The door from the garage to Mother's painting studio was open. The padlock was unlatched, and her silver key ring shaped like a longhorn steer and inlaid with turquoise still hung down from it. Mother sat in her mother's old rocker with her back to me. She was laying papers on a fire in the cast-iron stove. The white edges charred black and curled in. I knew not to speak. Above her on the wall, that big portrait of Grandma looked down, her stiff arms at perfect right angles. Mother had moved that portrait from the living room after the funeral, leaving the wall blank. It scared me to see Grandma Moore there gazing down at her.

There was a strange odor in the studio that day. On top of the regular head-opening sting of turpentine and oil paints, I made out either lighter fluid or the charcoal starter Daddy always used to fire up the Weber grill. In fact, after I hit the doorway, Mother reached down for a can next to the rocker and squirted clear fluid from it so there was a whoosh. Flames licked out the stove front before settling back into their low rumble. (Later on, I'd find a brown scorch spot on the vaulted ceiling. I also later figured that she was feeding the stove with all the mail that had come addressed to Grandma since her death—bank statements and seed catalogues and get-well cards from the Lubbock Methodist Church Ladies' Auxiliary.)

Anyway, Mother's back to me in that rocker conjured that old Alfred Hitchcock movie *Psycho* she'd taken us to in 1960. In the end, the crazy killer was got up like his nutty old mother with a gray wig. He rocked in her personal chair. Mother turned around slow to face me like old Tony Perkins. Her face came into my head one sharp frame at a time. I finally saw in these instants that Mother's own face had been all scribbled up with that mud-colored lipstick. *She was trying to scrub herself out,* I thought. Sure enough, the scribbles weren't like those on an African mask or like a kid's war paint. They didn't involve the underlying face that much. They lacked form. No neat triangles or straight lines went along the planes on the face. She looked genuinely crazy sitting in her mother's rocker with the neatly ruffled blue calico cushions in front of that blazing stove with the smell of charcoal fluid and her own face all scrawled up bloody red.

Then we're in the lavender bedroom I share with Lecia. The sun is going down, so there's a vine pattern through the wax-papered windows, the shadows of wisteria and honeysuckle. Mother stands before this lit window over a cardboard box by our open closet. She picks up toys one at a time off the closet floor and flings them into the box. We have left our room a mess, she says in a hoarse voice I don't think of as hers. But that's the only voice she has left, her drunk Yankee one. *I want to be a good hausfrau,* she says, which word I didn't even know meant *housewife,* but I fear the hard German hiss of it. Hausfrau. *That's my job. That's what I am—the wife of this fucking crackerbox house.* And into the box fly the one-armed Barbies and fistfuls of checkers and marbles and plastic soldiers and metal cars and board games and the marble chess pieces—all hitting the cardboard with a sound like splattering rain.

Once the closet's bare, she yanks off our bedcovers and sails them through the room. She drags our mattress on the floor, then lifts our bare box spring over her head. She looks like Samson in Bible pictures with one of those big stone pillars bench-pressed up when she heaves it. It hits the wall with a deep-throated clang at once primitive and musical. That's what starts me crying for the only time that night. I duck my head and bury it in the armpit of Lecia's bleached white PJs.

Next I can see, we are out behind the garage in front of a huge pile of toys and Golden Books and furniture heaped in a tall pyramid. I have been to football bonfires and beach-side pit barbecues with whole calves roasting on spits. Becky Hebert even once took me to a fish fry hosted by the Ku Klux Klan, where they were burning schoolbooks and drugstore romances in a pile higher than any of the houses around. This stack is almost as high as that. It's taller than Daddy, who's six feet in his socks.

I zero in on my old red wooden rocking horse. He stands not ten feet from me. He hangs all saggy now from his metal frame by these rusted springs. Mother is pouring gas out of the red can onto him, and he looks sullen underneath.

When she takes up the big box of safety matches, she waves Lecia and me back with a broad sweep of her arm, like she's about to do some circus trick. I start to stand so I can jump and catch her arm before she lights that match. But Lecia's hand clamps on both my shoulders to stop my rising. She shoves me back down onto the ground. I feel my legs buckle under me like they're the legs of some different girl, or even like the cold steel legs of one of those lawn chairs just folding up on itself. I sit down hard on the wet St. Augustine grass, the blades of which are stiff as plastic. That's my horse getting doused by the upended gas can. I knot my arms in front of my chest and think how I wanted to keep that horse for bouncing. It's supposed to be a baby toy, but some days when Lecia's out, I ride it with springs screeching and close my eyes and picture myself galloping across a wide prairie. Now that horse looks at me all blank-eyed and tired.

I scan around for a rock or two-by-four to conk Mother on the head with. But Lecia's hands won't let go my shoulders. She could be watching the weather on TV for all the feeling her face shows. I tell her that's my horse Mother's messing with. But she's bored with this complaint. So I let it go. *Bye-bye, old Paint,* I think to myself, *I'm a-leaving Cheyenne.*

Mother drags the safety match in slo-mo down the black strip on the side of the box, and the spark takes the red match head with a flare. She tosses the match toward the horse with a gesture that's almost delicate. For an instant she might be a lady dropping a hanky. Then flames surge up over my horse with a loud *whump.* For a long time inside the orange fire you can see the black horse shape real clear. But at some point that shape caves in on itself, gives way to the lapping fire that Mother pitches stuff into, no horse left at all. She upends the last box of toys and shakes it the way, earlier in our room, she dumped out each drawer from our highboy.

The fire is working hard. It climbs up and over every single object piled there. She's burning her own paintings too, some of them, the landscapes of the beach mostly. The canvases catch before the frames do, so lined up at different heights along one side of the pyramid are these framed pictures of flames. Fire burns wild inside the gilt frames and wormwood frames and slick, super-modern brass frames.

Then Mother drags across the grass the biggest, deepest box of all, an old refrigerator box we had been planning to cut up for a puppet theatre. Out of it she draws our clothes—culottes and sunsuits with shoulder ties and old pajamas with beading on the feet that make a clicking noise on the bathroom tiles and keep you from sliding around. A white shirt with a Peter Pan collar flies out of her hand and arcs across the black sky, and behind it comes a huge red crinoline petticoat I wore to can-can in. It always reminded Mother of Degas's dancers. Now it swirls from her hand in a circle and settles in the fire almost gently where it's eaten in a quick gulp. From Mother's arms tumble dozens of tennis shoes. They smother in a lump till the canvas of them catches, and after that, black smoke comes up with the wicked stink of scorched rubber.

After the shoes catch, she fishes out the dresses. She slips each one off its hanger the better to see it before she commends it to the fire. At her feet, a big thicket of hangers is piling up. Each hanger drops from her white hand into the pile with a faint ringing. That ringing sends her into heavy motion again. She holds every dress briefly by its shoulders like it's a schoolkid she's checking out for smudges before church. Then one by one they get flung away from her and into the fire. There sails my white eyelet-lace Easter dress, and the pinafore Grandma smocked and embroidered with French-knot flowers in pink. There's the pink peasant skirt Lecia got at the Mexico store in Houston. There's the green plaid jumper with yellow cowgirl ropes stitched around the pockets that we've both worn. Those dresses look like nothing so much as the bodies of little girls whose ghosts have gone out of them. (Epictetus has a great line about the division between body and soul—"Thou art a little spirit bearing up a corpse." When I read that line years later, I automatically pictured those dresses emptied of their occupants and sailing into the fire in graceful arcs.)

At some point the fire fades to orange background, and I stare only at Mother's face. It's all streaked up with lipstick and soot, so she looks like a bona fide maniac. Her lips move in a muttery way, but I can't make out the words. Nipper growls and yaps. He occupies that large circle of dark by the house that barely exists for me anymore. I can hear him lunge to the end of his chain, then get his bark choked off by the collar before he slinks back under the house. Mother's voice rises, so I can make out what she's saying over the fire and the whimpering dog: *Rotten cocksucking motherfucking hausfrau.*

If I keep my eyes unfixed and look through my eyelashes I discover I can turn the whole night into something I drew with crayon. The trees around us have bubble-shaped heads. The dresses flying into the fire are cut out of a paper-doll book. The fire is burnt orange and sunflower yellow and fire-engine red, with bold black spikes around it. The refinery towers in the distance are long skinny lines I drew with the silver crayon, using my ruler to keep them so straight. Their fires remind me of birthday candles fixing to get puffed out.

I don't know when all the fight drains out of me, but it does. You could lead me by the hand straight into that fire, and I doubt a squawk would come out. I can't protest anymore, and I can see that Lecia has been scooped pretty empty too. We are in the grip of some big machine grinding us along. The force of it simplifies everything. A weird calm has settled over me from the inside out. What is about to happen to us has stood in line to happen. All the roads out of that instant have been closed, one and by one.

I think about the story of Job I heard in Carol Sharp's Sunday school. How he sort of learned to lean into feeling hurt at the end, the way you might lean into a heavy wind that almost winds up supporting you after a while. People can get behind pain that way, if they think it derives from powers larger than themselves. So in the middle of some miserable plague where everybody's got buboes in their groins and armpits swelling and bursting with pus, people can walk around calm. So I know with calm how cut off we are from any help. No fire truck will arrive. None of the neighbors will phone Daddy or the sheriff.

I picture old Mrs. Heinz standing next door at her sink behind the window she cleaned down to the squeak every Saturday with a bucket of ammonia water into which she squeezed a lemon. She can see us out there. I feel her eyes on me. She's wiping off the last plate from the drainboard and watching us and wondering should she come out. But she thinks better of it. Mother's flinging things into the fire like one of those witches out of the Shakespeare play, and old Mrs. Heinz probably peers out from behind the ruffled Priscilla curtains that she copied herself on her sewing machine using dimestore gingham to look like the ones in the Sears catalogue. She probably takes one long gander at that hill of flaming toys and furniture and the picture frames of living fire and Mother stirring it all with a long pole and thinks to herself, *Ain't a bit of my business.* Then she lets the pink-checked curtain go so it fell across us.

The other neighbors have done the same. I feel them all releasing us into the deep drop of whatever is about to happen. Each curtain falls. Each screen door is pulled tight, and every door hook clicks into its own tight eye, and even big heavy doors get heaved closed in the heat, and all the bolts are thrown. I can almost hear it happening all over the neighborhood. TVs get turned louder to shut out the racket of us. Anyone might have phoned Daddy and said, *Pete, looky here. This ain't none of my bi'ness, but . . .* (The thought that burdens me most today is that somebody did call Daddy to let him know, and Daddy—gripped by the same grinding machine that gripped us—just stayed in the slot that fate had carved for him and said he planned to come on home directly. Or he said kiss my rosy red ass, for Daddy could turn the volume on any portion of the world up or down when he had a mind to. I can very well picture his big hand setting the phone back in its black cradle. The men on his unit might have been frying up some catfish they'd caught. From high in his tower, he could have looked out that curved window across fields of industrial pipes and oil-storage tanks, past the train yards to the grid of identical houses—in the yard of one of which Mother was setting fire to our lives—and maybe Daddy just decided to change the channel away from that fire to the sizzle of cornbread-dipped catfish floating in hot lard. *Boy that fish smells good,* I can imagine him saying.)

When Mother gets done emptying stuff into the fire, she goes back inside the house, and we follow like herd animals. We don't run to some neighbor house calling, *save us save us.* We wouldn't leave Mother alone in this state. We cross the sopping lawn from the fire's scorch and into the humid damp of the dark yard and unlit house. We traipse up the concrete steps and into the kitchen at an even pace. She walks down the long hall to her bedroom, and at that moment, some spark of something must catch inside Lecia, some desire to get us both loose, to disembark from that wild ride we've been on, because she nudges me to our end of the house. I go where she pushes like a blind calf.

Our room is scrambled and holds no order. That box spring tilting against the wall scares me big league. I can picture Mother heaving it and hear it hit all over again. There's a gray-and-black quilt Grandma once stitched together from a book of men's suit samples she got from some tailor. Lecia spreads that out like we're on a picnic. I lie down on it, and she draws the white chenille bedspread over our knees, which we bend into mountains. The chenille is nubbly as code. We roll on our sides and face each other. The quilt squares stretch beneath us. We hopscotch from square to square in finger tag—black gabardine to charcoal flannel to gray pinstripe, like farmlands seen from up high. Mother earlier smashed all the lightbulbs in our room with a broom handle, so it's dark. You can't quite decipher the individual pieces of furniture tipped over and flung around, just the right angles that poke up making a jagged mountain landscape around our floor pallet.

I can hear Mother in the kitchen now. She must be dumping cutlery from the drawers because the noise of metal crashing explodes then stops, explodes then stops. If I close my eyes it's like a great battle right out of King Arthur is taking place in there. I can picture knights in armor bringing their swords down against shields, arrows flying into battlements, lances striking the breastplates of horsemen. When I open my eyes, though, there is only the dark plain of the quilt we lie on divided up in squares by the neat grid of suit samples. Next to me Lecia's face is long and white under her spiky bangs. She looks baleful as a basset hound. She has stopped hopscotching and now presses her index finger against her lips to show me not to say anything, but what might I say? A long rectangle of light spills over us from the open door.

Then a dark shape comes to occupy that light, a figure in the shape of my mom with a wild corona of hair and no face but a shadow. She has lifted her arms and broadened the stance of her feet, so her shadow turns from a long thin line into a giant X. And swooping down from one hand is the twelve-inch shine of a butcher knife, not unlike the knife that crazy guy had in *Psycho* for the shower scene, a stretched-out triangle of knife that Daddy sharpens by hand on his whetstone before he dismantles a squirrel or a chicken, though it is also big enough to have hacked through the hip joint of a buck. It holds a glint of light on its point like a star, so that old rhyme pops into my head: *Star light, star bright, first star I see tonight. I wish I may, I wish I might, have the wish I wish tonight.* Then I don't know what to wish for. Lecia's finger stays pressed to her lips. Her eyes are big but steady on that figure in the doorway and on the knife. I wish not to scream. Screaming would piss Lecia off. I can tell. A scream is definitely not what I want to happen to me right now. It's part wish and part prayer that zips through my head and keeps me from howling.

No sooner do I choke down that scream than a miracle happens. A very large pool of quiet in my head starts to spread. Lecia's face shrinks back like somebody in the wrong end of your telescope.

Then even Mother's figure starts to alter and fade. In fact, the thin, spidery female form in black stretch pants and turtleneck wielding a knife in one upraised arm is only a stick figure of my mother, like the picture I drew in Magic Marker on the Mother's Day card I gave her last Sunday. I wrote underneath it in pink block letters that I decorated with crayon drawings of lace, "You are a nice Mom. I love you. It has been nice with you. Love from Mary Marlene." That Sunday morning when she'd opened that card up and read it, she cried racking sobs and hugged me hard so her tears streamed down into my ears till Lecia showed up at Mother's bedside with a vodka martini she'd mixed saying, *Here, sip at this.* Then there was another martini and another. Della Reese was singing "Mack the Knife" on the record player. She kept saying *My poor, poor babies* and *This isn't your fault.* By the time I got my nerve up to sneak in the kitchen and upend the vodka bottle down the sink, there was only an inch left anyway.

That was Mother's Day a week ago. On my card, I had drawn a stick-figure mom wearing a string of Ping-Pong–sized pearls around its stick neck. Now in my mind, that stick figure is what Mother becomes. She's just a head like a ball and curly scribbles for hair. But there the likeness to the figure on my card ends. This stick figure holds a triangle knife with a star glinting off its end. My stick-figure sister is breathing deep in the chest of her white PJs, and I match my breath to hers. We lie there in that cartoon of a room for what seems like forever, and then out of nowhere Mother roars *No!* like a lioness, her mouth shapes itself into a giant black O with real definite pointy teeth for what seems like a long time. The black *NO* sails out of that mouth in a long balloon with the tail of a comet streaking past us and out the wax-papered windows into the flaming night.

That's how God answered my prayers: I learned to make us all into cartoons. That stick woman in the center of the big black page with her eyebrows squinched down in a mad V over pin-dot eyes is no more my mother than some monster on the Saturday cartoons. She just isn't. I lock all my scaredness down in my stomach until the fear hardens into something I hardly notice. I myself harden into a person that I hardly notice. I can feel Lecia cock her head at me, like she wants to know what the hell I have to grin about.

Now the stick-figure mom sets down the knife on the floor to dial the phone. I count the seven turns of the dial, feel it unwind under her stick finger. She's crying, the stick mommy, with sucking sobs. A whole fountain of blue tears pours from both pin-dot eyes. I guess it's Dr. Boudreaux who answers on the other end, because she says, "Forest, it's Charlie Marie. Get over here. I just killed them both. Both of them. I've stabbed them both to death."

CHAPTER 8

After they took Mother Away, I sank into a fierce lonesomeness for her that I couldn't paddle out of into other things. Nor did anyone come into it looking for me. By this I mean that Daddy never mentioned the night of the fire. Nor did he say when Mother might come home, other than pretty soon. Maybe our own silence on the subject—Lecia's and mine, for we didn't bring it up either—was meant to protect him somehow, so as not to worry him overmuch. If we failed him by not telling him all about it, he sure as shit failed us by not knowing how to ask.

At school, I cleaned up my act. There wasn't cussing or fighting, and I won not a single exile to Frank Doleman's office for chess. My final report card for second grade shows my getting "Satisfactory +" in both Conduct and Citizenship. Which was for me a first. No doubt, I was operating under the notion that being completely good in the eyes of all authorities might urge Mother back.

At home, I also picked up my side of our bedroom, and grudgingly helped Lecia make our bed with military tucks on the sheet corners. There my housekeeping stopped, though she pulled off a whirlwind scrubbing of the whole house every Saturday, down to the insides of the toilets. She wrought particular hell on Daddy's ashtrays. He couldn't thump the ash off a Camel without her swooping down to wash and dry the ashtray before he got his hand drawn back good.

Without real data on Mother's psychic health (or lack thereof) Lecia and I cooked up some fairly worrisome scenarios about her. On TV one night, we watched a movie called *The Snake Pit*. It starred Olivia de Havilland as this fairly nice if somewhat high-strung lady who wore over-baroque brooches and belted dresses when vacuuming her house, but who, nevertheless, had a twitchy mouth early in the movie that foreshadowed her hellacious, capital-B Breakdown later. The film's title captures how the mental ward got portrayed. There was an icy bathtub in which one maniac got dunked under wet canvas, and a description of shock treatment that went something like this: "Then the electrodes are fixed to the temples and ZZZZZZT—thousands of volts course through the brain!" Finally, poor Ms. de Havilland got locked in a padded room and belted into one of those long-armed strait-jackets that forced you to hug yourself all day and besides which looked really hot. All the while she was hallucinating snakes crawling all over. That was the picture of mental-ward life for the full-blown Nervous that Lecia and I promptly settled on. It was all we had.

The neighbor kids gave little comfort. Like us, they ran short on real data about psych wards, but they were very long on mean-assed idiom. To this day, it's a peculiar trait of Leechfield citizenry that your greatest weakness will get picked at in the crudest local parlance. In fact, the worse an event is for you, the more brutally clear will be the talk about it. In this way, guys down there born with shriveled legs get nicknamed Gimpy, girls with acne Pizzaface.

My daddy even worked with a guy whose teenaged son had gone berserk with a twelve-gauge shotgun and marched one summer day into the junior high, where he shot and killed a guidance counselor while the principal (the alleged target, we later heard) hid in the school safe. The men on Daddy's job right away nicknamed this kid the Ambusher. The week the local paper carried a story about the boy's incarceration and lobotomy in the state hospital at Rusk, the guys at the refinery pitched the kid's daddy a party complete with balloons and noisemakers. I shit you not. Daddy claimed that the card they gave the poor fellow read: "Here's hoping the Ambusher can finally hang up his guns!"

This kind of bold-faced ugliness was common to us. The theory behind it held that *not* mentioning a painful episode in the meanest terms was a way of pretending that the misery of it didn't exist. Ignoring such misery, then, was equal to lying about it. Such a lie was viewed as more cruel, even, than the sad truth, because it somehow shunned or excluded the person in pain (i.e., in the above case, the Ambusher's daddy) from everybody else. Plus ignoring such a grotesque event as the lobotomy of one's only son would suggest that the guy was somehow made weak by it or "couldn't take it."

So neighbor kids talked to me in language meant to toughen me to the cold facts of my life. I heard how Mother was crazy as a mudbug and nutty as a fruitcake. She didn't have both oars in the water. She had been slam-dunked in the loony bin, the funny farm, the Mental Marriott, the Ha-Ha Hotel.

I got my ass whipped three or four times by jumping like a buzz saw into kids popping off this way about her. Finally, Daddy urged me to start biting down hard on any kid getting the better of me. He knew that to back up would bring a steady stream of ass-whippings, and my size precluded any bona fide victories. "Lay the ivory to 'em, Pokey" was how he put it. Even if I got whipped after, a bite left a mark that'd stay with a person. That summer, I bit to draw blood seven or eight times. But the time I took a good chunk out of Rickey Carter's shoulder ultimately led to events that cinched my reputation as the worst kid on the block.

The red-faced Rickey, who was twelve and couldn't bear having busted into tears in front of the littler kids after I'd chomped on him, scanned around for a way to get even, and then jumped on Lecia. Jumping Lecia always proved a mistake. Rickey was older and way bigger, but she was tough as a boot. She couldn't walk into the drugstore for an ice cream without some roughneck pointing at her and saying, "That there's Pete Karr's daughter," which praise always caused some guy's eyebrow to cock itself north a notch. Anyway, Lecia had pinned Rickey pretty quick when his baby brother Philip came up behind her with a ball bat and brought it down with all his might between her shoulder blades, knocking her out. At the crack of wood against spinal column, the whole gang broke running back to their separate yards. Lecia toppled, and a few minutes passed before her cheeks flushed and her eyes fluttered open.

The next day right after dawn, I pulled down my BB gun from the top bookshelf and went on a rampage that prefigured what Charles Whitman—the guy who shot and killed thirteen people from the tower at the University of Texas—would do a few years later. I stuck a can of hot tamales with a can opener in a paper bag and fixed myself a jelly jar of tea. While all the other kids were still sitting around in their pajamas eating their doughnuts with powdered sugar and watching cartoons, I was sneaking across the blackberry field behind our house. There was a lone chinaberry tree at the field's center, and I shinnied up it, then pulled my BB gun after me to wait for the Carter kids. They'd planned to berry-pick that morning so their mama could make a cobbler. I'd overheard talk about it.

I didn't wait long. The sun had gone from pink to hot white when the whole Carter clan clamored across the grassy ditch circling the field's edge. Their daddy was leading them; they straggled behind, each with a saucepan or bait bucket. I lifted the BB gun and sighted through its little V as close as I could to the white glare of Rickey's glasses. I fully intended to pop him between the eyes. I repeated Daddy's injunction to pull any trigger slow: "Don't jerk it, Pokey," he always said. I didn't, and after the satisfying little zing, a miracle happened. I saw Rickey Carter slap his neck, like he thought a wasp had stung him.

My next few shots missed. But Mr. Carter heard them skitter through the long grass and tracked the noise till he finally caught sight of my shape in the tree behind leaf cover. Even I could see the little bloody hole in Rickey's neck where I'd pegged him. Mr.

Carter yelled my name, then yelled was that me. But like Brer Rabbit, I just laid low. Then he yelled did I have some kind of weapon up in that tree, and Babby Carter dropped her pot and ran crying back to the road with Philip right behind her. Shirley took out running too. Her flip-flops slapped against her bare feet till she jumped the ditch and hit asphalt on the other side. Rickey put his hands on his hips like he was pissed off, but he stepped sideways so that his daddy stood between him and my chinaberry tree. *You pussy,* I thought, as if Rickey's not wanting to get shot were a defining mark against his manhood. Mr. Carter screamed to get down from there, that I could put somebody's eye out with a pellet gun. And I came back with a reply that the aging mothers in that town still click their tongues about. It was easily the worst thing anybody in Leechfield ever heard a kid say. "Eat me raw, mister," I said. I had no idea what this meant. The phrase had stuck in my head as some mild variant on "Kiss my ass," which had been diluted from overuse.

I stayed clueless a long time, even after Daddy had been phoned and ratted to, even after he'd spanked me with Grandma Moore's old homemade leather horse quirt, itself an insult. I may have actually cried.

The next day, I planned to picket the Carters' driveway, believing kids from union families wouldn't cross such a line to play with them. With Mother's oil paints, I wrote placards for Lecia and me to carry. Mine read, prosaically enough, "Down with the Carters"; Lecia's, "The Carters Fight Unfair." But Lecia talked me out of it. My morning as sniper won me a grudging respect. Kids stopped mouthing off about Mother. The anti-Carter campaign had brought me activity, and a parcel of relief. Without them to plot against, I sank back into my lonesomeness for Mother.

Daddy had only one Liars' Club story that told me about his own momma's meanness, and that dealt with the blistering quality of her whippings, which were such that he bragged about having stood them. "The old lady would stripe my ass too. Don't think she wouldn't. Just as quick as Poppa would."

We're cleaning ducks—Daddy and I, and the other fellows. By nine this morning, we'd bagged our limit. I'm scooping the guts out of a little teal duck, and Daddy is pulling feathers from the huge slackened body of our only Canadian goose. With one swipe of his hand he clears a wide path in the feathers. "Momma was tough as a wood-hauler's ass," he says, and that's high praise. Back in the logging camp, wood haulers drove mule-drawn wagons of raw lumber. Since their butts rubbed up against unstripped pine all day, they became badges of toughness.

"How many eggs ya'll want?" Ben wants to know. Everybody says three. He slides a big slab of Crisco into the black skillet. We stopped here at Cooter's one-room cabin to clean ducks and eat breakfast. It's on Chupique Bayou, just across the river in Louisiana.

"Not as big as a minute, my mother," Daddy says. "But mean as a snake if you ever lied to her."

Shug then says with a straight face that he can't imagine Daddy *ever* lying. He's quartering the ducks and wrapping the pieces in white freezer paper for us to divvy up when we're back in town.

Daddy tilts his head at Shug. "Last time she ever whupped on me was over lying. I had got big enough to figure I was too big to whup. Hell, my arms was that big around." He stares into the washtub full of duck carcass and feathers at his feet like it's some oracle his momma's ghost is about to rise out of.

When he's sure everybody's listening, he backs up to set the scene. "Had come a hurricane that August. Dumped umpteen-zillion gallons of water in the Neches River. High?" He glares at each one of us so we get the point. "Lord God, that river was high." The room sits quiet, the only noises the pop of eggs sliding in grease and Shug folding up the butcher paper. For a split second, the word "hurricane" sends roaring out of my own head at me a memory of the Orange Bridge during Hurricane Carla—how the railing had come rushing sideways at the car through the rain. I shake my head loose from that and get back to my teal ducks. It's sticky work.

"I remember that storm," Cooter says. He's got a little wire of excitement in his voice at the idea of actually being in on the story.

"Cooter, you was still shitting yellow back then," Ben says, "if you was drawing breath at all." He breaks the yolks with his spatula so the eggs fry up hard. To get eggs like this in a truck stop, you say to the lady, *Turn 'em over and step on 'em.*

"Well, I remember one like it," Cooter says.

"Hell, we all remember one like it," Shug says. He's about fed up with Cooter, who's been bossing him all weekend because he's colored. *Shug, get the outboard. Shug, you're shooting too soon. Goddammit, Shug, I was saving them biscuits for later.* Cooter is also just walking the edge of telling colored jokes. He uses *Polack* and *Aggie,* but everybody—Shug included—knows that if there wasn't a black man holding down a chair in this room they'd be nigger this and nigger that. Daddy says Cooter's just ignorant, never knew anybody colored before, so it's not his fault. But it seems mean how nobody ever says anything back directly. I mean, the guys do try to corral him a little and keep him from being overmuch an asshole. But nobody says flat out *You're just picking on Shug because he's colored.* It sometimes seems to me like we're not supposed to notice that Shug's colored, or that saying anything about it would be bad manners. That puzzles me because Shug's being colored strikes me as real obvious. And usually anybody's difference gets pounced on and picked at. This silence is a lie peculiar to a man's skin color, which makes it extra serious and extra puzzling.

Daddy's voice stops me wondering. "Anyways, Momma told me and my brother A.D. flat out not to go into that river. 'Stay out of that river, boys. They's boys drowned in that river.' And we said okay. But A.D. cut me a little look. And I know we thinking the same thing.

"Me and old A.D. go squat outside the window and talk real loud so she'll hear us. Say we oughta go down the sawmill. See if Poppa needs any help. We take off down that woods road, but soon as we hit the fork where she can't see"—he forks his fingers like a road he's arriving at—"we peel off and go yonder a ways. The rest of them boys was gonna be down at the water. So that's where we want to be too. We got there and stripped on down and dove just as straight in that river as a pair of butter knives."

Daddy's done plucking the goose and hands me the prickly pink body to gut. He picks up a mallard. Its head is an iridescent green. When Ben was toting all the mallards up from the duck blind earlier this morning, all their green shiny heads came together in his big red hand like a bouquet of flowers. But for their black eyes staring out, you could almost forget they're dead.

"And this was your oldest brother you was with?" Cooter asks.

"It don't matter who it was, Cooter," Shug says. "Goddamn, you're the asking-est sonofabitch I ever met."

Cooter twists around on the chair and stares at Shug. Cooter maintains a birdlike way of twitching his head around that makes me think sometimes that he's about to go clucking off across the room pecking at the floorboards. "It matters if I feel like knowing," Cooter says.

Daddy draws back the mallard in his hand like it's a ball bat he's fixing to swing. "I swear to God, I'm gonna flail both your asses with this duck if you don't shut up," he says.

"He started it," Cooter says, then sinks back down in his shirt collar.

Ben says to let it go. He's over at the stove, pouring off the extra grease from the skillet into the lard pot.

Daddy takes a few swipes at the mallard to get everybody's eyes back on him before he starts up again. "That evening we head down through them woods back home, and here comes Momma. She'd got her apron pulled around and tucked in her skirt so the brush don't catch it. And she always wore a old blue-flowered bonnet." Daddy fans his hands behind his head to show the bonnet. "The sun was going down to the west, which was her right side. So that bonnet th'owed a shadow across't her face. Kept us from seeing her. But I could tell by how she was stomping through those weeds that she was mad. Plus she'd already cut herself a piss elum pole about as long as she was tall. Like she'd got it in her head already to whup us. I whisper over my shoulder to A.D. not to tell her we went in. Just to say we watched the other boys. And he says okay.

"Not a minute later she stops square on that path in front of me. 'J.P.,' she says, 'you go in that river?'

" 'No'm,' I says, 'we just watched them other boys.' And she says fine. Then she reaches that pole around behind me and taps A.D. on the shoulder. Just light enough to get his attention. 'A.D., did you go in that river?' And damned if he don't say, 'Yes'm. I went in, and he come in with me,' And I thinks to myself, you sorry sonofabitch."

I watch Ben draw a cake pan of biscuits out of the oven. He uses a pointy bottle opener to pop a triangular hole in a brand-new yellow can of sugarcane syrup. I like to poke a hole in a biscuit with my thumb, then fill it with that syrup so it gushes out the sides when you bite down. I figure on doing that, which fills the back of my mouth up with longing for the sweetness of it. I'm still holding that sweetness like a thirst when Daddy starts up.

"Lemme tell you fellas, my momma at that time wasn't no bigger than Mary Marlene here." He jerks his thumb at me so I can prove his mother's tininess. I ignore this by faking big-time interest in slitting open the fat belly of this goose. "Probably didn't weigh ninety pounds with boots on, my momma. Anyways, she took us out on the screened-in back porch—we slept out there in the summer. Started in on him with that pole and like to have killed him. Brought it down on his back in one narrow swatch, like she was trying to cut a groove through his flesh. I'd laugh like hell every time his eyes caught mine. I figured she was getting wore out on him. So's my turn wouldn't be as bad."

Shug says, "My daddy beat me and my brother thataways. Taking turns, so one watched the other."

"Now you're interrupting!" Cooter says, slapping the table. "Why don't nobody stop him interrupting?" The veins are standing out on Cooter's neck. Ben tells him to get the plates down and stop feeling sorry for hisself.

Daddy drops the mallard in the tub like he's all of a sudden exhausted by thinking again about that whipping. The whole burden of it seems to fall on him full force. His shoulders slump. The deep lines of his face get deeper. Then he gets an unfocused look at the middle distance like the beating's happening right in the room, and all he has to do is watch it and report back to the other guys. "That pole of hers cut the shirt right off my back in about four swipes." His head drops lower, as if under the weight of that pole, which is getting easier by the minute for me to imagine. "I've had grown men beat on me with tire irons and socks full of nickels and every conceivable kind of stick. But that old woman shrunk up like a pullet hen took that piss elum pole and flat set me on fire from my shoulders clear down past my ass. And every time she said a word, she brought that pole down. 'Don't—you—lie—to—me—Don't—you—run—from—me!' Hell, I broke loose from her a couple of times. And I run to the screen door. But the pine boards on that old sleeping porch was swole up from that rain. The door was swole. So I couldn't pull it flush all the way, couldn't get the latch unhooked. I'd just about get it wiggled tight in the frame, and then that pole would find my back again. You could hear it come whistling through the air just a heartbeat before you felt it. And Momma behind it just hacking at me like I was a pine she was trying to knock over. I was scared to fall. Scared I wouldn't live to get vertical again. I promise you that. You think she was wore out on A.D.?" He squints at us, then picks up the mallard again and picks at a few of the quills like he's winding down. "Hell, she just warmed up on A.D."

"They hate that when you run," Ben says. He's sliding the last egg onto the platter. "My grandma was the same exact way. Running just dragged it out." Of course, I am famous for running in the middle of a spanking. It makes me proud that Daddy used to run too. I always figured only a dumbass would just stand still and take it. I have maneuvered my way over by the stove and am eye level now with the plate of biscuits, which have plumped up nice and brown on top. The slightest blink from Ben saying okay, and I will snatch the first one.

"I finally broke straight through the middle of that screen," Daddy says. "Left a outline of myself cut clean around the edges as a paper doll." Shug winks at me over the unlikeliness of this. He always keeps me posted as to the believability quotient of what Daddy's saying, even though I'm a kid, and a notorious pain in the ass as kids go.

Daddy sets down the duck again, and a smile stretches across his face, his eyes crinkle up, and his shoulders go square like the best part of the story just bubbled back up in him. "And old A.D. had hell to pay. Don't think he didn't."

"Wasn't Uncle A.D. a lot bigger than you, Daddy?" I am always trying to figure a way around my own skinniness. Uncle A.D. is a big oak tree of a man, white-headed and strong. In all the pictures of the Karr boys lined up, he stands close to Daddy and stares down his nose, like he's lording something over him.

"Don't make no difference, bigger," Daddy says. "Bigger's just one thing. They's a whole lot of other things than bigger, Pokey. Don't you forget it. Bigger's ass, was what I thought.

"I head out behind the shed," Daddy says, "and there's old A.D. hunkered down on the ground. 'Say, brother,' I says to him." Daddy's voice as he makes out talking to Uncle A.D. is smooth and sweet as melty butter. " 'I believe you made out pretty bad back there.' I tell him I got some burn salve may take that sting out. And A.D. he bends over. Starts picking at that shirt on his back where that fabric's stuck down in them sores. He's a-hissing between his teeth. Gets that old cotton blouse pulled up over his shoulder blades, then asks me does that look bad. And I say, 'Poor old you.' Course she cut the shirt slap off my back. 'Pull your shirt off your neck a little higher,' I says to him. 'I don't want to get this here salve on it. Piss Momma off any worse.' So he bends way over further. Gets bent double-like. His arms all hung up in them shirtsleeves till he's stuck like a snake in a sock. That's when I grab hold to him. Pour that old turpentine horse liniment down in them sores. Was a deep, purple-black liniment Momma made from tar. I held him still and smeared it in with the flat of my hand. And him wrassling me to break loose."

Shug stops wrapping bird carcasses a second. He tilts his head at Daddy, then says that his momma cooked up some horse liniment back then out of a tar base. See, Shug's from up in the piney woods too. "Hers was tar and pine sap, I remember right. Maybe she put some lemon grass in it, one of them stingy herbs." Shug's momma knew Daddy's momma. They were both pretty good country doctors, and every now and then Shug and Daddy ride back toward their mothers into that place to get to something like this liniment, or some other doctoring recipe. The looks on their faces grow so vaguely soft that I feel tears start in back of my eyes. I am verging on lonesome myself for these women I never knew.

Daddy says that sounds like the exact stuff. He stands from the washtub of feathers and sidles over to the sink to wash up. He seems pleased. Shug's knowing the very liniment proves that the world Daddy's telling exists. But Shug's brow has grown a furrow like it bothers him. He claims to Daddy that you couldn't get that stuff off you, not out of a cut or something. And Daddy says that was the very idea, to scald Uncle A.D. down to the bone for tattling on him.

This sets me wondering. I hear about Daddy doing this kind of meanness, and I see guys shy away when he strolls over to a pool table, but he handles me like I'm something glass. Even his spankings are mild enough to seem symbolic. When I got up cold this morning before we set out for the bayou, he warmed my socks over the gas heater before I pulled them on. (Lecia was sleeping over at a friend's that morning, having outgrown Daddy somehow, having also gotten agile at worming her way into families quieter than ours.) My daddy buys me whatever I ask for and laughs at my jokes and tells me he loves me better than anybody about fifty times a day. I've seen him fight, but I've never seen this sneaky meanness he talks about at the Liars' Club. I look at him scrubbing the blood out from under his fingernails with a pale blue plastic brush and wonder about it. He's laughing like hell over what he did to A.D. Daddy pats his hands dry on a dish towel. "I left old A.D. squirming on the ground. Scrabbling to get away from hisself."

Ben upends the pan of biscuits, which fall out of the tin in a perfect steaming circle. They're crusty brown on the bottom. He nods at me to tear one loose, and I do. But I have to hot-potato it hand to hand to keep it from burning me. Finally, I drop it on the counter and cup my hands over it in a little igloo that I blow on. When I look up from that, I see that Ben also has a dark look on his face, like he can't get away from the meanness of this story fast enough either.

Maybe it was Daddy's hint of low-lying meanness that kept me from asking him about Mother overmuch while she was in the hospital. His silence on the subject was a fence I wasn't supposed to cross. But I'd shoved past no-trespassing signs before.

So it was that one day when Daddy and I were riding home in his lizard-green truck my mind swam back to the night of the fire. By then, I had blotted out Mother holding the butcher knife. I had even blotted out the fire itself and her burning our clothes. All my mind hung on to was Dr. Boudreaux with his caterpillar mustache asking me where were the marks. I knew he'd checked Mother into a psych hospital. So I ventured out to ask about this place and why we couldn't visit. Daddy said that kids weren't allowed, being as how little bitty kids who saw their mommas on a locked ward with a flock of other folks in their pajamas just got scared. He turned away then, and shook a Camel loose from his pack and pushed in the cigarette lighter. That lighter was like the period at the end of a sentence. It was supposed to shut up my questions. I could feel my hair twist around on my head in the hot wind. Through my window, I watched the rubber factory slide by.

For some reason, though, I pushed past that moment. We were heading home from the Farm Royal, where the carhop always leaned against Daddy's window while I drank my cherry freeze. She never brought a check, either, even though Daddy downed at least three cans of beer. Maybe the beer might make him more apt to talk. I asked if he wasn't scared when he went to see Mother. Folks in that place, he said, didn't seem so much full-blown crazy as in really sad moods. They sat around over board games a lot, he said, not moving their tokens real often.

That one detail about the game tokens turned the hospital real for me. All of a sudden, some black fury I'd been hiding boiled up. I finally told Daddy I didn't want Mother to come home if she was gonna go crazy all over again, just because we hadn't cleaned our room.

Then he did something so apart from all I knew him to be that it immediately became the gesture that defined him most in my head. He turned the truck wheel sharp, so we bumped off the road shoulder into gravel. He slammed on the brakes. The truck fishtailed to a stop. Daddy didn't even turn to look at me. His eyes stayed pinned off to the side, either fixed on his own face in the side mirror or on the towers in the distance. This let me take in his profile—the sharp cheekbones and hawk's-beak nose. His eyes narrowed when he finally spoke. He said that if I kept talking about my mother thataways, he would slap my face clear into next Tuesday. We sat there in the violence of that threat a minute, for he had never slapped my face, nor even threatened to slap it. My face got overhot at the prospect. But I didn't make a chirp. After a second or so, he depressed the clutch and shifted back down into first gear, and we started back up the road.

Daddy did finally take us to the hospital, a low brick building that sat in a scrubby field, in blazing sun with no scrap of shade for acres in any direction. We didn't go in, but stood outside what must have been the dayroom. He'd arranged the time with Mother in advance. As we walked up, I could make out through the screen and the extra layer of chicken-wire mesh stapled to the window—to keep folks from running off, I guess—the wild tropical print of her lounging robe. Daddy had to hoist me up by my waist to reach that window. Even then, only my nose fit over the bottom sill. Mother put her hand on the chicken wire. It was very white, and I put my hand to match up with it, careful that I touched as much of hers as I could. The screen gave a little to let our palms actually meet through the chicken wire. Her face in the deep shadow of the room was just a pale oval without any features, but I could hear the crying in her voice when she said she missed us. She dabbed at that oval with a Kleenex and made snotty noises in her head. We took some more turns saying we missed each other.

Then I said something that caused Lecia to pinch my ankle: "I'm sorry you're all locked up," I said, which made her laugh. "Shit, honey," she said, "you-all are locked up, too. You're just in a bigger room." No sooner had she said that than from a far corner of the room, where I hadn't looked at all, there came a whole flock of giggly laughs that chilled me to the core. Peering over toward those laughs, I could see a vague knot of lady patients in blue nightgowns sitting at a large round table in a low gray cloud of cigarette smoke. It struck me that those were the other crazy people. But instead of being scared by their facelessness, I just felt disgruntled that they got to hang out with my mother all day. They ate meals with her and played gin rummy with her while I only got fetched up to the window like I was a big load of something she could hardly bear to see. My seeing them seemed to prompt Daddy to lower me back down from the window. I said, "I love you," and snubbed a little. Mother did the same, then gradually she slid out of my sight.

Lecia was taller, and so Daddy was able to heft her up higher. He locked all his fingers together into a kind of stirrup, then straightened his back so she rose to fill the whole window. It rankled me to see Lecia and Mother talking all whispery. I'd had to poke my nose over the window ledge like some kind of bandit or peeping Tom. Lecia had her whole face up next to Mother's. Plus I couldn't hear a word they said. Secrets had always moved between them. Nights, when Lecia was mixing her martinis or changing record albums for her, Mother usually fell silent when I came into earshot. Lecia also had the habit of shooing me away when the two of them conspired. She'd flap her hand at me as if I were some horsefly to get rid of. They had some special hookup to each other, those two, some invisible circle of understanding that they stood in together, while Daddy and I were exiled to a duller realm with which Mother had no truck.

Anyway, that day at the hospital when the white figure of the nurse finally came to stand behind Mother, the signal for her to go, I guess, Lecia craned up her head for a good-bye kiss. She pressed her lips right up against the chicken wire. I wanted to smack her on the ass of her cut-off Levi's, especially when Mother's lips appeared through the honeycomb mesh to meet hers.

When Daddy was backing his truck out of the gravel parking lot, the tropical print Mother wore came to fill another window. And she put her hand flat up against the mesh. It made me think of a very white orchid I had found once sprinkled with some powder and mashed between the pages of *Hamlet*. That one visit was the only time we saw her all that month.

That night I fell right to sleep for the first time in weeks. And the worst dream came to play itself on the back wall of my skull like it was wide-angle TV. In it, Daddy was hacking up some large, dead animal on the plywood table in the kitchen. I was walking across the dining room toward him, watching him through the rectangular window between the two rooms. I couldn't make out what kind of creature it was—deer or boar, something big. Plus, Daddy usually cleaned his kill on the back patio over a washtub, so he could hose the blood off the bricks when he was through. His T-shirt was spattered with blood. The veins on his hands were raised up from the strain of the work. At one point in the dream, he lifted the cleaver and brought it down hard. Then he wiggled it to get through some gristle, which he did with a click. I heard the cleaver thump clear through the bone onto the table's wood.

About that time, Daddy caught sight of me and said to go back to bed, he was busy. "Get on back to bed, Pokey" was how he put it. He hardly looked at me at all. I turned to go, but felt compelled to look back, as if magnetized by his task. He held up a part of the animal to study. Then the light changed. And he was holding an actual human arm, hacked off at the elbow. At the end of that arm was Mother's hand wearing Grandma's wedding band. The wrist was bent so the hand was at a right angle to the arm, as if Mother had held up the hand to say *stop* and it had frozen that way. I gasped up from sleep, my T-shirt pasted to my chest, snails of sweat collecting on my upper lip.

It occurs to me from this distance that Mother's chopped-off hand from the dream was in the same position as the hand she'd pressed to the hospital screen. But there was another hand from that time that also got seared into what I can remember. It was the hand of Bugsy Juarez's wife. It was covered in flour one morning she came to our back door. She pressed that white hand onto our damp breakfast table while she said to Daddy, *Please come quick, Bugs has shot hisself.* She'd been making biscuits when she heard the shotgun blast. He'd taken special care, she said, to cover over the garage floor with the plastic tarp they used for their lawn furniture, so it wouldn't be such a mess, and didn't we think that was kind of thoughtful, she said, as a last thing to do. She had a very dim smile on her face, thinking of it. Daddy didn't answer, of course. He was too busy dialing the sheriff. Anyway, I remember that white handprint of Mrs. Juarez stayed on that table all day like a ghost had touched it. It put me in mind of Mother every time I passed by, till Lecia finally sponged it off just before supper.

II. Colorado, 1963

A man's at odds to know his mind cause his mind is aught he has to know it with. He can know his heart, but he dont want to. Rightly so. Best not to look in there.

—Cormac McCarthy, *Blood Meridian*

CHAPTER 9

We moved to Colorado wholly by accident. We were crossing the state, headed for the Seattle World's Fair, when Mother, who'd been staring blankly out the Impala's window, cried out for Daddy to stop with such a screech that I figured she was carsick. They were both carsick a lot on that trip, plagued as they were by Smirnoff flu. We eased over. The road sloped down into a broad valley all embroidered with columbine flowers and pink buttercups and white Queen Anne's lace. Beyond that stood Pikes Peak, which, for a kid reared in the swamp, looked unreal. In my chorus book was a similar mountain on the page facing "America the Beautiful," a purple peak with a long wisp of cloud dragging across it and a snowcap. Stepping out of the car air-conditioning that day was like entering that picture. *How weird,* I thought, *the air's so cool,* for in Leechfield blue sky meant suffocating heat. Also, the smell of evergreen was dislocating, for it conjured the turpentine in Mother's studio.

Being a champion pouter on any car trip, I was pouting, in this instance because we'd stopped. I also pouted sometimes when we didn't, and would pitch my shoes out the car window to force my parents to stop, if, say, I was dead set on visiting some snake ranch or ice cream store, or didn't wish to pee squatting over the coffee can in the backseat with passing truckers peering down at my shining ass and pulling their ropes to toot at me like I was public amusement.

The outdoor pool at the Holiday Inn in Colorado Springs closed at sunset. All day, I'd nagged Daddy to get there in time. While we rode, I positioned my mouth about two inches behind his ear prattling in a low insectlike hum more or less nonstop that, should we get there too late for a swim, I was gonna pitch a screaming cuss fit right in the motel lobby. But Mother wanted to pull over to take in the view.

I chucked rocks at a tire's whitewall. In my head, I worked up the fit I'd throw in the motel: I'd tell the clerks this man wasn't my daddy at all, but had kidnaped me at knifepoint during a bank robbery. The thin air made me dizzy. I looked up. A hawk reeled overhead with a rodent squirming in its beak, close enough so you could see the bird's black shiny eyes. That set Mother snapping away with her Kodak while Lecia bobbed around like a simpleton waving her arm and yapping about the food chain. Daddy was lifting the hood to check the radiator level when Mother sashayed up to him. She tilted her head against his khaki shirtfront and asked could we stay for a while, honey, please, since this light made her want to paint.

I wanted to keep going. Lecia and I had unfolded the map from the Esso station to plot our course. We'd drawn red lines in Magic Marker between the black dots of Western towns to make a broad red lightning bolt across the U.S.A. clear to Seattle. I wanted to hit the Space Needle gift shop so I could send Peggy Fontenot a postcard. I'd worked on a draft in my cherry-red diary with the flimsy key that Mother had bought me at the drugstore before we left: *Dear Peggy, doesn't this just beat your old Vacation Bible School with a rubber hose?*

Daddy was occupied with whether to stay or go as he cranked the ignition, so the car bumped onto blacktop, and the china-blue sky started rushing across our windshield again. He finally winked at me in the rearview and announced that he wanted to keep heading west too. But Mother didn't. She argued, politely at first, and then in terms to make Lecia and me stopper our ears. In no time, the whole tone in that car had shifted away from whether we'd stop or not to more general terms—who always did this and who never did that. Finally, Mother threw a matchbook at Daddy, and he swerved off the road into a little town I'll call Cascade, where we wound up buying a house.

The stone lodge Mother bought hung off the side of a mountain like something from a Road Runner cartoon. Pictures confirm this. It looks like a good-working car jack or even a serious nudge with a crowbar on the far side of that house would send it toppling off its log stilts and rolling ass-end-over-elbows down the sharp dirt road into town.

The house proved how Grandma's money was fixing to boost our overall comfort level. Back in Texas, we'd had hints. Before leaving, Daddy braced air-conditioners in the window of every bedroom. When we donated our black-bladed fans to the Salvation Army, we moved into the county's upper echelon socially. Plus in Houston, Mother bought herself a real leopardskin coat with a matching hat like the Cossack on the vodka bottle wore. (Maybe that coat—a torture to wear in our tropical climate—proved Mother never intended to come back to Texas from that trip, though she denied any such plan.)

But our trip west itself drew the boldest line between our family and the neighbors. Daddy only had three weeks off. He planned to fly back—yes, fly, by plane, Mrs. Fontenot must have whispered across her apron lap of green shelling peas to the other ladies—leaving us without a man to squire us around. That was scandal enough, living in a distant town without your husband. Perhaps more damning was to travel so far in the first place. In fact, I'd never known a family to set off for points farther west than the Alamo or farther east than the crayfish festival in Breaux Bridge, Louisiana. New Orleans lay just three hundred miles east, but it existed solely in lyrics from "House of the Rising Sun."

The day we pulled out of the driveway pointed at Seattle, neighbor kids lined up the block—first to wave, and then to huck gravel by handfuls. Their parents stood stock-still on their porches as if having our old Impala chased after by marauding kids constituted some just farewell. The luxury of our vacation implied cheating on our part, a betrayal the whole town had every right to take personal.

In the same way, our mountain house seemed fancy. Nobody we knew had a second dwelling beyond a duck blind or river trailer. A Denver banking family had built the cabin for summers of roughing it. But for me it bespoke untold mystery. Granite stones in the foundation reminded me of some ancient castle. The root cellar would have been an impossibility in the Leechfield swamp, where digging introduced you to the water table after you hurled the first tablespoon of dirt over your shoulder.

The living area was long enough to bowl in. Right off, Mother bought new sleek and curvy couches in burnt orange, to break up the stretched-out, dog-run feel of that room. The stone fireplace at the far end stood almost as tall as Daddy. Within days, hired workmen clomped in to cut holes in the walls and install picture windows all around, till the house felt like an aquarium. The wood-burning stove got swapped for gas. Mother had new tiles from *Architectural Digest* grouted together over the bathroom's rough-hewn lumber.

For a few weeks, we lived like characters in a Disney movie. At night elk came down to rub their shredding antlers against the jack pine. Mornings, Lecia and I piled into my parents' separate beds to watch bears through their picture window. A mother grizzly ambled down the slope with her two cubs to root in our garbage every morning. Mother had left across that window the lumberyard's masking-tape X, looking past which always made me think of our house as a treasure spot marked on some map that bears carried around.

At first light I sat on Daddy's twin bed, next to his bony white feet poking from covers. The bottoms were tough as horn. I didn't want them rubbing against me, plus I resented being exiled to Daddy's inert form when Lecia got to cuddle with Mother. I was a moist, unwashed child. If I'd tried to slide in with Mother too, she'd have unwrapped my arms from her neck, saying I made her hot.

One particular morning, we heard the bears scrambling across the pine needles and dust on the forest floor. Then between the vaulted pines, the mother shape appeared in strobelike flashes. She walked with a long stride. Her great shoulder muscles rolled under her fur. My spine instinctively stiffened at the sight. I froze that way, only relaxing once the cubs came scampering into view behind.

The crash of the first garbage can roused Daddy from sleep. He roared up shouting. In his foggy head, he thought the bear's hunched-over shadow a burglar. Before I could grab his leg moving by, he charged straight at that glass and commenced to pounding on it while we all gaped, wordless. Maybe Mother said his name a few times, nothing much more than that. But he kept at it, mired in whatever dream he was acting out. He yelled at that momma bear to get the hell out of his yard with such power that her cubs skittered behind her, leaving a trail of trash and melon rinds.

This pissed the bear off. She sought to get Daddy's barking six-foot figure to back up. She reared to her full height, her ears slanted back, and she staggered toward that window, growling with her arms wide and with the great meat of her torso shimmying under glistening fur. For one brief second, she and Daddy stood about three feet apart, with only a sheet of glass and that masking-tape X between them. The bear's muzzle made a puddle of frost a good foot higher than his black hair, which was all cowlicked around from sleep, making him seem especially goofy. I dove under the covers and prayed us all back to Leechfield, where the Lord sent sneaking water moccasins and black widow spiders to kill you with slow poison.

At some point during my prayer, Daddy clicked awake, for when I peeked out, he was backing up from the window. The end of the bed hit behind his knees and made his legs bend, so he sat down. He looked addled. Still, the bear held her ground.

She growled and showed her teeth and lacquered claws. We all sat breathing shallow till she cocked her head at Daddy, as if making her mind up. Finally, she reeled around and fell over heavy on her front paws and went shambling back up the mountain, her babies scrambling to keep up.

At the mountain's base you could rent stable horses for seven dollars a day. Mother was paralyzed with fear of riding anything not equipped with factory air. Still, she sashayed one bright morning into the tack room of this stable where the owner, a young cowboy named Rick McBride, was bent over mending a bridle. She had on her leopardskin coat at the time. She let the tack-room door slam after her so the two of them were alone, which caused a lot of hooting and catcalls among the hands standing around the corral. When she came out, she'd cut a deal to buy the two quarter horses Lecia and I had already fallen in love with, half-brothers. Big Enough was mine and the smaller of the two, a chestnut bay with black points; Lecia got Sure Enough, a dark red roan with a deeper chest and a little more jump.

If there's a particular joy that marks that whole dark Colorado time, it starts and ends with those horses. Unless you suffer from a dire case of physical fear (as Mother, in fact, did) you cannot heave yourself on the back of a horse without some jaw-slackening wonder at the animal power of it. In pictures of the time, I look dumbly small perched on Big Enough. I had remembered myself as tall in the saddle, long-legged, and needing only the faint pressure of a knee and the slight flick of rein to turn. In fact, my legs didn't reach even a third of the way around the horse's barrellike girth. They practically stuck out sideways in the stirrups, which I always had to buckle up on the shortest length.

From my first whiff of that stall every morning—horseshit and mud, that pissed-on straw that smells so much like beer—I drew enough horse up into my lungs to be some form of drunk on it. If Mr. McBride was shoeing something nearby, you could hear horsehoe and hammer and anvil clanging together, or the steady rasp of his file against hoof. Otherwise, the only sounds were animal—the plop of green manure at odd intervals; a sleeping mare shifting its weight foot to foot; some pony's muzzle banging around in its empty feed trough, making a padded thump against the wood bin. We learned pretty quick to leave off the wearing of cowboy boots for the dudes from Chicago and Los Angeles, so my tennis shoes sunk down in the muck and then sucked up with every step. Mud tended to seep over the tops. It wet my white Ban-lon socks. I can still see Big Enough's shiny chestnut rump as I smoothed my hand over it (I had to climb a few boards up on the stall side to accomplish this) saying *easy, easy.* I spent some minutes with a currycomb on his broad neck before backing him out of the stall.

Horses are blessed with an alert expression, this despite the fact they they aren't half as smart as, say, a pig. Any halfway lonesome child who currycombs some rows in the dust caked on a horse's broad neck, or takes a minute to rub the white star on his forehead, is prompted by this look to feel that the horse loves and understands her as no one else. This myth is especially easy to fall into if the horse is steady and good-natured enough to take said kid on long rides without trying to scrape her off against a tree or otherwise showing fret over the burden of her.

I liked to ride bareback, with nothing more than a hackamore. But saddling that horse every morning was a public ritual that proved my competence to any bystanders. Maybe it was my first real competence at anything. I hitched Big Enough to the front stable post beforehand in case any of the cowboys wanted to watch me achieving this.

First you centered the Mexican blanket across his spine; then you heaved the saddle over that. Actually, I needed Lecia's help with this. We had to drag two chairs from the office to stand on. The weight of the saddle was such that we had to heave-ho together, so its speed would swing it up across the horse before it fell in the dust. Then you hooked the left stirrup onto the saddle horn in order to buckle the belly cinch, which with my horse always involved whacking him on the stomach a few times, for he had learned to fake a bloat for the tourists in order that the saddle be belted on loose. This caused folks to slide off mid-ride. A few whacks, though, and he'd suck in his gut so you could buckle up. You slipped the remaining strap through a small silver ring on the saddle's side. You looped this around and knotted a flat knot. Then you let the stirrup flap back down off the horn. Mr. McBride or his wife, Polly, always came around before I rode off to see how many fingers they could wiggle under the cinch, and to tighten the saddle accordingly.

The bridle came last. For the longest while the McBrides had to do that part. But I finally learned to get my horse to take the bit in his mouth by fishing from my Levi's pocket a sugar cube I stole each morning from the café where cowboys bought their eggs and where Lecia and I kept a running tab. I held the nickel bit inside a circle I made with my thumb and index finger, between which I also pinched the sugar cube. I can still conjure the feel of his mouth on my fingers: it was both blackly velvet and bristly from his whiskers. It gave off a clover smell when he'd go to bite, which was my cue to slide the bit between his teeth. After you buckled his chin strap, you were ready to head up the mountains.

That sense of trust I felt on Big Enough's back was new. Maybe because of that trust, I turned out to be a fairly decent rider. I was stupidly fearless and also had some innate balance built into me. I still have the red ribbon I won on the barrel races that July at the gymkhana. (Lecia took sixth in the Washington pole bendings, though she would have me point out here that the competition in her category was far stiffer than in mine, which was only little kids.) All summer Big Enough never threw me once, though he was spirited enough to rear at a chipmunk or gopher that crossed the trail, and would go into a wild buck at the sight and racket of a bulldozer on the road. A few times we got caught on the bridge that led back to the stable behind that kind of heavy equipment, and I got to fancy myself a rodeo rider. The fact of my never being thrown speaks more to how close I'd paid attention—I'd become a watchful child, prone to clutch the saddle horn at any sign of trouble—than to any real skill on my part.

We rode every day, higher than I now think was safe. We rode with neither guide nor map; the horses could always find the way back to water and oats. The landscape was various in a way that had never seemed possible under the empty East Texas sky. After every stand of trees, another vista opened up. There were wide meadows we could lope across, scaring up jackrabbits as we went, and narrow paths of rock that our horses took like ballerinas high-stepping. There was even a cave with a small muddy opening that widened out into a vast, cathedrallike cavern of red rock. We took bag lunches there, and flashlights we'd tied to the backs of our saddles. Once we built a fire with dead wood and pine needles and paper matches from the café. But at some point we figured that the squeaking and clicking noise above us came not from the few high nests of nocturnal birds but from a ceiling hung with fruit bats. The twin circles of light from our flashlights dragged across the mass of them chittering. They were red-eyed as the nutria rats I'd seen. Our Keds, when we finally backed out of that cave, made no more sound than the pair of Indian ghosts we'd been hunting for.

Another time, we hobbled our horses outside an abandoned mine, followed the cart tracks deep inside, where we found next to a solid wall of fool's gold a slackened rubber, which I mistook for the skin of a snake. In fact, I toted that rubber back to the stable like a trophy and made the cowboys laugh and hoo-haw. We stumbled onto waterfalls and clear mountain streams too cold for swimming but which we loved for wading and drinking, being a different order of water entirely than the brackish bayous and soggy Gulf of Mexico I'd known. You could see rainbow trout whipping around under the surface, and could drink from two hands till your gullet was full and your ankles and knuckles ached from the blue cold of it.

Of course, when trouble hit we were on our own. In one rocky pass our horses grazed while we watched a herd of wild goats. All of a sudden both horses started up from chomping in one jangled motion. Their ears pricked forward, and their necks arched high, as if they'd breathed in something evil and hoped to see it coming. At some point, Big Enough flattened his black ears up against his head. Sure Enough started crabwalking. A black cloud slid across the blue sky like some flat plate of steel. When the sky finally broke open, it brought down hailstones the size of baseballs making us double over in our saddles and spooking the horses even worse.

We dismounted and tried to wait out the storm under some trees. Lecia even taught me how to count that space in time between when the lightning hit and the thunder sounded. Since that interval was getting littler, she told me, the storm was moving toward us at a good clip, and should, therefore, pass overhead as fast as it had come. But when a bright white line struck a dead trunk in a clearing we could have spit at and hit, we fell to earth and covered our heads. The horses jerked the reins from our hands and went clopping away down the mountain.

We hiked three or four miles down that trail on foot, hatless, soaked through our jean jackets. The temperature had dropped. We got to the stable blue-lipped and shivering. I toweled off in the office. *What if we got hurt?* I asked Mr. McBride. He said the bobcats tended to drag the bigger bones and carcasses up past the timberline, but that buzzards and vultures would usually clue in a search team as to where to hunt.

Another time, we were racing some kids bareback—Lecia on a borrowed roan named George—when a nasty little tar heel hurled a garter snake at that horse, who reared and toppled over on Lecia, snapping her collarbone. Under the yoke of Lecia's white blouse, the bone poked the skin as if to pierce it. But when we found Mother sipping a vodka Gibson at the cowboy bar, she just offered Lecia some baby aspirin from her purse. Doctors would no doubt screw it up, she said. She didn't think that bone could be set anyway, and would we like some cherry Cokes, to which we said no thanks. I can still see Lecia's face—pale and tearless, with a streak of amber clay along her jaw—when it dawned on her that nobody was fixing to take up the cause of that busted bone. She held that arm in front of her like it was a piece of furniture.

The bartender in that place was a handsome, black-haired Mexican named Hector, who had been reading Mother's palm when we came in. He set Mother's hand down long enough to make Lecia a sling out of a bar towel. That towel stank faintly of sour gin and had a candy stripe of red grenadine up the front. Hector also punched open the register and gave us quarters for the jukebox. But we took them the hell out of there and bought bombpops back at the stable instead.

Other than times like this, when we wanted a straight-thinking adult but couldn't find one, we felt safe enough. We also stopped keeping such close watch on our parents. I failed to notice, for instance, that we never saw them together. Daddy sometimes hung around the stable to drink coffee with Mr. McBride, for Daddy could tell a mare's age by staring into her mouth, guess a stallion's weight within twenty pounds, and reckon how many hands high a gelding stood. Daddy had broken cutting horses as a young man, and this earned him a measure of cowboy respect, despite his being Texan, which was reprehensible to most of the hands. Mr. McBride even loaned Daddy his very own blue-spotted Appaloosa free of charge one day to take Lecia and me riding into the mountains.

We tied our horses before a country store with an honest-to-God cracker barrel inside. Daddy paid the man to make us roast beef sandwiches on Wonder bread. He used grainy mustard and thin slices of red onion. We also bought tins of pink salmon eggs and rented fly rods and waders for trout fishing.

Which remains about the only sport I've ever whipped Lecia at right off. Whatever reflex makes her sharp with a gun (she can still pluck a dove from a tree) made her restless in the water. Standing around just bored her. She needed more to do.

That afternoon the canvas bag I'd slung around my neck quickly filled up with the shining bodies of flopping trout. When I could no longer carry it, I waded back to the bank to leave it with Lecia, who'd given up and broken out the sandwiches. I nearly laid down my rod too. That would have been a mistake, for the last fish I hauled out of the water that day must've weighed five pounds and was all fight.

Daddy laughed like hell when it hit. My rod bent double. I staggered out into deeper water hollering for help. He had to wade back to the bank first and get rid of his pole before he could reel the fish in for me. I did manage to get the net under it myself. Together we dragged it flopping on the grassy bank, where it smacked its tail and made Lecia sidestep with an odd daintiness. She actually said *ick.* Daddy grabbed its tail in two sure hands to whack its head on a rock.

Then it lay still, eyes staring ahead. Its gills puffed in reflex. It was not, like the old fish that poet Elizabeth Bishop once wrote about, "battered and venerable and homely" with the long mustache of a mandarin. Nor did it have the bulk that thrilled Hemingway in a tuna. But as fish go, it was close to perfect, being clean silver in the sun with that rainbow stripe all pink and blue and yellow-green melted right into its unnicked scales, and not a square inch of moss or tatter to mar it. It resembled some rare Chinese artifact—the way its scales overlocked so neat, like some jeweler had taken a soldering iron to assemble it one scale at a time. Daddy didn't even suggest I gut or scale it. He wanted to haul it back whole to the country store, figuring the old man who'd rented us our gear would get a kick out of it.

Daddy even carried that fish dangling by the gills into the store, and spread it flat out on the fellow's meat counter. He put both his hands on my shoulders and said that Pokey here had caught that one. The man nodded and called his wife from the back, and she nodded. Then we all stood around nodding a while till the man started giving the names of various taxidermists, at which point Lecia said could she have an Eskimo pie. Even after Daddy bought the ice cream for her, she was all sulled up, arms crossed tight across her sweatshirt. Her lower lip stuck out about two inches in front of her chin, and it was that lip led us out of the damp store into the bright afternoon.

That evening, Daddy gathered kindling for a fire on a boulder about fifty yards up the mountain behind the house. Night was falling. He put Lecia and me in charge of puffing on the little fire he'd lit till it blazed, while he went down to the house for a skillet. We squatted on our haunches and played Indian. I can still make out the loose-limbed shape of Daddy as it came to me through the smoke of that green kindling. He moved between the trees toting the iron skillet up the mountain. He was long-legged and surefooted and made no sound.

Once the fire was high, Daddy swamped each little fish carcass around in a pie tin of cornmeal, then fried it in Crisco. I was hungry as only a day on horseback can make you. A canopy of evergreens waved overhead. Stars were bobbing into view in between. The fire kept popping to send whole handfuls of sparks skittering up the air.

We ate with our fingers off paper plates. The cooked trout gave off a steaming crunch, for they were small and crusty. I kept spitting out the spiny bones. The night air was cold. You had to cool every bite down to a chewable temperature by taking that air in between your teeth with a hiss. This made a nasty noise. Lecia said I sounded like a mule with a feed bag hooked over my ears, and Daddy said, *Talk about the pot calling the kettle black.* And what might have been a fight evaporated right there, rose up with the smoke and dispersed through all those waving evergreens.

He saved my big fish for last and made a ceremony out of cooking it, which he had to do in halves to fit the pan. Even then, the tail looped over the edge and burnt. It was the meatiest fish we ate that night, with the greatest proportion of white flesh to spiky bones. Lecia and I ate it while he worked up a skillet full of thin-sliced red potatoes along with Vidalia onions he'd quartered.

I can still see Daddy scraping at those potatoes, which would keep the smoky fish taste from the lard. He was singing "Goodnight Irene" under his breath, staring into the skillet with that faraway look. Watching the sky arch above us through pines, I thought about a passage I'd read in the encyclopedias Grandma bought us, how the Rockies were formed by glaciers sliding across the continent to rake up zillions of tons of rock. I pictured one moving slow as white silk across where we sat. *Maybe God dropped that boulder off right there,* I wrote in my diary the next day, *for us to cook on.* (Comfort makes fools of us that way, and a kid gets faith back quick.) At one point Daddy said to hush, and through the far pines, lit by a three-quarter moon, we made out the blunted antlers of a moose, which struck me as noble in its big-jawed ugliness. It chewed in profile slow as a ballplayer. Sometime later, a bobcat even yowled, close enough to make me scoot up under Daddy's arm, which fear made him laugh and say nothing was going to bother me. And I believed him.

After we ate, Daddy stoked the fire again. He lay back on a jeans jacket he'd balled up and sipped at a silver whiskey flask. Lecia and I undid a couple of wire coat hangers for marshmallows. I roasted three at a time, dipping them right in the fire. They blazed and cooked black outside, but inside were nothing but goo. Lecia was more even in approach: she toasted them singly to a pale gold color. She even bent one end of the hanger, so it had a rotary handle she could turn like an honest-to-God spit. For once that difference struck me okay without sinking me into a swamp of worry about how it might augur about my character, or lack of character. She even told me while she sat twisting her spit that mine was one helluva fish, and Daddy agreed.

We fell asleep beside him on that unlikely cold stone, both full as ticks on fish and potatoes, each snuggled under an armpit, our heads on his chest. He still smelled of horse. A few times some coal crumbling in on itself caused me to jerk awake; then I saw sparks surge up in a tower and felt Daddy draw our football jackets up over our shoulders. Otherwise, he lay still, the flask balanced on his breast bone at the perfect angle so he could sip steady without lifting his head or spilling down his chin. I don't recall his scrubbing the skillet out with sand and pine needles, nor getting carried down the mountain.

I can only guess what Mother was up to that night: reading, maybe. That was her Russian history summer. The jacket photo on her Rasputin biography showed him wild-haired and googly-eyed above a bird's-nest beard. But she could also have been bellied up to the cowboy bar in town ordering shots of tequila. Or she often sat for hours at home in the Adirondack chair on the front porch that poked out over a sharp drop, sipping vodka by herself in the dark. She did that a lot, drinking and staring down the mountain. If I'd had a penny's worth of sense, her sitting in that deep, downward-sloping chair wrapped up in a serape and sucking down vodka would have struck me as a bad sight.

The night my parents announced their divorce, Lecia and I hadn't even been home for the buildup to it. That always struck me as a moral failure on our parts, like we might have talked them out of it. But the stable held night rides up the broad, easy trails for cookouts. The stablehands would bring out a few guitars and lead the dudes through "On Top of Old Smokey" and "Ninety-Nine Bottles of Beer" before we rode back down. I'd been extra happy that night too. I rode down the mountain with the moon hopping along beside me through the pines. I fell asleep at some point in a saddle slump. The horse rocking me as he picked his way over stones had a rhythm like the Gulf, which until that night I'd never once thought of. It was a fetal rhythm, I guess, the kind that sneaks under your heartbeat and makes your brainwaves go all slack and your eyelids seam themselves together.

I'd started drooling down my sweatshirt when Big Enough reached the trail's end and startled. The clomp of his hooves on asphalt woke me up flailing. I clutched at the saddle horn just before he broke into a light trot at sight of the stable. There, in the headlights shining across the empty stalls, stood the lanky, big-handed figure of Daddy in loose khakis. He had on a baseball cap with *Lone Star State* embroidered on it. Under that logo was a yellow star that caught just enough moon to make itself seen. I rode toward that star. Under the brim lay a broad pit of dark. His face stayed in that dark, and the quiet that came with it, all the way home.

Mother sat on the curvy living room sofa in front of the fireplace heaped with ashes. The screwdriver she'd been drinking had gone watery. She had on black stretch pants and one of the white shirts we gave Daddy from Sears every Christmas. This one had just been unfolded, I could tell. A little tab of cardboard stuck out like a priest's sprung collar. The new deck of Bicycle cards on the table was untouched, its seal unbroken.

I can't recall how they announced the divorce. Daddy just sat heavy on the far end of that curvy couch. He was leaned over with his elbows on his knees, his big rawboned hands dangling toward the floorboards. His head hung down at the angle a bull's does at the end of a fight, when he's lost a lot of blood and the shoulder muscles have been picked at and stabbed so he can no longer lift that head to make a charge. Big tears fell from Daddy's eyes onto the floorboards. He didn't even bother to wipe at them. Every now and then he dragged the back of one hand across the bubble of snot that kept starting from his nose. The tears left dark drops on the wood floor. I studied the splatter of them a long time to keep from watching him cry. They were some connect-the-dots picture I couldn't make sense out of.

On the other end of the couch, Mother stayed dry-eyed. That's no testament to how she felt, mind you. Maybe she held down a wellspring of ache, or maybe not. She wasn't really there, of course. The enormous screwdriver had taken her Away, which was its purpose.

They point-blank asked us who we wanted to live with. Mother was staying in Colorado; Daddy had to go back home. They spread those facts before us as if setting out two ice cream flavors we got to pick. Which would be better to have—a daddy or a mother? Or we could divvy up ourselves if we wanted, so each got one.

Lecia called me into the kitchen for a powwow then. She claimed she'd slap me senseless were I to shed a tear. But I was nowhere near crying. I wanted to curl up in a ball.

We peeked around the doorjamb into the living room. The backs of our parents' heads poked over the sofa back. They sat not speaking like strangers on a subway. That one would go forever Away seemed impossible. I pictured the globe with its dividing meridians. I knew how far it was from Texas to Colorado. But it wasn't just geography I was picking. I eeny-meeny-minied between their two heads a second. I considered a coin toss. In my head, I zigzagged between swamp and mountain, between impossible heat and blue cool. I still wanted to lie down on that floor with the Italian tile against my hot cheek and go noddy-blinkems till the bears woke us up. While I fretted, Lecia's gaze went very level, as if she'd seen this choice coming across the far sky like a weather front.

She chose, finally. If we left Mother by herself, she'd get in capital-T Trouble. But Daddy would just go back to work at the Gulf, so we'd always know where he was. The logic seemed solid enough. *Let's go back in there and break it to them,* she said.

Daddy left the next day about dawn. Mr. McBride's truck lunged up to the house. He stepped out on the running board and left his motor going and said no to coffee when Mother asked. Daddy came out to heave his army duffel bag in the truck bed. I'd tried to zip myself up into that bag in the middle of the night. I buried myself among the flat-folded hankerchiefs and balled-up socks. I fit pretty well, too. But I'd stopped the zipper right under my chin, being basically a sissy about the dark.

That's where Daddy found me asleep in the morning. He smelled like Old Spice. His weathered face was nicked up. There were red polka dots of blood on which he'd stuck white squares of toilet paper. He squatted down with his brown leather dopp kit in one hand. *Get outa there, Pokey,* he said, drawing the zipper down to my belly button. *God sakes, you'll break a fella's heart.*

Then Mr. McBride's gray Chevy truck was drawing Daddy away down the mountain. His head got smaller in the window, till it was no more than a black dot, like one of those towns on the map we'd once been in such an all-fired hurry to get to. All across Texas I'd ridden behind that head. I knew every comb mark in it. Daddy's leaving never even dimly occurred to me as possible on that trip, though Mother's was a constant, unspoken threat. But Daddy was the guy you set your watch by. He woke in the same humor every morning, asking did you want oatmeal or eggs. And now Mr. McBride's truck was winding him away from us in hairpin turns down the mountain. I finally stopped watching for glimpses of the truck to break through the dark spaces between trees and put my head down and ran hard down the dirt road. I kept running till the dust gave way to asphalt, even though that vehicle had long since disappeared.

Back at the cabin, Mother pulled the rollers out of her hair in about three swipes of her hand and announced that she felt like a freed slave.

We drove to a vast and canyonlike Denver department store where she bought what she called an honest-to-God cocktail dress, along with church dresses for Lecia and me (though we'd rather have chewed linoleum than gone to Sunday school). The place gave me vertigo. The glass cubicles were sharp-edged. They gleamed, displaying impossibly bright scarves, jeweled cigarette cases, real gold chains for the sole purpose of holding your glasses around your neck. The smell of new dye from the clothes made my eyes sting. Metal escalators meandered between floors and threatened to eat my toes off at the end.

We all got fur coats. Mother's white shirred beaver was softer all over than the inside of my arm. It had a lining of pale beige silk that felt on my bare shoulders like the menthol lotion you get smoothed on for sunburn. Around the heavy swirling hem of that coat ran a wide strip of black lace. The parkas Lecia and I picked out had rabbit fur around the hoods and pockets deep enough to squirrel extra dinner rolls in.

That afternoon, we flounced into a grand hotel's great marble lobby hung with chandeliers. The guy running the elevator had on the brass-buttoned uniform of a naval officer. He drew a steady paycheck for nothing more than pressing buttons all day, he said. That caused me to speculate on how the union in those parts must play hell with the hotel companies. He and Mother laughed at that like old pals. He was still laughing when she pressed five dollars into his white-gloved hand.

That night in the dining room, our table had a whole starting lineup of spoons. Still our waiter brought eensy baby forks with our shrimp cocktails. He wore a tuxedo and claimed the potato soup was cold on purpose. There was another guy with a gold cup tied around his neck who tasted Mother's wine before she got to. At the end of the meal, the chef himself came out of the kitchen in his puffy hat with a skillet of chopped-up bananas he set fire to right at the table, then ladled over our gold-plated dishes of ice cream. Mother ordered a bottle of Dom Pérignon and crystal glasses for us to share. We ratholed the cocktail forks in our skirt pockets to steal as souvenirs. Mine looked like a devil's trident belonging to a tiny little devil, I told Lecia, and she nearly wet her pants laughing. We clinked our glasses to staying in that hotel like princesses forever. Meanwhile, the waiters in their black clothes took our plates away and scrubbed crumbs off the table with silver-backed brushes they maneuvered using wrist movements too strict to seem natural.

All this time, Daddy had fallen out of my head completely, which must have been Mother's plan, of course, But when the fact of his absence came rushing back through me like a train, it brought a whole coal car of evil feeling.

I was lying under emerald satin covers with a leather-bound breakfast menu tilted on my middle. Lecia was still a lump on the bed's far side, but the drapes held a line of light at their bottom that made it morning. Hunger wasn't bothering me, but I was wondering intensely what a Belgian waffle was when out of nowhere, my last sight of Daddy came sliding fast through my head. Mr. McBride's gray truck vanished behind a stand of evergreens. The menu dropped from my hands. How could Daddy's going have slipped my mind? I'd always measured my loyalty in unshakable terms. My head brimmed with tortures I could endure for noble causes, comrades, family honor. But I'd been bought off cheap: a rabbit-fur coat and the stolen fork of a baby devil had shoved Daddy clear from my mind.

By the time Mother started keeping company with a cowboy from the stable, a fellow named Ray who had the small and peg-like teeth of a rabbit, I'd stopped riding Big Enough. Colorado and the horses took Daddy Away. I vowed to prove myself worthy of his return through deprivation, thereby luring him back. So I spent my days reading and trying to write poetry, which I did in the cool comfort of the Christian Science Reading Room. Here's a bona fide excerpt:

Grandma used to wear a scarf
Upon her silvery head.
I thought that she would wear it
Till she rolled over dead

One afternoon I'd nodded off over my volume of e. e. cummings and been poked awake with a pointy finger-bone by the reading-room matron, who suggested that I wobble myself home to nap.

And it was there I found Mother, shirtless, lying flat on the floor before the fireplace with old Ray astraddle her like she was a pony he was fixing to break. He was kneading her shoulder muscles. His cowboy hat sat perched on the sofa back, and his brown hair looked specially greasy and mashed down. In fact, his hat had left a dent all the way around his skull as if it had a flip top. I stared at him, my copy of cummings clutched to my chest. Of course, Ray leapt upright. He was grossly bowlegged. (In Leechfield parlance, he couldn't trap a hog in a ditch.) Meanwhile, Mother patted her hand around till she laid hold to her bra, which she demurely slipped under her torso and hooked in back with one sure hand, still facedown the whole time. Ray said, *Well, hello there, Slow Poke.* His voice was loud and rusty. And I corrected him right off: "Pokey," I said without blinking. "My daddy calls me Pokey, not Slow Poke. Slo-Poke is a brown sucker you buy that breaks your teeth." Mother pulled her shirt over her head and said she was glad I'd come home for lunch for a change. That lie wounded me worse than the shirtless fact of my mother stretched half-naked under a cowboy. She wasn't one bit glad to see me.

Ray quit his stable-hand's job the next week, disappearing for parts unknown. His leaving was coincident with Mother's solo trip to Mexico. "Acapulco, here I come," she'd said, promising to buy us both sombreros. But when Mother returned from that trip to pick us up (we'd been staying with the stable master's family for pay) the man who stood from the car was distinctly not Ray. He was too tall and lanky and black-haired.

I was walking two lathered horses around the corral at the time, and the sight of that male figure by the car made something quicken in me. He stood through the cloud of dust the Impala kicked up. He wore gray slacks and what might have been a short-sleeved white shirt from Sears. I dropped the reins of both animals, prompting Mr. McBride to yell, *Don't leave them horses wet.* But I was sprinting toward that tall figure with all the hope of a kid on Christmas morning. I did not, however, skid to a stop in front of my daddy, whose large hands I'd already imagined lifting me light as a ghost to whirl my feet above the dusty stable yard. No, it wasn't Daddy standing on the passenger side of Mother's car. It was Hector, the barkeep from the cowboy joint. Mother leaned over the car roof holding out a hand weighed down by a diamond solitaire ring. I stopped in my tracks. *Say hello to your new daddy,* she said. And I could hear Lecia close the gap behind me, her spurs clanking while I took in Hector's alligatorlike grin, and Lecia whispered what I was already thinking: *Oh shit.*

CHAPTER 10

One Sunday after Hector came, Lecia and I walked down to the stable and found the tack room still locked up, though the sun was high enough to show behind the mountains. Somebody had been and gone already. The stalls were all mucked out, with clean straw strewn around. And there were oats in the bins and fresh water in the troughs. But the McBrides' truck wasn't parked in the dirt driveway in front of their trailer. Banging on their aluminum screen door brought no face to stare down at us. I crossed the bridge and peeked in the café window. Not a soul perched on a single counter stool. I told Lecia it was like that *Twilight Zone* episode where space guys had kidnaped everybody on the planet except this grouchy old teacher, who wound up being sad that she'd always been such a jackass to everybody.

We sat on the cinder blocks in front of the café. The owner had lined those blocks up there to stop drunk folks from plowing straight through the plate glass. Lecia pulled our sandwiches out of a paper bag. Bologna on Wonder bread—mine with mustard, hers with mayo. Going home wasn't an option. Mother and Hector had tried one on (that's how we heard the phrase "tied one on") the night before. They'd doubtless either still be passed out or coping with the morning whirlies. Hector had concocted a hangover remedy involving raw eggs, vodka, and Pepto-Bismol. I called it a Dismal Flip. The very sight of it tipping up to his lips sent Mother scurrying to the bathroom with the projectile heaves. So mornings with the newlyweds were something we tended to miss. In fact, since Hector's Florsheim shoes first crossed our threshold, we hadn't piled into that bed a single morning to watch the bears. I know for my part, I wouldn't have gone into Mother's room before noon on a dare.

I ate only the middle of my sandwich, in a nibbled circle that pissed Lecia off. She hated me doing anything eensy. She said that was how squirrels ate, and then she pitched my leftover crust at the sparrows. Not a car passed while they pecked it up. The sun got a notch higher. Otherwise, nothing. After a while, we gave up hoping the McBrides would pull up to unlock our saddles. We played a primitive form of kickball with the wadded lunchbag across the bridge and back to the stable.

Lecia found a pair of hackamores hanging from a nail, and we took our horses for a short lope along a narrow, roller-coaster length of trail with a dip in it that made your stomach drop toward the end. The horses got lathered doing it. We walked them in figure eights through the corral, then brushed and watered them. We killed the rest of the morning snake-hunting in the field behind the stable. There were two or three grass snakes writhing across each other in the bottom of an oat bucket when the McBrides' truck finally lumbered across the bridge and set us running for it.

Mr. McBride said hey, and we said hey back. He asked me didn't I know what day it was. I said Sunday, from the look of things. Then Polly stepped down from the running board and swung around to face us with their new baby girl balanced on her hip. That baby's face stays in my mind as having an uncanny resemblance to Winston Churchill. *That's a sad face,* I was thinking, *for a girl to bear forward through the world,* when Polly said hadn't we even sent our daddy a Father's Day card.

The question doused me quick in cold shame. Lecia barged right in over my quiet and said sure we had. Plus we'd sent him a whole tackle box of hand-painted lures from Denver, a bag of red rubber worms, and a new Zippo reel with hundred-pound test line. Mr. McBride said he didn't think there was a hundred-pound test line, not in nylon anyways. But Lecia would have backed him straight to the wall with that lie before she'd have let it go. She said that Colorado trout were much bigger pussies than East Texas bass. That meant that Yankee tackle stores didn't need to stock heavy line. Down in Leechfield, she said, hundred-pound was about the lightest line you could get, the biggest being as big around as her wrist, which she held out for Mr. McBride to study as proof. Everybody around the stable had gotten way sick of Lecia's Texas-this and Texas-that. That morning Mr. McBride just squeezed her shoulder before heading to the office to open up. His kids spilled out of the truck and scattered, me hating every one of them for having a daddy. I wanted my own tall daddy to come there and make a me a patch of shade with his big cool shadow.

I thought back to the morning he'd unzipped me from his duffel bag, how I later ran after the truck that carried him off. I was dead certain that I'd die without Daddy around. But I hadn't died, of course. Oh, I hadn't started calling Hector "Daddy" like he'd asked me to. ("That'll be a cold day in hell," I'd said.) But neither had I written Daddy a letter every day, like I'd promised. I'd fired off five or six letters the first few weeks. But all I got back was a postcard of the Spindletop oil gusher. Daddy had scratched out some lame joke about how rich he was getting by being "in oil." He'd put "Ha Ha!" after it, which seemed pitiful to me. And he'd closed off with "Love from your best Daddy." That made my eyes tear up, the best Daddy part, like a whole slew of others were lined up to daddy in my direction.

Plus another thing niggled at me: I wasn't entirely sure Daddy knew about Hector. It had gotten harder to write stuff without mentioning him. Maybe we were supposed to fake in letters that Mother was moping around lonesome like one of those country-song divorcées. I had the good sense, of course, not to write about old bowlegged Ray rubbing on Mother's nude back. But between not mentioning Hector and not knowing whether to sound cheerful or like I was suffering without Daddy, writing him got harder. I spent a lot of time staring around the Christian Science Reading Room. Or I'd try to chew my tooth pattern into the yellow paint of my pencil so the marks lay exactly even all the way down. Sometimes a whole morning slid out from under me in that musty room with not a "t" crossed nor an "i" dotted on my Big Chief tablet.

That Father's Day Lecia and I crossed from the stable to the pay phone booth at the Esso, which was hot as blue blazes from taking in early sun. Unfolding the glass door let loose a blast of hot air like an oven. The silver floor was crusty, littered with wasps and moths that must have just dropped mid-flight from heat and lack of oxygen. I stood in the doorway so as not to smush them on my shoe bottoms. But Lecia just crunched right over them to the coin slot and dropped in her dime. The black receiver got held an inch or so off her cheek, to keep from scalding her, I guess. She told the operator to dial a collect call to Woodlawn 2-2800. After it rang about a zillion times with no answer, the operator broke the connection. On her next try, the switchboard lady at the Gulf wouldn't accept charges or put her through to Daddy's unit. Lecia said in her most quavery voice that it was a medical emergency, then she called the woman a nasty-assed bitch and slammed the phone down so hard it bounced right out of its little silver catch and spun from the cable, whapping the phone-booth glass.

Lecia busted into tears after that. She buckled up like something broke inside her, sliding to the bottom of the phone booth without even checking the coin return for change.

We wound up making two Father's Day cards from blue construction paper. We put "Dad" in cursive on front of both using sky-blue glitter and Elmer's glue. I went with a flag motif on mine, adding red stripes in crayon. The silver stars I drew went a dull, gunmetal gray instead of looking sparkly like the Crayola itself did. Staring at the end product rankled me. No matter how swell some drawing looked in your head, it always got cobbled up into a ratty kid-thing by the time you were through.

Mother set both cards on the mantel to dry. Lecia's at least was clean. Mine had glue scabs all over. Plus she was hell on coloring inside the lines, which I was a long way from at that time. Still, old Hector swayed in front of both like they were the Holy Fucking Grail. He had this bleary, dog-faced look that I now realize was as much myopia as drunkenness. He slurred out a sentence about how he hoped someday we'd make him something for Father's Day, to which Lecia said, "Don't hold your breath." That made me feel sorry enough to hug him before bed. My arms squeezed quick around his middle, which was wishy inside the slippery nylon of his shirt.

The next morning Mother dragged out of bed first thing to hit the post office for stamps enough to mail Daddy our cards. Motoring around before her blood alcohol level got adjusted was no small act of will. She'd brought a Bloody Mary in a tumbler with a lid on it like a baby would sip out of. She sat heavy behind the wheel in front of the P.O. rifling through her brown Coach bag for her wallet. Her hands shook. She finally plopped the whole thing in Lecia's lap, saying just take it.

Left alone in the car with Mother, I saw for the first time how drinking had worn away at her looks. She'd bleached her hair platinum for some ungodly reason. She also wore dark sunglasses in daylight. Something about the vast difference between those colors—the hair like scalded grass and the shiny black of the glasses—yellowed her complexion. She had also draped a white chiffon scarf around her head and neck like some bandage too loose and sheer to do any good. Her big square hands trembled even when she did something definite with them, like dumping the ashtray out the window. I was silently scrambling for something to say. But no sooner did a possible sentence scuttle through my head than I could picture the tired scorn Mother would meet it with. She liked to say her bullshit meter went off pretty easy in those days. I only knew I bored her. I watched her sprinkling salt in the sippy hole of that tumbler using a Morton's picnic shaker she kept in the car. I finally told her maybe she needed a whole block of salt like what we put out in the horse pasture. She pinched her mouth into a stiff little asterisk at that.

Mother's bleach job put me in mind of an obituary picture I'd seen of Jayne Mansfield, who apparently got her head cut slap off in a car wreck. I was prone to grisly images at that time so it was no strain at all to picture Jayne Mansfield's head—still wearing cat's-eye sunglasses with rhinestones all around the edges—all lopped off at the neck and sailing up across the blue air like a fly ball. The image vaporized when Lecia shoved out the glass door into the sunlight. That big Coach bag over her shoulder bumped at her like a soldier's duffel.

For a week or so after mailing off the Father's Day cards, Lecia and I stopped at the P.O. morning and evening looking for a letter back. She drew the mailbox key from the string around her neck to open the tiny brass door, whose actual number is nothing but a smudge in my memory. Daddy wasn't much of a correspondent. It always sat empty as a little coffin.

In all fairness to him, divorced men back then just surrendered their kids to the moms and forgot about it. Like a bad litter of puppies you'd tie in a potato sack and fling from your speeding Ford off the Orange Bridge, kids just got let loose. I wouldn't have thought such a vanishing possible, not where Daddy was concerned. We'd shot too much pool together. We'd caught too many fish and eaten too many good gumbos. He always spouted stoical-sounding promises about his loyalty. At the first hint of lonesomeness for him, those promises could start zooming through my head like bad reverb: "I'm not a rich man, darling. But I can still walk. And when I walk, I walk heavy. And I swear to God, anybody messes with you, I'll walk just as far and just as heavy as I ever did for the U.S. Army. I guarangoddamntee you that."

Sometime that summer, Lecia lost the mailbox key riding. Then it just seemed too much trouble for us to stand in line at the counter and ask for the mail twice a day.

My final campaign to woo Daddy back that summer relied on the Green Stamps we'd never bothered to save before. Stores used to dole out these stamps according to the amount of money you'd just spent. Say you got twenty stamps for every dollar you paid for groceries, something like that. You then pasted the stamps in trading books, and took those books to a Green Stamp center to swap them for "free" stuff.

The stamp product catalogue was thin, like the circular a hardware store might send out for its President's Day sale. But it lacked order. Kid stuff got scattered in with flashlights; housewares, with fire extinguishers. For ten books of stamps you could get an off-brand of the Chatty Cathy Doll, one that would stop talking after a week of tugging on its string and just gibber a kind of high-pitched monkey language. A hundred books might get you camping gear or a croquet game that fit on a little wheely wooden cart. Thousands of books would buy something as big as a clothes drier, or a La-Z-Boy recliner. Back in the Leechfield grocery, the lady shoppers had fallen like vultures on the long ribbons of stamps Mother held up at the end of the checkout lane. "Anybody want these?" she'd holler, waving them in the air. The carts would converge four deep where she stood, all those ladies grabbing across their chicken parts and lettuces and fat babies in the riding seat with their stubby legs jammed through the square metal holes like so many rolled roasts. Mother didn't believe in Green Stamps or coupons. They were a trick to keep women hunched over their kitchen tables after their kids were asleep, not unlike darning and embroidery—things Mother excelled at but refused to do. Nor would she drive a block out of her way to get gas for two cents cheaper. Mother had transcended thrift, even before she got Grandma's money.

Still, when I started stuffing those stamps in the tin metal coffee canister with a rooster painted on it, Mother didn't utter a word to mock it, which must have taken some big-league restraint. I spent my evenings at the kitchen table licking stamps and then smoothing the sticky sheets into savings books. When my spit ran out, I took up the sour-smelling blue sponge from the sink. On the pages of those books lay neat grids spelled out in menthol-green lines. I worked sloppy most of the time, but it pleased me no end when I did manage to line up a strip of stamps exactly within those borders. Lecia asked me on a nightly basis if I'd gone slap-dab crazy. But there wasn't much venom in her voice.

Days, I hung out at the grocery store in town, just inside the magic doors. People sometimes pulled their stamps out of the paper sacks to hand over to me before shoving their carts onto the black rubber runner that ticked open those doors with a hum.

Garbage day was my best haul. People tended to stuff grocery sacks in those armored-looking metal cans. Often as not, the brown sacks came in a neatly folded pile on top of all the yucky stuff. Only a few times did I have to dig past coffee grounds and melon rinds to get at them. And in those sack bottoms, you could sometimes find Green Stamps by the yard that somebody's husband or teenager forgot to draw out. The few doctors and business people from Colorado Springs who kept weekend places up there didn't mess with stamps at all. I hit their small, neat garbage cans first.

At the end of all this foraging and licking and counting, I had dozens of full stamp books stacked in a vodka box. Lecia had to help me scoot it over the pine needles and gravel in the driveway to the car. Mother then heaved it in the trunk. She drove me clear to Colorado Springs, to what the Green Stamp marketing wizards had named the Redemption Center.

The Indian woman behind the counter wore a polished turquoise stone on a fine silver chain inside the deep shadow of her serious cleavage. That cleavage stays with me because I stood eye-level with it a long time. Finding something I'd X'ed in the catalogue actually on the shelves turned out to be a problem. There was no new rod and reel looking just like a Zippo. There were no gold cufflinks shaped like horseshoes with diamond chips for nailheads. The lady offered to send to Ohio, which would take six to eight weeks. But my daddy didn't raise me a fool. Just as I knew not to buy on credit, I damn sure knew not to pay for something I couldn't lay my hands on, not unless it was from Sears.

The lady was nice about looking through her inventory book, though. We spent the better part of her shift at it. I'd read off the product number from my dog-eared catalogue, and she'd check for it in her three-ring binder. The notebook was tethered to the counter with twisted cable, and had a dusty blue cloth cover like the ones high school kids carried. As time wore on, the inventory book came to hold all the power of a sorcerer's spell book. It had Daddy's gift somewhere inside it, and locating that gift on its onionskin pages was the last leg of a long journey that had started back when I'd chased after Daddy down the mountain. Whenever the lady stopped flipping past the staggered dividers and started running her fingernail down a single page, I'd cross the fingers on both hands for luck.

All this time Mother stood chain-smoking back by the glass door. I could hear her stamp out each cigarette butt. The toe on her high heel wiggled and made a raspy noise against the concrete floor. No sooner had one been stamped out than another got lit. I'd hear that lighter flip open, then the rough click of the flint sending out a spark. A few seconds later a double lungful of Salem exhaust would drift up to us. She also sighed out heavy smoke every time the clerk shook her head no.

Not a single thing I'd picked was in stock. That shocked me. I'd lain in bed night after night picturing Daddy stepping down from his truck after the long drive to Colorado, how he'd scoop me up in his arms while Lecia stood tapping her foot. Behind him on the truck seat would sit the box in which the new fishing reel (or tie tack, or ebony domino set) had been shipped. Luring Daddy back had—in my mind—edged over the line from being a wish into being a fact. I even fooled myself that *not* having everything in stock augured well. Fate itself would pick Daddy's present, rather than running the risk that I'd get something half-assed.

Mother headed up the aisle toward us. I heard the measured click of her heels, which told me she had the red-ass over this whole undertaking. She announced to the counter lady that the catalogue didn't say word one about them not shipping stuff till Kennedy was out of office. She said her baby (meaning me) had worked like a field hand getting all those stamps stuck in books. I tugged the elbow of her beige cashmere jacket to slow her down, but she jerked away. It was a rant I'd heard—the Goddamn Lying, Republican Bastards who'd ever thought up the miserable, niggardly business of stamp-licking. The lady misheard the "niggardly" part and herself got steamed, saying she wasn't colored, she was an Indian, to which Mother replied, "I don't give a great steaming pile of dogshit what you are—"

I somehow herded Mother outside under the forest-green awning. A fine rain had started to fall. Great gray clouds rolled down the mountains. The street was wet and black. I'd left my box of stamps on the counter and would have fried in hot lard before I'd have slid into Mother's Impala without something in my lap for Daddy, however small and wrong that gift might wind up being. But I knew better than to say it that strong. You couldn't draw a hard line in front of Mother, ever, could never set down an ultimatum. Doing so only made her bow up—as Daddy always said—like a cut worm. She would spend her last breath calling you a cocksucker before she'd back down. I hedged. I suggested. I finally watched her skitter through the rain on her heels across the wet street to a bar with a red neon sign in the window, the Black Cat.

For what seemed like hours I walked the wide chilly aisles of the Redemption Center. The shelves rose all the way up to the twenty-foot steel-beam rafters. Most of the grown-up stuff was inside boxes the color of dirt, so I kept going back to the front desk. But the clerk—dead sure, I guess, that Mother had called her a nigger—wouldn't let me handle the inventory book hitched to the counter.

After a while, the toy aisle drew me. There were Ping-Pong tables and pool tables, an inflatable swimming pool deep enough to go swimming underwater in. I almost blew a batch of stamp books on a plastic toy factory that used a heat and vacuum process to sculpt from small squares of plastic the kind of bright-colored doodads you got out of gum machines for pennies—baby footballs and squatty dolls with loops on the tops of their heads to string them around your neck. The picture on front showed a clean-scrubbed boy and girl about my age operating a roadside toy stand. They were taking fistfuls of dollar bills from a whole herd of toddlers clambering around to buy their toys. I'd read a comic-book biography of Henry Ford and fancied having my own assembly line—a union shop, of course. For a full twenty minutes, I stared at that toy-factory box thinking of all the dollars I could generate at ten cents a pop selling geegaws to the rich tourists at the stable.

When reason finally struck, it fell over me with the harsh neon light from long bulbs high among the metal rafters. It was a light the color of horse piss. I knew that no kid in her right mind would shell out real coins for that crap. Daddy's voice ran back through me. He's always talked back to the TV commercials. "Now how did I live fifty some-odd years with no Veg-O-Matic to make me julienne fries? Confound my bad old luck!"

I wound up getting him a ceramic statue of a pot-bellied monk with a bald pate and a crown of hair made of real brown felt, fuzzy to the touch. The monk carried a bamboo fishing pole with a line of gold braid. A mug of frothy brown beer sat at his sandaled feet. I also got Mother an electric can opener, which impressed me most for the built-in knife sharpener it had at the back.

When she lifted that can opener out of its box there under the red Coca-Cola clock in the Black Cat Lounge, she was tickled over it in that loopy drunk's way. I could have given her a rat turd in a bucket and gotten the same amount of gush. She planted a lipsticky kiss on my cheek and passed the can opener around. The cowboys lined up at the bar handled it too gently. They turned it over in their rough hands in a way that made it seem shoddy. The barman even unplugged his blender to test the sharpener on his lemon knives. The shrill grinding sound it made on steel was crazed as a dentist drill.

The monk got wrapped in newsprint and shipped. The coffee canister got filled up with Green Stamps again, almost by accident. But the very prospect of them made me tired. One night I stomped on the trash-can pedal so the lid popped open like the jaw of something, and I upended the stamps in there.

On what felt like the last day of summer, we helped Mr. McBride and all his saddle hands herd the stable horses to winter pasture. Dusk was coming on. The constable had cleared the main road of cars for the time they figured it would take. He even blocked off incoming roads with black-and-white-striped sawhorses.

I don't know why they let Lecia and me ride along, because even Mr. McBride's kids—all champion riders—were forbidden. Once the corral gate got thrown open, the herd hesitated before trotting out. Only after they'd crossed the stone bridge did they seem to twig to where they were headed. Then they ran in a single, faintly weaving body at full tear. Their big necks strained forward, their long backs seeming to follow behind. If I'd fallen, I'd have been stomped flat before anybody even noticed the empty saddle. Still, I mostly wasn't scared. The whole scene was like something from a cowboy movie. Much of the road was packed dirt instead of pavement, and the dust was enormous. A great cloud wrapped around us the whole time. Even Lecia's face bobbing seemed blurry as a cheap newsreel. All I could make out for yards in any direction was the bare backs of those horses—dun and chestnut and blue-spotted Appaloosa—stretching out for rows and moving in such perfect unison that I could sometimes convince myself I was standing still in the undulating roar of it. To ride in the midst of that filled my skull with thunder and made me dumb. At some point, I watched a little paint pony break loose from the herd. He skirted up somebody's lawn, leaping first across a sidewalk, then over a low hedge into another yard. Mr. McBride finally galloped up the incline and folded him back in. That single horse cutting out brought home to me in a great rush how fast we were traveling in that streaming tide of animal. My own velocity gave me a rush of stark fear. I bent over my saddle horn and locked my body down over that fear, then got swept back up in the surge of horses again.

The next day, Mr. McBride's truck pulled up to the house dragging a hired trailer with our horses inside. That's how we figured out we were leaving town for the school year.

We headed west again, into even higher altitudes, toward a black dot on the map that Mother had circled in red ink—her own idea of winter pasture, I guess. She'd bought herself a bar as an investment. If your mother's drinking worries you, and she buys herself an entire bar in a town you've never heard her so much as mention before, you might respond with big-eyed quiet. She did try to soft-pedal the bar aspect of the move. In her speech at the time, she claimed the Longhorn Bar was no different than a sock you'd stuff with your gambling stake and pitch deep under your bed where dust bunnies rolled around. Hector had some family in the new town. Also, if we stayed in the mountain cabin, Lecia and I would have to catch a bus to a Colorado Springs school at six on winter mornings. *Who'd relish that?* she said.

Lecia and I carried some clothes in round Barbie travel cases. I watched the cabin get littler behind us. Then a grove of aspens came between us and it, blotting it entirely from view, and the car started to hairpin down the mountain.

I knew we'd never get back there and said as much to Lecia, who claimed that was the least of our worries. I looked at her serious profile while she watched the trees tick past. She had a way of tucking her chin in. Her head dipped down like a gull's would facing a steep wind, so her brown eyes peered up at the world from a definite slot under her blond bangs' sharp border. She drew her chin back further into her neck's folds. That was her way of digging back into herself, of getting down deep in the solid foundation of what she was before another change swamped over her. Seeing her profile go all chinless in the car, I felt a whole flood of dark fill me up, cold as creek water. Daddy wouldn't even know where to come get us when he got ready.

We drove all day across the high plains. All the while, Mother was babbling about how small our life in Texas had been, a town with no music but country and zydeco; no books but the Sears catalogue, which ladies I grew up with called the "dream book." The only thing a woman might dream for there, Mother said, was a deep-freeze filled with deer meat she'd cleaned and dressed herself; or a fat vinyl ottoman to prop up her swollen feet on at day's end. At one point, she just pitched her black beret out the window. I watched it tumble to a stop behind us and lay there like roadkill.

At a Western store, we ordered blue-plate specials for supper: meatloaf, and mashed potatoes that Lecia and I molded into volcanoes. On the way out, Mother bought a man's Stetson with two long quail feathers sloping backwards out of the band, and a pair of snakeskin cowboy boots. She also paid a hundred dollars for a squash-blossom necklace. It was made of leaded silver heavy enough to feel like an ox yoke when you put it on.

By the time our pale Impala began to rise off that plain back into the mountains, the sun had gone red. Dark settled in. The speedometer glow got noticeable. I stood between their heads, Hector's and Mother's. His saggy, reptilian profile as he slouched behind the wheel—he always put me in mind of an alligator—showed no response to Mother's new cowgirl motif. Hector was, to my mind anyway, in the deepest way possible along for the ride. Mother stretched out on the shotgun side of the car, her cowboy boots propped on the front dash. She'd taught us an old cowboy song earlier. I fell asleep to her singing it alone in her tuneless whisper:

I'm an old cowhand, from the Rio Grande,
But my legs ain't bowed, and my cheeks ain't tanned.
Well I know all the songs that the cowboys know
'Cause I learned them all on the ra-di-o.
Yippee-ay-yo-ky-yay . . .

CHAPTER 11

Our headlights streaked across a billboard announcing that we'd crossed into Antelope proper. The town fathers hoped to catch the ski crowd, who drove straight past that sign—painted in chubby red cursive like you saw on ice cream trucks—to Telluride up the road. Antelope was founded during the Gold Rush, though very few nuggets of gold got sifted through the screen mesh of many miners' pans back then. Somebody did pickax up great streaks of silver and copper, but after those mines played out, Antelope had no clear means of keeping its citizens alive. Lecia was slumped on my shoulder, and I elbowed her to scope the place with me.

Mother had geared us up all our lives for a great city. The bedtime stories she told were full of such places: Athens in the age of Socrates, before the Cynics started running things and folks got to opening up their wrists longwise in the baths; the Paris of the twenties; Vienna when a sick and sweaty Mozart was scribbling out the notes to his own requiem. Not least on that list was Mother's own New York in the forties. Such a city was our birthright, we'd been told. But when we eased along Antelope's main street that wet fall night, the squatty buildings and storefronts were lit only by a few beer signs. No marquees blinked.

No long awnings were guarded by officious doormen with gold taxi whistles around their necks.

By daylight, the landscape was capital-B Beautiful. But something grim and Gothic hung around the place. The mountains seemed to lurch over the town. Plus that fall the sky stayed gray, not unlike the skies I'd read about in *Dracula*, vaulted over by the Carpathian Mountains with their bare trees clawing out.

I'd founded a vampire club at the time, myself the only member. I wrote out the initiation ceremony, which was lengthy and painful, in my red Big Chief tablet. You started by poking your finger with a straight pin to swap blood with all the other members. With Lecia watching, I jabbed both my own index fingers, to prove how serious I was about the whole deal. You were also supposed to douse your hand in lighter fluid and set a match to it, afterward patting it out fast on a wet towel—a trick I'd seen back in Leechfield on Halloween. (This I postponed actually trying till there were more members to wow with it.) Then came the written vampire test. You had to spell out the three or four Transylvanian words from Bram Stoker's book. (*Vlkoslak* was the one, I think, that meant vampire.) These would serve as passwords to enter the clubhouse I never got around to cobbling together. Once you'd passed these trials, you got to mark your carotid artery with two red dots from a laundry marker. Lecia refused to endure this even when I offered to waive the initiation rites and promised she could be my vice president—then president, with myself as Igor.

But truly, Antelope suggested such things—secret clubs, demonic rituals. The German market still hung sausage by twine from the ceiling. The first time I pushed open the heavy door that set the huge cowbell overhead banging, I was horrified to look up and find all those fragrant, inert hunks of meat in blood-colored casings swaying over me. They reminded me of some medieval etching I'd seen in one of Mother's art books—dozens of heretics hung by the Spanish Inquisition. The bodies had swung off this giant scaffolding in some town square and just twirled rotting in the breeze, arms falling off, eyeballs popping out. The guy who owned that market was named Olaf, no less. He ran the place with his twin sister, Anna. They were both about a hundred years old, their arthritic spines seeming to curve them more deeply in on themselves every time you went in. Each cast a shadow like a bulbous question mark on the scuffed and streaky linoleum.

They scooped penny candy from drugstore jars and gave out samples of their own garlic cheese spread, which was a Day-Glo orange you never came across in nature. There was stuff on the shelves that had been sitting there since Eisenhower. The cans of bathroom cleaner they sold had faced the sun in their display pyramid for so long that their front labels had faded from lime green to pale lemon. The mouse-print instructions about not eating the stuff could no longer be read. "If swallowed—" each of the cans said, then there was just a wordless scorch mark as warning.

At first we stayed across the street from that market in an old stucco resort hotel painted a stale pink. For breakfast and lunch, Anna slapped together sandwiches from greasy salami, and ham with white rivers of fat and gristle running through it. They were huge Dagwood sandwiches. She spiked them together with flat toothpicks. You had to disassemble one entirely for even the smallest bite. Then the white bread itself was so tough and dry I needed the better part of a grape soda to wash down a mouthful. After a while, I skipped the bread entirely and lived on papery salami slices and leaves of iceberg lettuce sopped in mayo. I picked this stuff off other people's sandwiches along with big mealy tomato rounds. That caused Lecia to swat my hand a lot and say I was fixing to draw back a bloody stump.

Nights, we ate in the town's one steakhouse, a damp ill-lit place specializing in sprawling slabs of prime rib. There were martinis or Gibsons (plural) to start, burgundy with dinner, and finally a cognac that Mother likened to silky fire going down. Walking across the main street after one such meal, I watched the streetlight bob in the wind blowing down off the peaks. What a godforsaken country, I thought. Mother leaned on Lecia and

Hector on me to cross. The sole driver whose headlights slid off my face must have taken Hector, lurching across the road like Frankenstein, for my daddy, which made me want to tap on his windshield and explain things.

Back at the hotel, they passed out, and Lecia nagged me to brush my teeth. "You don't want those scummy green teeth like Ray back at the stable," she said. And I said no ma'am, I didn't. In the mirror, I saw the wooden button from Hector's peacoat had pressed a half-moon dimple into one cheek where he'd been leaning on me. I'd always wanted cheek dimples, like Shirley Temple. Lecia spent some time trying to fix a matching one on the other cheek. First, she pinched with her thumbnail till I squealed. Then she pressed the toothpaste lid in the flesh while I counted to a hundred. But we never got the marks lined up right.

Mother rented a colonial house turned out in chintz and claw-footed mahogany. It belonged to the town's last bank president (who'd gone to jail, if I remember right, for embezzlement). Lecia and I had never been in a two-story house before. We walked through it whispering, craning up at the high ceilings, the long drapes tied back with silk tassels. We curtsied to each other before sitting stiff-backed on the very edge of the rose love seat to pour fake tea.

The house had scope. The dining table was long and dusty enough for us to write our names on, with room left over. I pointed out that the twelve matching chairs were like for the Last Supper, minus Jesus. They were deep as dentist chairs, with padded bottoms in royal blue satin. Comedy masks grinned down from the carved corner moldings. In the living room, a baby grand piano sat under a chandelier whose glass teardrops had gone a dull amber. French doors led from there to a small parlor, where Hector and Mother set up their bed, so we'd be less likely to pad in.

Upstairs, Lecia and I had our own bedrooms for the first time. Mine had a tall cherry highboy with drawers deep as culverts so even the clothes Mother ordered from Denver seemed paltry once I'd wadded them up in there. Lying next to it at night, I always expected one of the drawers to slide open and some midget corpse to sit up. So I got in the habit of crawling in with Lecia. She stayed asleep even if I was bold enough to weave my fingers in with hers.

The first day of school, we walked till we reached a stretch of black graffiti on the sidewalk. Somebody named Ken blew dead bears, it said. Behind this sentence stood Antelope High, a building of gray cinderblock that was the town's only school, serving all grades.

You had to walk past a gaggle of high-school kids smoking to get up the steps. Boys had carved their hair into large doo-dah rolls. The girls wore cat's-eye liner and beehives. You could smell the hair oil and peroxide ten feet away. In Leechfield the older boys had been crew-cut. Most had worn button-down shirts and cardigans like the teenagers on TV, except for a few farm kids who showed up in clean overalls and brogans. These Colorado kids seemed older somehow. The girls smoked right in public, instead of hiding in the bathroom or behind the skating rink like they had back home. Somebody's transistor radio hidden in pocket or handbag was playing what sounded like "Louie Louie." A black-haired girl with unbelievably precise ebony spit curls on both her pale cheeks was doing the Dirty Dog to this song right in front of everybody. She humped the air and held her white frosted lips pooched out. I'd only seen that dance done in Texas at a slumber party by somebody's wicked cousin from Louisiana. I moved past her all slack-jawed, for I judged that dance the moral equivalent of a strip show.

We walked up waxed entry stairs to a wall covered with brass hooks screwed floor to ceiling at exact intervals. Sleds were stacked off to one side, next to low shelves for boots. For the first time, I realized I'd get to see snow there. There'd be snowballs and lumpy snowmen and sledding like I'd only seen in books. I resolved to fatten up, maybe even get some Wate-On, which was what Junior Dillard's brother had ordered from the back of a comic book to beef up for football. He'd later complained that it turned his teeth gray. But I was sick of shopping for baby clothes when vast circular racks of dresses marked "Chubbies" got picked over by the bigger girls. Gray teeth or no, I wanted to make more of myself.

Lecia tipped my face up with a finger under my chin. She said if I got in a nickel's worth of trouble that day she'd snatch me bald-headed after school. Then she glanced around to be sure nobody saw before smashing my arms against my sides in what was supposed to be a hug. She went clicking off in her new patent-leather shoes.

She needn't have bothered threatening me, for there were no teachers around to get in trouble with. The school had taken up something called self-paced learning, which meant kids worked independently through a progression of reading folders and math folders. Student monitors oversaw the classes. The teachers stayed in the lounge all day smoking and eating from big Tupperware containers they took turns bringing in—brownies and cupcakes and cookies by the boatload. I was put in the fourth grade. But though I could at this instant rattle off my second- and third-grade seating charts without missing anybody, I couldn't name more than a kid or two from that class.

The teacher did show up that first day to lead us through the pledge and take attendance. I can still feel the cool weight of her hand—which smelled faintly of Jergens—on my shoulder when she introduced me to the class.

At my old school, a new kid would have had instant celebrity merely for being from somewhere else. Texan kids would have blitzed her with airplane notes and swarmed over her at recess. These Western kids were more wary. I stood in front of the teacher watching them. Their faces looked back at me blank as dinner plates. By recess, nobody but the classroom monitor—who happened to be the principal's daughter, a blue-eyed girl with a shiny Dutch-boy haircut the color of brass—could have told you my first name, much less where I'd come from.

Also in Texas, a whole wad of fourth-graders left unattended for long periods would have upended desks, scrawled nasty words on the board, lit fires in the trash cans. A scapegoat would have been chosen and picked on. Still, that teacher went sidling up the hall away from us with no more than a backward glance. In Antelope, even the dumb kids stayed immobile at their desks for the better part of the day, as if everybody had been given some powerful narcotic. The kids were pasty-faced and indistinct. No one talked, since that got you demerits from the monitor. Too many demerits got you detention, which came in fifteen-minute increments and meant staying even longer in the vacuum of that classroom while the red second hand circling the huge industrial clock face swept away the daylight hours.

Most kids bent their heads onto their notebooks and tried to sleep. One boy gauged the quality of his day by sleeping on graph paper, then drawing a circle around the drool spot he'd made and comparing it for size and integrity to his drool spot from the day before.

For a while I went through the reading and math folders to pass time. It was a stupid system, where you moved from one level to the next wholely unsupervised. You even got to grade the tests you'd given yourself. The monitor handed out the answer key and a red pencil stub for x-ing mistakes. So far as I know, nobody ever even checked over my work. But I wouldn't have bothered cheating, for the tests were first-grade easy. One I remember went something like this:

> Apples come in different colors. Color the apples in the tallest tree green. Color the apples in the next tallest tree red. Color the apples in the shortest tree yellow. How many apples are green? How many apples are red? How many apples are yellow?

Even I could figure out that you didn't need to color them in first before counting them. The lessons seemed full of chores like that you could skip. Passing the test for one folder just led to another folder, and so on, into what seemed like an eternity of folders. There were trains traveling at sixty miles per hour toward Cincinnati; there were twelve stalks in each bundle of corn Farmer Brown was selling.

The teacher can't have actually stayed in the lounge the whole day, of course, but that's what I recall. Once some boy stuck a paper clip up his nose and started a great gushing nosebleed. The demerits monitor tended to it. She tipped his head back and balled up his own gym sock over his nostril, an act that brought a brief scurry of *ooooh*'s from the other kids because the sock was supposed to be rank. I was selected to fetch Mrs. So-and-So from the teachers' lounge. That involved navigating some concrete stairs down into the boiler room, which was like those horror-movie basements that always got you screaming to the girl in the movie holding the candle, *Don't go down.* The furnace clanked when I passed it. The twisty pipes overhead were bound here and there with rags and still dripped sweat. Beyond all that stood the lounge door with a round frosted-glass window like you'd expect to find on a submarine. I put my hand on the brass knob and pulled.

Inside, the place was solid smoke. All the teachers at that time were women, and stout women at that. Their broad backs faced me, their zippers straining to hold them inside their pastel dresses. Their enormous bottoms spilled over their wooden chairs on both sides. When their faces turned my way, I could see that each lady teacher had an aluminum ashtray all her own. Each had an empty paper plate with a white plastic fork that had been licked clean. And in the table's center sat the remains of a gargantuan chocolate sheet cake. The piece of baker's cardboard it had been squatting on resembled a big muddy football field torn up by cleat marks or claw marks. My teacher got to her feet when she saw me, and walked me back to the classroom.

I moved eighteen reading levels and twelve math levels the first week, a new school record, achieved as much from boredom as ambition. They announced it on the loudspeaker one day after the pledge. I briefly felt that old surge of pride in my chest. But looking around, I caught a lot of eye-rolling from the other kids. Maybe there was some secret class pledge about not achieving overmuch, so as not to up the ante for the other kids.

At recess that day, a sixth-grade girl everybody called Big Bertha behind her back strode right up to me where I stood in line for the water fountain and slapped my face. She'd drawn back good before hitting me. So I saw the hand swinging at me from a ways off. But the oddness of it kept me from so much as ducking. Once she'd whacked me, it took another second to sink in. I stood there holding my cheek. If I'd been more ready for the blow, I might have fallen down just for dramatic effect. My cheek finally started stinging under my hand. Meanwhile, the water-fountain line dismantled itself. The kids of varying heights gathered on one side of us in a jagged wall, to block us from the teachers' view.

Big Bertha's little pig eyes squinched together with the rest of her features in the center of a vast Moon Pie face. She eventually let on that she'd hit me for making her little sister look dumb in my class. I didn't even know who her sister was. But I couldn't resist such a clear shot. So I said her sister didn't need any help in the looking-dumb department, nor did Big Bertha herself, cow that she was.

Hearing her nickname spoken right to her face, she backhanded my other cheek. This time I flew into her big body, kicking and flailing. Lecia was at the far end of the playground swinging at the time. She later told me that it looked like a windmill had broke loose from its stalk and hurled right into the soft middle of old Bertha. She was slow, but eventually started landing some good blows upside my head. I was ready to quit when out of some wild instinct, my hands shot up to grab the collar of her blouse. I yanked down hard. And through some miracle, every single white button on that blouse popped loose and fell with whispery little plops into the grass. At the time, Bertha had both her hands dug in my hair, so the rubber bands from my pigtails tore at my scalp. My eyes were slanting up to my ears. My mouth felt like one of those astronaut training pictures in *Life* where the wind pressure blows his mouth open to show his wisdom teeth. Bertha was so busy shaking my skull that it took her a minute to look down. When she did, she saw that her white training bra stretched over her poochy nipples was laid bare to the whole school, at which point she let me drop and bolted toward the cafeteria doors.

The upshot of that fight was my right eye going black—the result of her boyfriend's chunky high-school ring glancing off my face. Mother sent one of her barfly slaves over to the market for a T-bone to press on it and take the swelling out. Then she patted foundation around my orbital bone, and dusted the whole mess with talcum from her fluffiest brush.

Deeter the bartender was polishing the lipstick smudge off a beer mug with what seemed serious thought. Behind him, the bottles staggered up on their little choir risers—amber and green and clear bottles, and one bottle of luminous yellow chartreuse shining out of the back line like some brand of rocket fuel. I looked across the bar and caught in the mirror on the back wall a long view of my pudgy eye, misshapen and caked with powder. *Daddy would have been proud of that eye,* I thought, and slid off the stool.

In the unheated bathroom, you could actually see your breath. I wiped Mother's makeup off with a glob of toilet paper I'd wetted down using tap water. Then I used the hand drier fixed to the wall to blow my face dry, as much to warm up as anything. Standing there by myself, with my eyes closed and that hot wind huffing down on my features so I could feel my hair stream behind me and some blood start seeping back to my bunged-up eye, I had a sudden flood of homesickness. Once I'd ridden in the back of Daddy's truck all the way from the beach. The sun that day had made even the nailheads on the floor of his truck bed hot enough to scald your bare foot if you set it down on one. The back of Daddy's head in his red Lone Star cap had been fixed like an icon in the rear window. I'd turned from him to lean my face up to the sun. The wind itself was hot but somehow kept me from sweating awful much. Still, that night I had a blistering sunburn on my face, which Daddy patted cool with Noxzema. The memory clicked off with the drier, as if the power on it got cut too.

I hoisted myself up the sink's edge to check out that bruise again, using the rectangular mirror on the towel dispenser. The eye had swollen back up glossy blue-black, with a streak of green at the edge. Daddy would have called it a kick-ass shiner.

Later when I lay half dozing on the banquette in the bar's darkest corner, I could almost see Daddy taking form from the vast ether of alcohol fumes and smoke. Finally, he sat next to me. Or a ghost of him sat, for I wasn't crazy enough to have believed that the Daddy-shape I'd conjured was actual. I knew full well he wasn't. Still, it comforted me to see him assemble through the veil of my own lashes. He sat gangly inside his creased khakis. "You gotta keep your guard up," he finally said. He drew a smoke from the tight line of Camels lined up like organ pipes. The glass on the black tabletop was only a little more transparent than he was. I told him I was missing him awful, but he just shrugged that off. "And lead with your left. Then she can't reach that eye. Lemme see that." His thumb pad pressed around the bruise, testing it for tenderness. "Hell, you'll be all right."

My eyes burned. I wanted to rest a minute with only Daddy keeping me suspended in the world, the way his big wide palms had when I'd learned to backfloat at the town pool. That's how I felt listening, buoyed up in my own tiredness by Daddy's presence. I fell dead asleep lying in his ghost lap.

Moving too fast through the folders had one other side effect even worse than Big Bertha clocking me. The principal wanted to talk to Mother about my skipping another grade.

The principal's name was Mr. Janisch, and other than the fact that the kids called him Janbo, I remember not one distinct feature of his. He was a looming blur in a light-blue three-button suit and striped tie. Mother flounced toward him, holding out her hand. She wore her sheared-beaver coat. Gordon escorted her in. He was one of the barflies she paid in drinks to drive us to and from what she called the three poles of our being (school, bar, home). He steered her by the elbow from Mr. Janisch's desk to the brown Naugahyde armchair in the corner.

Gordon's being there embarrassed me. He had white girly hands. His skin was a mass of acne pits and scarring. Some poet wrote once about "the young man carbuncular," and that was Gordon. That day, he wore rumpled camouflage fatigues with black combat boots. Mr. Janisch asked about Gordon's branch of military service. Old Gordon just ducked his head in fake modesty and lied through his beaver-like front teeth that that was a matter of national security. I knew for a stone fact that Gordon had been 4-F during Korea for something, being flat-footed or somehow nutty. Gordon's whole military act was made extra pathetic by the fact that he had a big, soft ass like a woman's. He tried to hide this by wearing his shirt pulled out, but that was the equivalent of wearing an I-have-a-fat-butt sign. In short, he was pompous and soft at once, and even having Mother explain that he was our chauffeur made me wince.

No sooner was Mother seated than Gordon lit her cigarette with a butane lighter that sent up a flame about a foot high. He pocketed the lighter, then leaned his butt against the window ledge and opened a magazine he'd brought along, the cover of which showed a cartoon Nazi, skinny and with a long ferret-like nose, squinting his eye to hold a monocle in place. This Nazi was pinning back the arms of a large-breasted blonde dressed in a shredded nurse outfit. The intensity Gordon brought to studying this magazine made me feel even worse than the fact that Mr. Janisch could see the sleazy cover.

I guess I concentrated so hard on Gordon that day, because I almost couldn't bear to look at Mother. She'd become the picture of somebody nuts. For one thing, she'd tried to dye her hair red that fall, but wound up with a substance less hair than pelt. It was the overall color and texture of dried alfalfa. For another, she hadn't bothered actually dressing for the meeting. She'd just stepped bare-legged into her cowboy boots, smushed some muddy lipstick on her mouth, and thrown that fur coat on over her peach silk nightgown. But the scalloped hem of the gown kept peeking out her coat bottom whenever she crossed her legs, and it seemed to me she crossed her legs a lot that morning. Maybe she was trying to show her legs off to old Janbo, a man on whom good legs might well have been lost. He just rocked back and forth in his office chair, nodding politely over the vast green expanse of his desk blotter.

I tried to keep a stiff smile welded on my face the whole time, even when Mother invited him and his wife down to the bar for drinks on the house any afternoon. She called the Longhorn "a family place." She bragged that her own "brilliant" daughters—she smoothed my hair at this point—sat studying at a cocktail table, while the jukebox played classical music. I distinctly recall ducking my head out from under her hand. (Something about the small betrayal of moving away from her still gives me a stab of guilt.) I knew that old Janbo knew that the Longhorn was a sleazeball dive, and I didn't want to sully myself any worse by seeming to back up such an obvious lie.

Lecia and I did go to the bar after school. But instead of homework we played this electric game, a mix of shuffleboard and bowling, where you slid a hockey puck down a long glossy lane to whack up some bowling pins. Or else we sat at the bar sipping cherry Cokes and learning bar tricks. I knew how to build a house of playing cards, and could throw dice from a cup so they came up nothing but sevens. I could also follow the slick moves of a shell game (I was still too clumsy to execute them myself), or fold a bar towel so it resembled a huge erect horse penis that would set all the customers laughing themselves into a blended chorus of drunk donkey snorts. The only classical piece on the jukebox was Ravel's "Bolero," unless you counted the music from *Exodus*, which made the Irish bartender weep. Mother carried a screwdriver around in her purse to jack the volume of that box up or down depending on her mood and whether she felt like dancing. Mostly we listened to Tennessee Ernie Ford singing about mining sixteen tons of coal or following the wild geese with his heart.

Certain steady customers hadn't moved for so long there were practically cobwebs stitching them to their bar stools. I'd seen the paintings of Edward Hopper, the washed-out misery of people slumped in diners. Mother had a book of them, one portrait more gray-faced than the next. The Longhorn was broke out in that kind of person.

Gordon and Joey were the most animate regulars, being young enough to run errands for Mother when her headaches were too blinding for her to get behind a steering wheel.

Joey survived on disability. He picked up a monthly check from some lawyer in Colorado Springs for the black lung he'd contracted mining, which didn't keep him from sucking down cigarettes all day and night. The index fingers on both his hands had brownish stains from nicotine. Unlike Gordon, Joey had once been handsome. He was a Mexican-Indian, small but broad-chested and narrow-hipped. He had a square jaw and black eyes Mother liked to call soulful. Those eyes had saggy pouches under them, though, and his straight black lashes stayed at half-mast all the time, the result of codeine painkillers and Valium (which Mother had also asked his doctor to prescribe for her). Plus the coughing fits he went into several times a day lasted a good five or ten minutes and stopped any bar conversation dead. He was clearly fixing to blow a lung. I patted Joey on the back when he coughed, like he only had a fishbone stuck in his throat, asking, "Did it go down the wrong pipe?" while Lecia fetched him a glass of water from behind the bar. She could be very patient, Lecia, holding out a frosted collins glass while Joey wheezed. He always left a pile of cocktail napkins he'd coughed into. Once after last call, I unfolded one and found a buckshot pattern of blood speckles that made me drop it to the floor, like it was radioactive, before Deeter swept it up with the swizzle sticks.

Gordon was sturdier-looking. He lived with his mother on the edge of town and had a pasture where we boarded our horses. "What do you do for a living, anyways?" I asked Gordon one afternoon. At the time, he was trying to teach me how to flip a filbert nut off the back of my hand and straight into my mouth. "Business interests," Gordon said. That caused Joey to laugh his way into a hacking fit. I was patting on his bony back when Mother pulled me into the bathroom to explain it wasn't nice to ask what people did. That was opposite from what I'd learned in Texas, where a job was a person's lowest common denominator, maybe even more defining than sex. You knew people based on what plant they clocked in at, which unit in that plant, and what union took their dues money—pipe fitters, Teamsters, or the OCAW.

In the morning when I'd pad downstairs in my socks, I always found either Joey or Gordon passed out on the parlor sofa. My task was to wake one and send him shivering out to warm up the car before driving us to school. We could have walked, of course. But Mother fancied our being driven. I made a habit of setting the gas flame under the kettle for coffee before I even poured myself cereal. That was meanness on my part, since the shrill whistle of that kettle woke any sleeper within range into a wincing misery.

One bright cool Sunday, Mother sent them both to Gordon's pasture with us to catch our horses. We'd been begging for that since we'd hit Antelope. I'd torn my hair in numerous tantrums over it.

What finally inspired Mother about the project was some rodeo rider who'd dropped in the bar one Saturday night trying to sell a pair of show bridles. He was on his way to Wyoming and needed extra cash so he could ask his girl to marry him. He flipped open his hand-tooled billfold to show us her homecoming queen picture in its scratched-up vinyl window. She was wearing a rhinestone tiara in her blond flipped-up hair and smiling out at us with more straight white teeth than I'd ever seen in a human mouth. One look at her and at this cowboy's sorry, mooning face, and Mother bought drinks all around. Then she'd rung open the cash register for a stack of bills and gone outside to buy those bridles right from his truck bed.

Joey and Gordon drove us to the pasture the next day right after dawn.

There was a hard frost on the ground when we set out across the field. The sky was dark blue. The horses stood feeding at some unbound hay bales near a ragged shed. I suddenly remembered the sleek power of being high on Big Enough's back, how I'd steered him around the barrel in that gymkhana, almost lithe for once, dipping out of the saddle to grab the flag from the sand bucket in a single balletic swoop that saved me seconds and won me the red ribbon. It took all the restraint I had that cold morning (I was not given to restraint) not to bolt at him. I moved easy. I started the low clicking noise Daddy had taught me to stop a squirrel on a branch.

The horse had seen me right off, of course. The minute I'd slid under the barbed wire, he stopped tearing at the straw. He lifted his long neck and pricked his black ears toward us. He nickered, which I read as a nod of greeting. Then Sure Enough stopped eating and high-stepped a few yards away, watching. We must have made a sorry procession: Lecia and I clanging the bridles, the long reins dragging on the frosted ground behind us; Joey and Gordon in their thin trench coats and scuffed-up dress shoes, both stinking of old drink. Still, I actually believed that those horses would gallop toward us, the way National Velvet had toward young Liz Taylor. But the alert look in Big Enough's round dark eyes was not, in fact, joy at my return. It was dread. He'd gone green as a colt. His expression was some equine way of saying *not her again.*

Eventually, Gordon and Joey took off after both horses. They got sick of how patiently Lecia and I held out handfuls of stiff grass, waiting for them to trot over. But the men didn't know horses. The bridles looked odd in their hands. Gordon squatted down to my eye level and drew his assault plan on his palm like a football captain. Lecia and I were supposed to herd the horses toward the two men. But I knew the animals wouldn't fall for it. They were faster than us by double, and way more nimble, not to mention that neither Joey nor Gordon had ever stuck a bit in a horse's mouth.

Lecia and I gave up helping pretty quick. We watched the men chase those horses for the better part of the morning. Gordon was lumbering and slow on his feet. Joey was quicker, but more and more hung over as time wore on. His blood alcohol level must have plummeted sharply at some point, for once he abruptly sat down in what turned out to have been a manure pile, so there was a fresh green shit stain on the butt of his tan raincoat. The horses themselves seemed tickled by the whole game. They'd lope hard a while; then, when the men flagged, they'd slow up.

The horses led the men the whole length of the field that morning—God knows how many acres. After a while, Lecia and I went back to the car to eat packets of soup crackers from the glove compartment. It was also warmer out of the wind. We played scissors-paper-stone with our hands the rest of the morning. The winner got to whip the inside of the loser's arm—the tenderest, whitest part—with two fingers. You licked your fingers with spit to make the sting worse, then smacked them sharp against the skin. By noon, both our arms had welts all up and down them. The men stood behind the horses far out where the field gave up to rock. The animals started climbing, and the men turned back, Gordon limping slightly, Joey stopping to hack his convulsive cough every few steps.

CHAPTER 12

Fall slid into winter. There were some light snows, but nothing you could sled in. Mother got a local doctor to order her up diet pills. She zipped them in the inner pocket of her Coach bag where she'd always carried baby aspirin before. The "bounce" she claimed they gave did stop her from spending whole days laid up drunk in bed. Her Empress Days, I called them, for she spent them doing nothing more than ministering to herself in small ways. I mean, she'd drink from a bottle of Smirnoff she'd made syrupy in the freezer and cut back her cuticles. Or she'd smoke while paging through back issues of *Vogue*, some blues record in the corner moaning the whole time about how shitty men were. But those days had never worried Lecia and me overmuch. If anything, we found comfort in them, for they kept Mother safe in bed. The diet pills took those days from us.

They also shot a sliver of pissed-off into Mother's voice. Even my asking for lunch money—if it struck her as off the subject somehow—could send her tearing around in search of a misplaced wallet, slamming doors behind her, or lead her to scream at the always sleeping form of Hector that he was a lazy sonofabitch. Don't get me wrong. Mother didn't go off every time you asked for something, and she had always been prone to temper fits. But on the diet pills a smaller spark could set her off. And the rages could carry her further. When Lecia and I finally figured out how to pronounce the magic word on the diet-pill label—methamphetamine—we used it in a jump-rope rhyme:

Meth-am-pheta-mean,
Diet pills will make you scream.
Meth-am-pheta-mean
Keep you fighting, keep you lean.

Mother did get thinner. She used an ice pick to poke extra holes in her alligator belt. Plus her tolerance for alcohol—always high—seemed to go up. She drank all day and night without throwing up or passing out. The Yankee accent that had always cued us in to how drunk she was turned into her standard manner of talking.

Even scarier was the fact that she never slept. I don't mean that she didn't sleep much, or slept less. I mean all those months, we never saw her asleep. Ever. No matter how late I woke and went scooting downstairs on my pajama butt past the winding stair rods, I could find her downstairs drinking, usually alone with a book on her lap.

She read more and more books by guys with more and more unpronounceable names, saying existentialism was the philosophy of despair. Lecia took to hiding what I called those "French-fried" books down deep in the magazine rack, for they got Mother talking in a misty-eyed way about suicide. She would gaze up from the page and say that for some folks killing yourself was the sanest thing to do. And the rare calm in her voice those times must have set Lecia fretting about the specter of Mother offing herself. We never spoke that worry out loud. But if Mother lingered too long and too quiet in the bath, Lecia might take up a post outside the locked door, her head cocked, listening with an intensity that always put me in mind of my cousin's hunting dog at a stand of quail. Lecia seemed to hold her breath those times, listening with her whole self for the slightest scuttle to suggest something alive.

If I went scampering down the hall humming to myself and ignorant of her worry, she'd wheel my way and press her finger hard against her lips to shush me, her face twisted into a mask of anger. Speaking a word like "suicide" aloud was unthinkable. We didn't dare give it breath for fear of invoking it.

In fact, we'd become superstitious enough to stop playing with the Ouija board. After the spirit of Grandma started spelling out how she was broadcasting to us from H-E-L-L, Lecia stamped on the planchette till it splintered. I pitched the board into the field of nettles behind our house. We both started any meal off by tossing salt over our shoulders, even times we hadn't spilled any in the first place. And walking to school, we skipped every sidewalk crack. I kept the fingers of my left hand crossed all the time, while on my right-hand fingers I counted anything at all—steps to the refrigerator, seconds on the clock, words in a sentence—to keep my head occupied. The counting felt like something to hang on to, as if finding the right numbers might somehow crack the code on whatever system ran the slippery universe we were moving through.

Mother's misery was also sneaking up inside me somehow. One night after Hector passed out, she found me lying wide-eyed in bed next to the lump of quilts that was Lecia. She sat down on the mattress edge and read to me by the hall light from *The Myth of Sisyphus*, her bible at the time, by Albert Camus, whose name she taught me to pronounce right, so nobody at any future cocktail party would ever tease me for a hick.

Sisyphus had it way worse than all of us, it seemed to me, being doomed to sweat and grunt pushing a boulder up a mountain all day and night without rest. The punch line was that once he got to the top of the mountain, the rock just rolled back down. So he had to push it up again, over and over. This happened forever, Mother said, closing the book. With my head lying deep in the trench of my pillow, I was still waiting for some moral, or happy ending, a reward for all that work. I must have said as much, for at some point she tucked a strand of hair behind my ear and told me there was no more point to Sisyphus' task than there was to washing dishes or making beds. You just did those things endlessly till your body wore out, then you died.

The first French sentence I learned might well have come from that book. *Il faut souffrir,* one must suffer. For some reason, suffering got lined up in my head not with moral virtue or being good, as it had with the Baptist kids back home, but with being smart. Smart people suffered; dumb people didn't. Mother had said this back in Texas all the time. We'd be driving past some guys in blue overalls selling watermelons off their truck bed and grinning like it was as good a way as any to pass an afternoon. She'd wag her head as if this were the most unbelievable spectacle, saying *God, to be that blissfully ignorant.* Daddy had always countered that message, for he took big pleasure in the small comforts—sugar in his coffee, getting the mockingbird in our chinaberry tree to answer his whistle. Without him, Mother's misery was seeping in. Happiness was for boneheads, a dumb fog you sank into. Pain, low-level and constant, was a vigil you kept. The vigil had something to do with looking out for your own death, and with living in some constant state of watchful despair.

Meanwhile, the world was draining itself of color before my eyes. The sky was grayer than ash, clouds close and vague as chalk smudges. Trees lost their leaves. Through the venetian blinds in our parlor Lecia and I watched autumn slip into winter like a slide show. For several days our neighbors raked, their kids jumping into the piles with dogs of various sizes bounding on the edges. It was like something from a Kodak commercial. Then the piles got burned in culverts and trash cans in front of the big colonial houses all up the block. Wasn't it weird, I said to Lecia in the bath one night, how we thought of trees having leaves as being "normal," when in fact six months out the year they were necked as jaybirds.

At school, I looked around at the dazed and sleeping kids, my peers—one boy drooling onto graph paper, another folding together a cootie-catcher. Even the monitor, the principal's daughter, who was supposed to be the smartest kid in class, was at that instant blissfully outlining her own hand in pencil. They didn't seem to mind being there so much, which I couldn't for the life of me figure, for it was all I could do to tromp through a day without screaming or breaking all my pencils or just kicking somebody hard in the shin.

Mother and Hector went away twice, both times to Mexico, I think. She'd cooked up a scheme to buy a tract of land down there for the purpose of founding an artists' colony, some new place for her to paint, though she hadn't hit a lick at a canvas since we'd got to Colorado. The truckload of art supplies she'd ordered sat untouched in a spare room. I was itching to break the seals on the new tubes of oil, dozens of them lined up by shade in a leather briefcase, but knew better. The clean brown palette with the hole for your thumb never got a single, bright turban of color squirted on it. The sable brushes of all sizes kept their paper wrappers on. The canvases she'd bought already stretched and primed white sat around the edges of that room like windows on nothing. Lecia and I made up titles for their emptinesses: "Polar Bears in a Snowstorm" and "Talcum Powder on the Moon." She never painted in Colorado, and they never bought any land in Mexico. They just drank and fought and flew back both bent over double from diarrhea, which Daddy had always called the green-apple shits.

The first time, they left us with Hector's cousin, a girl of about twenty who was cheerfully raising two toddlers by herself on welfare. We called her Purty. She was small and birdlike, with a tumbling mass of black hair that she tried to tame by rolling it on soup cans at night, and still it frizzed and seized up in waves around her heart-shaped face. Purty's kids were easily the world's most miserable toddlers, which she didn't mind one bit, being tickled silly by every blubbering fit one threw. "Poor nanito," she'd coo, when all I could think was how to smush a pillow across its face to stop its breath altogether. They weren't twins but have landed in my memory as exact replicas of the same baby, both slobbery-mouthed and worried-looking. They also had freakishly huge heads that wobbled on their necks and whapped into table corners, or could pitch them forward off-balance from sheer weight. Lecia learned quick how to plug one up with a pacifier or a bottle of cold milk. Me, I pouted, reading in the corner.

The second night we were there, Purty's roving husband showed up drunk and pounding on the back door. He was raving in a slurry Spanish I could barely make out that he'd come to claim his kids, whom, by the way, I would have been hard-pressed not to part with. But Purty yanked the soup cans from her hair so bobby pins scattered all over the dark bedroom with a skittery noise that put me in mind of East Texas roaches scrambling. She shoved Lecia and me under the bed with the babies to keep them quiet. She said he'd kill us all if we made a peep. Lying under that bed, I watched her fuzzy pink scuffs slide her away from us into the strip of light from the kitchen.

Quiet was hard for me. I'd rarely played hide-and-seek without being first found. Plus, the baby I'd been charged with keeping still hardly fit under my arm, being fat and squirmy and smelling—through the powder and baby shampoo—like nothing so much as clabbered milk. There were spiderwebby threads hanging from the bedsprings right in my eyelashes, and the floor through the cloth of my pajama top was a clean slab of ice.

While the voices got louder in the kitchen, the baby got squirmier and noisier. Lecia finally elbowed me in the head to do something, so I clapped my hand over its sloppy mouth. In the course of this, though, my index finger somehow poked between its lips. For a second I felt a few stubs of tooth in what otherwise seemed like endless slippery curves of gum, the baby's fat tongue writhing like a slug. Something about my finger in that mouth seemed so grotesque that when the baby set to gnawing on my knuckle like a teething ring, I reached down my free hand and pinched it on the thigh, pinched it with all my might, which amazingly enough, made it fall quiet lying under me. Under the backwash of guilt I instantly felt about having hurt a baby was a deep pleasure at such blatant meanness, the soft flesh giving way between my fingers like Play-Doh. No sooner had I done it than I longed to do it again. I didn't dare, of course, for fear the baby would start wailing again, instead of just making the low-level sniffle I'd decided was okay.

After what seemed a long time, a tremendous crash came from the kitchen, glass shattering. Footsteps headed down the hall to the front of the house before Purty broke out screaming "Murder, Murder!" Her husband's car peeled from the drive.

He'd shoved her face through the back-door glass, it turned out. But that scene has melted from my head. We must have rushed in and found her bleeding and screaming, and the babies must have hollered something awful. Still, I only keep a picture of Purty very patiently explaining to the red-faced highway patrolman exactly how her husband had choked her throat, then smacked her face into the glass, so she'd heard shattering around her ears and felt the rush of cold air from outside. Her face was all nicked up, and tiny spangles of glass had settled around the flowery yoke of her pink nightgown. The ambulance guy was rigging up a butterfly bandage on a gash that had severed her arched eyebrow into two neat wings.

The next time Hector and Mother traveled, we stayed with his sister Alicia, whom I'd have guessed was too old and fat to fight with her husband, Ralph. She wore long gray braids twisted over her head like an opera singer and stood close to the ground, being about as wide as she was tall. But sure enough, she was standing at the stove frying tortillas one night and bickering with Ralph about car insurance when he lunged at her. Alicia was quick, though. She hit him square on the forehead with the iron skillet's bottom, and that stopped him in mid-lunge. When he finally swiveled down to the floor, it looked like an afterthought. At breakfast the next morning, Ralph had a blue knot on the center of his forehead like a goat's horn trying to break through.

After that last fight at Alicia's house, I flat pitched a wall-eyed fit over the prospect of being left overnight with anybody, which tantrum killed Mother's trips to Mexico. She wore down staying in Antelope. She even began to pace window to window the way she had in Texas.

I wandered downstairs about three one morning and found Mother sitting in her peach silk wrapper at the piano. She'd twisted pin curls on the top of her hair, the slightly longer part, so the short sides stuck out and put me in mind of duck feathers. There was a long-stemmed glass of red wine on the piano bench next to her, a Salem burning cool blue smoke from the crystal ashtray. Her ragged copy of Jean-Paul Sartre's *Nausea* was propped on the piano's music stand.

She mixed me some burgundy topped off with 7UP, to help me sleep, she said. She brought it from the kitchen in her fanciest bone china cup, the one with gasolinelike rainbows somehow fired into the white background. It had cherries painted on it—inside and out—and gold on the rim where you put your lips, and even swirls of gold down the handle and around the saucer edge. Mother set that cup next to me on the square resting spot above the keyboard. The 7UP bubbles rose through the red wine like lava from way far down in the earth's core.

Before that night, I'd had lots of liquor—real champagne even, at somebody's wedding. And I'd cared for it not one whit. Oh, on a hot day with oysters, I liked a taste of Daddy's salted beer okay. But more than a few sips left me dizzy. And whiskey or scotch, even mixed with Coke, scalded me inside like poison.

Also, my parents' drinking was bound up in my head with their screaming cuss-fights. Many were the nights in Leechfield when—with the two of them raging behind their bolted bedroom door—I sneaked into the kitchen and gathered up their bottles (whiskey for him, vodka or scotch for her, single malt when she could afford it). Dumping those bottles down the sink drain, I always craned my face away. Keep in mind that I was surrounded by poisonous stuff that didn't bother me the least. From my front porch, you could see an iron refinery tower flaming black smoke into the air. With eyes closed in a moving car, I could tell by smell alone whether the stink was from the rubber company, or the open waste pits of the chemical plant, or the clean-earth odor of heated crude from the refinery. None of those made me pinch my nose. But that brown liquor seemed dangerous, even a breathful.

My first sip from Mother's bone-china cup changed all that. I'd heard her tell a hundred times how the monk who discovered champagne had likened it to drinking stars. Suddenly, that made sense. The wine and sparkly soda set my mouth tingling. I thought right off, *Drinking stars.* Whole galaxies could have been taking shape in there, for the taste was vast and particular at once. I'd taken too little a sip, though, and had to have another to see if the same small explosion happened. It did. I drank down some more. Besides its tasting good, the wine seemed to go down deep in me, not burning like it had before, but with a slow warmth. A few more sips set that warmth loose and rolling down my limbs. I actually felt a light in my arms and legs where the alcohol was spreading. Something like a big sunflower was opening at the very center of my being, which image I must have read in a poem somewhere, for it came to me whole that way.

When the cup was empty, I set it down in its saucer with a chimelike clink that told me the world had changed. I looked down at my bare feet dangling out of my nightgown. They seemed far off and pale as a marble statue's, elegant almost. I looked up at Mother. The pin curls with her hair spronging out didn't look goofy anymore, or scary like Medusa's snakes. In fact, the close cap of pinned-down hair seemed elegant. The bones of her face suddenly held all their old beauty. Her forehead was smooth and high, her cheekbones winged out. Her green eyes and pale skin were actually glowing, held in a dim halo. This, it dawned on me, was what people drank liquor for, even though it could make them puke and slur their words, could bring a man to throw a punch at somebody bound to whip his ass, or cause an otherwise clear-thinking woman to drive fast into a concrete wall. Alcohol could actually make life better, if only by making your head better. I thought of all the fairy stories that talked about magic potions, of Shakespeare's witches from *Macbeth* with their cauldron bubbling.

Later, I lay in bed a long time feeling woozy. If I closed my eyes, I felt the the mattress tip sideways like a raft at sea. Only staring steady at something could chase off those whirlies, or at least soften the incline that I felt myself sliding up and down in the waves I was dreaming under myself. I fixed on a small portrait on the far wall. It was Mother's last painting, a guy she called "Mack the Knife." She'd toted it all the way from Texas. That puzzled me since it wasn't even of somebody we knew, being a black-haired Frenchman with almond-shaped eyes. Actually, maybe he wasn't French. But to me, he was the spitting image of the nauseated fellow on the Sartre book jacket, the one Mother had told me wanted to puke just from being alive. Mack the Knife wasn't exactly handsome in the technical sense, being sallow-complected and puny. But it was a good painting. His eyes rested on me easy, and the light coming in sideways from the street gave him a sad, knowing look. Plus, he took the whirlies away, merely by being constant in the great roiling of that room.

When I said my prayers that night, which I did only after I was sure Mother was back in the parlor out of hearing range, I directed them as much to that sorry-looking fellow with his sallow cheeks and black turtleneck suspended in a sea of red and black swirls as to any father who might have been installed in heaven. *Dear Mack, please keep me from horking on these covers. And keep Mother from finding her car keys in the ivy pot. Amen.*

Other nights were occupied with Mother and Hector fighting. The litany of his innate low-lifedness got seared into my skull during this time. Hector was a pussy, was her main gripe. Also, he lacked gainful employment, which meant Mother accused him of sponging off her all the time. But if, of a hung-over morning, he lamely started scanning the want ads for bartending jobs, she'd coo up next to him don't bother, because if he was working they couldn't make love in the afternoons.

Hector was also the planet's sloppiest drunk. He staggered and slurred and forgot stuff. He fell down and threw up. One morning, I overheard her screaming that for Christ's sake, he'd wet the bed again. Another time with Gordon and Joey standing in the kitchen, she'd hollered that Hector couldn't even "get it up right." She rapped the wooden countertop with her knuckles. "Pete's dick was always as hard as this. Always." I didn't know how to take this news, but watched Hector sink down under the weight of it, staring the whole time at the bottom of his lowball glass like it was a crystal ball.

For some reason, Mother was just springloaded on pissed-off, which made her want to harm herself. Once, for instance, when our car was winding home from a particularly nasty dinner in town, Mother just threw open the car door and pitched herself out on the road. Suddenly, the black night was rushing in across the place where Mother had been sitting a few seconds before in a sullen drunk's quiet. The Impala's dome light had flown on. The heavy door bumped and scraped against the snowbank piled on the road's shoulder with a noise like breaking Styrofoam. After a few swerving yards, Hector finally pulled over and threw the car in park. We watched him stagger away from us along the icy road in his unbuttoned peacoat, disappearing in the dark beyond the red taillight. In a few minutes, he staggered back into view with Mother on his arm. She was wearing a white cashmere coat that night, and the flared bottom was splattered with mud.

She was okay, it turned out. She'd just hit a snowbank and rolled. In fact, they both piled in the car laughing like hell. But I noticed that a scary calm had fallen over Lecia's features. It was a look I'd seen in *Life* snapshots of old soldiers heading back into battle, while the young ones still wore their fear openly, with sweetness. Then the starless night went back to sliding off the car windows again.

More nights scrolled past, and days so gray and grainy that not one stands unblurred from any other, till I get sick one day and the grown man who allegedly comes to care for me winds up putting his dick in my eight-year-old mouth. In fact, the whole blank winter sort of gathers around that incident like a storm cloud getting dense and heavy.

It's early afternoon. I've stayed home from school, really sick with a fever. I've been sleeping, and now my forehead is sweaty and cool. There's a headache way back in it. Whoever's supposed to be peeking in on me has left a bowl of Campbell's chicken noodle soup, all peppery the way I like it, on a wicker bed tray. That soup is way cold. I can tell by the globules of oil at the edges.

I'm sitting in a shaft of sunlight on the Oriental rug in my room reading *Charlotte's Web* for the hundredth time. It's the part after the spider Charlotte dies, which happens from her having woven an egg sac and then filled it full of baby-spider eggs. Making those eggs took her last ounce of strength. She knew it would kill her, but she did it anyway. Mother has explained to me how that makes her Noble, according to Mr. Camus. Charlotte left the sac in the care of her pal Wilbur, himself a pig. In the weeks since Charlotte last lifted her spiny leg to Wilbur in good-bye salute, he has been laying in the mud bawling. He's still bawling when all of a sudden the eggs get ripe enough to hatch. Baby spiders start crawling out of the sack, I mean by the zillions. They're eensy as punctuation marks and scramble out right in front of his blurry eyes.

The fact of them being actually alive makes Wilbur feel better, the way—it occurs to me in that shaft of afternoon sun—people talking about the cycles of nature get to feeling better; the way Baptists talking about the Lord's Mysterious Plan feel better. But no sooner have those spiders said hey to Wilbur to cheer him up than they begin flying away from him on silky little parachutes. They scatter across the sky over the barnyard like so many seeds. They're going to make their webs somewheres else, so you think for a minute that Wilbur's gonna sink back into his porcine misery all over again. Then three of the baby spiders pipe up from the high corner of the open doorway over the pen that they've decided to stay with Wilbur. They want to make their webs right over him, just like their mother did.

The story more or less ends there, though the writer—Mr. E. B. White—lets you know that when those three spiders grow up, they're gonna lay some eggs too. And you know that this sad-eyed pig will have a steady stream of spider pals, each with the vocabulary of a college professor, to edify himself. Sure, they'll die after they lay their eggs, too, the girl spiders, just like Charlotte did. But the point at the end of the book is that Wilbur will never have to be lonely.

I can spend the better part of a day moving between the sad part of this book, where Charlotte dies, then paging ahead to read about the three baby spiders wanting to stay with Wilbur. I cry a little, then cheer myself up. (Later, I'll learn that's the structure of an elegy: lament, consolation; bad news, followed by good news.) The sun feels so warm on my bangs all straight and shiny across my forehead, and the thought of those three baby spiders spinning out the first silk threads to make new webs over the grinning Wilbur laying supine in his muddy wallow fills me with such light that I want to tell somebody about it. I shout downstairs through the open door for my sitter to come up a minute and get a load of this.

When he stands next to me in that circle of sun, I tell him about it with my whole heart. About Charlotte and the babies and Wilbur. I remember so much that I think Daddy would be proud of my telling. My sitter nods all slow and serious. At the end, he says how being special friends with somebody keeps you ever from being lonesome. And do I want to be his special friend?

That sets me scampering around the room in search of my Big Chief tablet, the one with the vampire club rituals in it. My bare legs are prickly cold under my gown, but somebody willing to be a vampire club member is a rare thing.

I find the tablet and plop back down in my spot of sun to start explaining the initiations. But when I look up from the sloping page, to see if he's buying it so far, the whole mood of the room has shifted. The zipper of his chinos is level with my eyes. And inside that zipper his pecker is making that bulge, the bad words for which zoom through my head—Hard-on, Boner, Stiffie. I think it is testament to my badness that I even know such words.

Once I spent the night with the principal's daughter, and when I asked her if she knew what "fuck" meant, she said no. When I explained it to her as nice as I could, she broke out crying, though

I hadn't even used a single cuss word, sticking instead to those words you find in the encyclopedia under A for Anatomy, with the sheer glassy pages of muscle and vein and bone assembling into a man body and a woman body side by side in TV-family clothes. Still, the minute I got to the end of telling the principal's daughter about the baby being born, her face just collapsed in on itself in a big pucker. She screamed that her parents would never do something that nasty, even trying to have kids. "Then where do you think you came from, dumbass," I said. She ran caterwauling out of the room at that point. A heartbeat later, her mother popped in all grim-faced. She led me by the hand into their dusty foyer, where she zipped up her parka right over her bathrobe and stepped barefoot into her galoshes. She hoisted me up still in my pajamas with my coat thrown across me and walked through the cold night back across the street to our house. That was the end of spending the night with the principal's daughter.

Maybe grown-ups know I know words like Hard-on from looking at me. "You got a smart mouth, little girl," Mrs. Dillard back in Leechfield always said, narrowing her eyes at that pronouncement. And I said that a smart mouth was better than a dumb one anyday. Still, sometimes I think being smart just makes certain words go scooting through your head, leaving some bad-word vapor that a mean man can pick up on. In fact, maybe this man, now, who's dragging down his zipper in slow motion, the little brass teeth unlocking before my eyes like the fangs of some sea monster, can hear that word Hard-on bouncing around inside my head. It invites him almost, draws him to me, actually draws on his dick like magnetism and makes it swell up inside the cloth of his pants.

I think of how the vampire couldn't cross into the girl's window unless she herself took the crucifix off that window and opened it to him, saying come on in. And still people did it, even when they didn't mean to. They hung up those garlic ropes at bedtime. They looped the rosary around the window handles. They full well meant to shoo that evil away when it came flapping all liquid at the glass. But by the time the vampire actually floated there in the creamy moonlight, the girl in the gauzy nightdress was so awestruck by his hunger—the sheer largeness of it—that she'd unloop all the stuff she'd fixed up to stave him off. The garlic ropes slipped from the brass handles, and the windows swung wide so the curtains billowed over them as he gathered her slender self up into his cape.

This whole scene is rushing through my head when my babysitter's zipper hits bottom. His hand fishes into that zipper and farther, into the shadow of his shorts. The seriousness of that reaching keeps me even from breathing regular. I'm also afraid to make him mad somehow, and even more afraid that any move I make or any word I speak will seem like welcome. So I sit still and pretend not to be home inside myself. I worry worry worry though about what's about to happen.

I think of that old neighbor boy laying me down on the cement sack in the Carters' garage, him on top of me bucking. Probably I don't even have a cherry from that. I didn't hear it pop inside me, because I was so busy thinking for him to hurry before I got in trouble. Whether I have a cherry or not, though, I can feel how marked I am inside for being hurt that way.

The high school girls always say in the bathroom that you can tell who's been fucked by how she walks. Lecia told me that a slew-footed girl—one whose feet splay out—has been getting it for sure. I take comfort in that, for I have the worst pigeon toes in school. Really. Back in Leechfield, I got kicked out of the yoga class that Mother wanted me to take at the Theosophical Society. Here I got kicked out of the Antelope ballet school. *No hip rotation at all,* the teacher told Mother, then suggested tap dancing for me. But stumping through a tap routine is for fools. The other girls at the barre mirror looked so graceful. They bent their knees down in plié, their frail arms sweeping as they rose. They moved all together like flowers in some Disney cartoon. I knew in my heart I'd never look that way.

The man's dick springs forward fast to get out of those tight britches. It's red like somebody's mad face, swollen like it hurts. The mere fact of it makes me seize up inside. The man pushes it down a little, holding it at its base so it points right at my face. I never saw a dick this big, this close. The little pee-hole surprises me, how it's cut longways like a vent in a pie. This man's not stroking his dick up and down, though, the way that neighbor boy did. He's just holding it gentle, the way you'd show a kid a hamster or something. Still, every now and then his pecker seems to jump of its own accord, as if it had an idea. Inside the tent of my nightie, I have buckled up my legs and pressed my thighs press together, hard. I have seamed myself shut down there. Somehow a small voice rises up from my belly and asks that dick all whispery not to hurt me.

This makes the mask of the guy's face smile down at me, the way you'd look down from the cutting board at a dog begging scraps. He reaches his big hand out to place it on my head, cupping my skull. It's like the gesture Jesus makes in my Bible picture, where they've written *Suffer the little children . . .* in the caption. But I won't raise my eyes to see if this man is Jesus, because all the while he's patting my head, that pecker of his is staring right at me with its slitted eye. From higher, the man's voice very gently says that he wouldn't hurt me for the world. No matter what. He would never, ever hurt me. We're special friends. He loves me. This—he runs his hand up his dick so it shivers to itself—means he loves me. He points his pecker at me again.

What I wonder is not where to run or how to lunge past him. I know that's impossible. Besides, even if I beat him scrambling downstairs to the phone, what would I say? I have a vocabulary for my own wrongness. All kids do, I think. It's the result of being smaller than, less than, weaker than. No, I can't get out of this by running. Instead, I wonder why somebody doesn't appear in the doorway to lift me out of range of that big, one-eyed dick staring me down. If God made the world, the way Carlita Defoe's catechism teacher said, then why doesn't He send some Christian soldier rushing in with a sword unclanging from its scabbard to stab this man, or to lop this pecker off at the root? And I know Carol Sharp would say that this right here is God's plan for me.

Or it's punishment for some badness I did—scaring Daddy off, maybe. Or not having the guts to go with him. Or weighing on Mother's mind till she couldn't paint a lick and flat lost her mind and set fire to the whole world.

The man's voice goes into a scary whisper, more secret-like. It tells how I should put my lips on that dick in a special kiss. Which I do. Smooch. And that's not so bad as you might think, if you keep your eyes closed and think of the dick as a little bald man. I should also point out that there is something deeply familiar about a hard-on, even when the fundamental feeling coursing through you is that this is wrong wrong, and you are wrong wrong for having been selected for it. Through all that wrongness shines a sense of something you know already. And the fear in your stomach—vampire fear, roller-coaster fear, pants-pissing fear—has a tickle to it like falling from up high, the bottom dropping out of yourself.

After I kiss his dick, I draw my head back, open my eyes, and see that it's no little bald fellow at all, but really a grown man's swollen outfit. The man's voice floats down to me again, saying why don't I poke my tongue out. Try to lick it like a Popsicle. And this time when my face comes closer to it, I draw in a breath and find the pecker itself doesn't really smell bad, not like a bathroom toilet or anything. Really, it smells like fresh baked bread, all yeasty and alive. There's a tear taking shape in the peehole, too.

I'm not going to hurt you, he says. Those words hang there in a cartoon balloon above my head. They are an obvious lie, given the man's voice, which has grown an ache in itself, a pleading. *Just open your mouth a little baby.* I try that. The fleshy head of the pecker parts my lips, easing forward. I open my jaw a little, but am shy of it. My teeth wind up scraping the pecker, so it pulls back with a jerk. *Watch your teeth baby,* he says. Then he says that I need to open wide and say Ah, and at the same time try to pull my lips over my teeth. I do my best at this, and must have done okay, for he says *That's it* and *Yes* before his breath gets ragged.

Then for no reason, his hands clap down on the back of my

head. All care and gentleness go out of him. I sense that even the voice has gone out of him. Which puzzles me, for I'm doing the best I can here. I haven't even cried boo-hoo crying, though tears are streaming down my face. But I'm not making any noise or sobbing, or calling out, so these tears seem like somebody else's, the tears of a different girl, or a baby doll on TV. The pecker pushes forward and seems to have swollen hard as stone to fill all the space in my mouth. It rams against the back of my throat, so I can almost feel it bump deep in my skull where my old dime-sized headache had up until then almost gone out. At the same time, there's a burning, tearing feeling in my tonsils, like the time I had strep throat. Plus the fleshy head of that pecker seems to block up my windpipe, for the air chokes off. My gag reflex kicks in.

All this takes not more than a second. Just when I can't stand it anymore, though, he pulls back. Which is a relief. He's still holding my head in a clamp, but for a second the dick itself backs up from my throat a little so I can suck in a half-breath. I stop gagging then. My eyes are watering hard. Surely this is the end of it, I think, for more than this would kill a person. But no sooner has that thought scuttled through my brain than he pushes down on my head again and shoves his pecker forward again, the head of it like some soft mushroom swelling to block off the back of my throat, and I gag again.

Then, worst of all, something wet and warm spurts out of the dick itself. He's peeing in my mouth. I'm sure of it. Back in Texas, during a Scout jamboree, a boy I knew peed in his sleeping brother's mouth, and neither one could live it down. But this pee is thick as cream rinse and not coming in a steady stream but pumping in a slow pulse I try to back away from. All the tendons in my neck get tight while I fight to raise my head out of his lap, but his hand holds me down. The dick pushes up. Then my throat fills with a salty chemical taste like the chlorine from a pool mixed up with salt gargle.

Later, when he's all done, he backs way off and gets gentle again. The flat of his hand rubs my back while I'm vomiting down the front of my gown. I am grateful for the warm rubbing of his hand, like whatever I did bad he's forgiven me for. I vomit again till my stomach seizes up on its own hurt, and he's patting on me bent over there. He's saying I'm okay. I did good, though it's clear down in the core of me that I'm no way okay.

That night in bed, I look at the window and wonder about Dracula taking shape on the other side of the heavy drapes, waiting to be asked in. I myself shouted down to the baby-sitter to come up to me.

After a long time, I get up and put on my school clothes. I sit dressed on the straight chair in Lecia's room, feet not brushing the floor—sit still as a statue, the way you have to when bird-hunting, or bass-fishing with rubber worms. You let the worm drop down to the river bottom, and just scoot it through the silt every now and then. Otherwise, quiet, for you don't want to thump around in the boat.

When the curtains get light, Mother comes in to scrub at the vomit stain on the rug. She has made a little paste with water and baking soda in a cereal bowl and is working that paste into the nap with a toothbrush. She asks me do I need to stay home again, seeing as how I earped yesterday. And I say no way. Lecia sits up in her heap of bedcovers, blinking. I've got my plaid satchel in my lap. I've matched my Ban-Lon socks and folded them to the exact right length; I'm immaculately turned out in my school clothes like I've never been before. Really, I say, I feel lots better. There's stuff at school I'd rather eat a bug than miss.

CHAPTER 13

Maybe if Mother hadn't taken it in her head to shoot Hector, we'd never have got back to Texas. But the sight of Mother green-eyed drunk on the other side of a nickel-plated pistol with a pearl handle—a weapon like something a saloon girl might pull out of her velvet drawstring bag to waggle at some mouthy, card-playing cowpoke in a bad Western—proved too much for Lecia. She got us the hell out of there. However, had she been polled in advance, Lecia might well have come down on the side of shooting Hector. So would I have. In some basic way, it was as good an idea as any that bobbed up that whole dark time.

They'd been staying at the bar a lot, Mother and Hector, leaving us home. I kept a late watch for them every night. The bar sat only a few blocks away, but Mother seemed a prime candidate for plowing drunk into something with more molecular density than herself—a slab of concrete or brick wall, maybe. After last call, I stood in my stripy Sears PJs at the upstairs window waiting for the Impala to surge up the snowy drive. I rubbed a fist-sized clear spot in the glass frost so I could better study the garage, its square black mouth like some toothless set of jaws. The driveway could lie unmarred by headlights and tire treads for what seemed a zillion heartbeats while I watched.

Lecia and I stopped hanging out at the Longhorn when guns showed up there in the palsied, uncertain, and sometimes liver-spotted hands of the Longhorn patrons and help. A robbery at the steakhouse up the block led Deeter to get fitted with a small shoulder holster. He wore it under his barkeep's apron. A few days later, Hector set out for the pawnshop to pick up a .22 pistol for his cousin to keep her husband at bay. Then he got his own Colt .45. All one afternoon he sat at a cocktail table fiddling with it. He'd sight down the barrel at a pedestrian trotting down Main Street. This was troubling. In Texas any four-year-old knew you didn't point a firearm at a live creature unless you wanted it dead. Even a busted, empty gun got handled like a snake.

Mother's pearl-handled job struck me as silly at first. I'd seen a cigarette lighter shaped much like it at a roadside joke shop once. It hung in a plastic bag from a spinning rack of other gags, including a small pink puddle of plastic dog vomit I spent my last nickel on.

Mother swore to keep the pistol tucked safe in her Coach bag. She just wanted it, she said, in case anybody ever tried to bother her. *Who*—my eight-year-old head wondered—*would ever dare mess with Mother?* I knew for a fact that she would have smacked the dogshit out of any yahoo who even approximated getting ready to bother her. The gun was—in a word I pinched off Lecia's sixth-grade spelling list—superfluous.

Guns per se didn't worry me. Every pickup in Leechfield sported a National Rifle Association sticker and rifle rack in the back window. I'd fired my first pistol way before kindergarten. Two-handed on New Year's Eve, I'd leveled Daddy's .22 over the garage roof and straight at the pie-faced moon. At the stroke of midnight, I squeezed the trigger. My hand flew up a good half yard, but I barely flinched at the blast. When the moon itself didn't go hissing across the black sky like a plugged balloon, I busted out crying. Later, my BB gun took down all manner of sparrows and blackbirds. By second grade, if Daddy braced himself behind me, I could shoulder and shoot a four-ten shotgun without the recoil knocking my arm out of socket. That meant I waded into the black marshes during duck season in winter, and spring found me trotting behind while the men bagged brown morning doves for gumbo.

Still, the sudden appearance of those guns in that bar set a shimmer of anxiety going in some watery place in my middle. They rested in the hands of people who'd never held firearms before. Fools, to a one. Like Hector, Gordon would draw his Magnum like Wyatt Earp for a joke, then shoo me off, saying the safety was on, or the chamber hollow.

One night Joey fell into a crying jag at the bar. His poor poppa had died in the mines at forty, and he pressed Mother's pistol to his temple, that shallow place where his hairline was starting to back up. After that, we'd stopped going to the bar, Lecia and I. But Mother hung on to her joke pistol. The night she decided to shoot Hector, it appeared in her hand fast.

Lecia had been playing the piano when Hector two-stepped out of the bedroom sloshing scotch. He stood behind the bench all misty-eyed. After a few bouncing renditions of "Alley Cat," he asked her to play the national anthem. She said she didn't feel like it. Hector even dug down in his trouser pocket and hauled out a wadded-up ten-dollar bill. He smoothed it flat on the keyboard. He said that money was all hers if she'd only play "America the Beautiful." I pointed out that "America the Beautiful" wasn't the national anthem, which insight caused Hector to smile blurrily at me while Lecia wadded up his ten-spot and pitched it onto the strings. She banged down the keyboard cover and stood up. She wasn't playing diddly-squat, she said.

Usually, that would have sent old Hector sulking off to bed. But for some reason, he took offense. Maybe because at dinner he'd been talking about the brother he'd lost in World War II. Hearing the national anthem got all balled up in his mind with that brother's funeral—the flag folded neat in a navy-blue triangle some officer handed over to his mother, the fistful of dirt Hector himself had tossed down the oblong hole onto the polished box they lowered by hand on straps.

Anyway, Lecia stood, and Hector's face worked itself into a

twist we'd never seen. He wound up calling Lecia a spoiled little bitch. Now, nobody would dispute we were spoiled. But the "bitch" part hit some string in Mother, and the next thing we knew she held that pistol.

Night had blacked out the bay windows behind her. She had on a silk slip the color of mayonnaise. Underneath that slip was her long-line conical bra, which turned breasts into something not unlike artillery. Hector slumped in the rose chintz armchair. His head bobbed down, so folds of neck skin gathered around his chin like a basset hound's. He said go on and shoot, his life wasn't worth a nickel anyway.

I got the idea to fling myself across his body. I was betting Mother wouldn't plug me to get at him. And the move did draw her up short. She squinted at me as if I were a long ways off. When she waved the gun sideways to motion me out of the way, her arm looked boneless and wiggly as an eel. *Scoot over,* she said.

Lecia begged her not to pull the trigger, while I draped the length of my body down his front like a lobster bib. He smelled of Burma-Shave and scotch. His belly was wishy under all the knobs and angles of me. I sank into that softness a notch, then craned my head back to see what effect I was having on Mother.

A mist from somewhere inside her skull seemed to skitter behind her green eyes. She was considering. Her hand even dropped a few degrees from its straight-on angle. *My poor, poor babies,* she said. Then the lines of her face drew up and hardened into something like resolve. *Get offa him, Mary Marlene,* she said. Hector's breath was wicked sour when he pleaded back to her, *Honey . . .* to which she said shut up.

Lecia took her place at Mother's elbow. She stared up with an expression that struck me as lawyerly, like Perry Mason's at the jury box. At any second she might've drawn out a pointer and clicked on an overhead projector, the better to list her arguments, which, by the way, struck me as real obvious. If you shoot him, you'll go to jail, maybe forever—that sort of thing. This didn't trouble Mother one whit. She tossed her head and squared her shoulders. *At least I'd have done something worthwhile,* she said. *Kill-*

ing that low-life sonofabitch. She studied Hector like he was some worn-out farm mule she was fixing to plug. She waxed lyrical about what a worthless sack of shit he was.

Her talk ground Hector down worse. He sighed a lot, sour air whooshing out of him. I practically scanned his neck for the nozzle that had come unplugged, for with every sigh his whole body sagged a level flatter. So I sank deeper into him, the softness of him. Had this progression gone on forever, he might well have melted to nothing but a puddle under me. I stared at his ear, long and leathery with a few stiff white whiskers tufting out of it.

Hector stopped not caring whether Mother shot him or not and started to lobby actively for it. Like getting shot was some kind of solution. Big alligator tears rivered down the folds in his face. *She's right,* he said. His voice had a crimp in it. *I ain't never been worth a damn.*

I turned from where I lay on him to Lecia, who'd dropped her lawyer pose entirely. She was off on another tack. The look in her brown eyes under the shiny blond shelf of bangs was no longer set. It was weary. And the accent she used next was pure Texan, straight from what you might call The Ringworm Belt. *He's not worth the bullet it'd take to kill him,* she said. She wasn't talking to Mother like some Yankee newscaster anymore. She was buddying up, appealing to Mother's fury, which she'd apparently adjudged immovable. *Jesus, lookit him,* Lecia said. She rolled her eyes. She might have been Mother's cocktail waitress, off-handedly doling out comfort while picking through change on her drink tray. *If Hector was on fire,* Lecia said, *nobody'd so much as piss on him to put him out.* Mother said that was dead straight, and under me Hector seconded the idea.

Then Lecia grabbed my foot and tugged. She wanted to lay across Hector too, she said. That seemed a sisterly gesture, helping out with a chore, as if she knew how gross it felt breathing in his whooshed-out scotchy fumes. She heaved herself up beside me as onto some squishy raft bobbing under us in the Gulf.

I saw she'd transformed again. The tired frown she'd carved

with her mouth was unbent. Her forehead had given up its furrow. Her round face was the only accurate barometer for the subtle atmospheric shifts in the room. And that face had gone blank and white as dough. Lecia had slap given up. I glanced back at Mother, who was sighting the short length of that nickel barrel as if to draw a very fine bead around us at Hector.

Somehow I'd buried any real fear till then. The whole scene had struck me as goofy. Sure I was anxious, but a low thrum of worry ran through me more or less constantly like current. Anxiety made me a nail-biter, a restaurant fidgeter, the kind of kid liable, in a given day, to spill at least one glass of liquid. But the deep fear that draws all air from your lungs and sends the world into slow motion hadn't pulled on me for weeks. I'd submerged it till that very instant when Lecia took her place beside me looking wholly empty of herself.

She was telling me to run. But in her pass-the-butter voice. Run across the street to the Janisches' house. Mother was fixing to shoot Hector right that second unless I could fetch some grown-up to stop it.

Sure enough, Mother had shifted into her ghost self, holding that very real gun with a hand so pale you could practically see through it. She didn't hear Lecia tell me to go fetch somebody, for she was past hearing. Her lips moved in a whispery way, as if she was praying. But her gun arm stayed straight. Her hair was spiky wild, and her jaw set.

She didn't move to stop me dashing by. I might have been a cockroach that scuttled past for all the notice she paid. And I didn't look back. I couldn't have seen my sister laying so deep in her ten-year-old body, stared at by that silver pistol's round and careless black eye, and still been able to run off.

Or so I tell myself outside, where time starts to shift. The night itself seems heavy. It drags against my shoulders and keeps me from running as fast as I'm able.

The fresh snow on the street I step into is blue as pool water. I don't even feel my bare feet go cold in that snow. Nor do I note under my white gown the constellation of gooseflesh that must break out down my stick legs. Even the fact that my legs are pumping doesn't fully register. I can only see the still street bob, which phenomenon reassures me that I'm running. The Janisches' mahogany front door with its wreath of holly jerks closer to me one stride at a time, in stop-action.

Their porch light is gold, their doorbell lit like a bright period at the end of some long dark sentence I've crossed. The finger pressing that doorbell must be mine, for there are my nails, square, with slivers of dirt underneath. A shape moves across the window lace. Then, where the door was, there's a rectangle of light holding Mrs. Janisch in her blue duster.

What I tell her is a mystery, though I can feel my jaw working. It's sharp cold, I think, for my very words to get eaten soon as they leave my mouth, before I can even hear them myself. Then Mr. Janisch appears wiping a clear path through the shaving cream on his jaw with a gym towel. He's wearing a T-shirt and dress slacks. And dangling around his neck is a tin medal of St. Jude, the patron saint of lost causes. If you can't sell your house, you buy a statue of Jude, get the priest to dab holy water on it, then bury it upside down in your yard before dawn. And by suppertime, you'll be knocking your for-sale sign over with a hammer.

That's the fact that must for a while occupy all my available brain space, for next thing I know, I'm not at the Janisches' anymore at all, but back across the street on my own porch, at my own front door with a breathing presence behind me that must be Mr. Janisch. The padded arms of his parka make a *whipe, whipe* noise when he moves. I can still smell his mint shaving foam.

I feel dumb knocking instead of just walking in yelling hey. But he insists. After nobody comes, though, I watch my raw-looking little hand start slapping flat on that door over and over.

Mr. Janisch grabs my wrist with his leather-gloved hand to stop me, but I twist loose and bang again with both fists. I've neglected to listen back on Mother's house. I was across the street, sunk deep in my own task. So my house has gone grinding through time minus my vigilance.

If, for instance, a gun went off, I'd have missed hearing it. Two or three shots might have been fired. This thought causes me to kick the door with my numb bare foot, so hard that later the big toenail will go black.

Suddenly there sails through my head a hand-lettered banner that used to hang in front of Central Baptist Church back home: *Prayer changes things,* it said. So if I can eke out the right prayer before that door opens on everybody sprawled around dead like deer you'd line up for a Polaroid before strapping them over the truck hood, maybe I can change the scene we'll find. I have to pray fast and get it right the first time. God'll want a convincing trade, not just that weary promise to be good I always back up on.

Then in a flash, the idea comes. How Abraham was ready to cut his own son's throat solely because God said to. Thinking that, I let one bullet have its way. I give God that bullet killing Hector the way you'd spot points in football when you got only the puny kids on your team.

But God's counteroffer comes in a backwash. I halfway wanted Hector dead from the git-go anyways. So that bullet may not count as offering enough. In church back home, Deacon Sharp always says—while he slips the offering envelope from his shirt pocket to drop in the prayer basket that's swooping up the pew on a long stick—he always says to give till it hurts. The real choice is between Mother and Lecia. Mother lying sprawled on the floor in that creamy slip. Or Lecia in a hump across Hector in the chintz armchair.

I would like to claim that I worried the bone of this choice a long time, but I did not. In an eyeblink's time, I killed the very sister who'd taken my place in the bullet's path. No sooner did the choice present itself than I chose. I just begged *please God.* Then I pictured Mother standing upright, the gun having fallen from her hand.

And God must have heard, for Mother did answer the door, and not even wild-eyed like a TV murderess in her slip. She had on her black turtleneck and stretch pants, and a little beret like a black pancake over her weird hair. She told old Janisch we were just having a family argument. You know how kids exaggerate. Guns, for God's sake? Her husband didn't even hunt. She shook her head at me. *Mary Marlene,* she said, wearing her TV housewife smile. I'd never seen Mother's face so completely free of irony. *Mary Marlene has such an imagination,* she said. Then you won't mind, Mr. Janisch said, if I come in. Mother stepped aside.

There Hector sat in the same parlor chair, Lecia wedged in by him. She had a Nancy Drew mystery on her lap. Mr. Janisch shook Hector's trembling hand, then looked down at me and said he'd be seeing me at school.

From the doorway, Mother and I watched him stride across the street. She drew me under one arm, to warm me in my eyelet gown. It was then I felt the pistol, sticking out from where she'd jammed it in the waistband of her pants.

That was the night Lecia called Daddy collect. She waited till Hector was passed out and Mother was making popcorn in the kitchen. I could hear the pot bang against the stove burner and the explosions inside it like firecrackers on a string.

What Lecia said to Daddy stays with me, for she was suddenly issuing orders again, first for the operator to put us through, then to the daddy absent so long I faltered on conjuring his face. Here's exactly what Lecia said: "Daddy, you need to get us two airplane tickets back down there from Denver." She didn't ask. There was no *maybe* threaded through her voice, no sliver of doubt. Had I been making the call, I would've told about Mother's pistol and laying across Hector and fetching the principal. The whole story would have rolled out. Daddy would've wanted whys and wherefores. Watching Lecia, I knew no further wangling would take place. She doled out a few cursory yessirs and nossirs. But Mother wouldn't get summoned to the phone to check was this okay. In short, it was a done deal.

That hits me funny, now. Here you had a fifty-year-old veteran of one major war and innumerable bar fights taking orders from a girl whose age had only recently nudged into the realm of double digits. Daddy didn't go along with Lecia's plan because it made sense. It didn't much. Maybe he'd been missing us so bad that he was set to grab us any way he could. But even that doesn't explain it. No, what moved him was Lecia, her sudden solidity and power, the sheer force of her will.

I was coiling the phone cord around my index finger when this knowledge settled on me. Lecia's eyes were the same calm brown as always, her blond bangs were still lacquered straight above dark brows. But her voice held less waver. By the time she handed me the phone, the small space between us had stretched into some uncrossable prairie. She'd moved forever away from me. For my part, I was still skidding around in the slippery, internal districts of childhood. I still half-wondered whether Mother might shoot us as we slept. But Lecia had stopped wondering about such things, had let go wonder altogether. She was set on enduring, no matter what. She'd harden into whatever shape survival required. From that second forward, she had to figure what-all she'd have to lose for that survival, what-all and who.

The receiver was warm on my ear. Daddy wanted to know one thing: "You 'bout ready to come on home, Pokey?" I told him I'd *been* ready. To which he said him too.

Early the next morning, we washed our faces. I brushed each tooth with the neat circle stroke Captain Kangaroo had instructed me to; then we buttoned ourselves into church dresses. By dawn, we stood side by side in the full-length mirror. Lecia had tied the hood of my car coat too tight under my chin, so I felt like a sausage in oversmall casing. Her face floating next to mine in the mirror would never again be the face of a child.

Mother must have squawked about our leaving. She would have yelled or wept or folded up drunk and sulking. I recall no such scene. Nor can I picture Lecia announcing our leaving, as she must done first thing that morning. Mother would have been smoothing Ben-Gay on her shoulder. The Sunday *Times* crossword, each box with a penciled capital letter, would have lain between Mother's body and Hector's. (She tended to come up with some kind of answer for each square fast, then erase mistakes later, so the puzzle always looked done but seldom was.)

But I'm making this up. The French door on that scene never swung open. Any talk with Mother after Lecia's call was siphoned clean from my head. Mother herself was clipped from my memory, though some days went by before we actually left, and I must have said good-bye to her. We must have wept, being a family of inveterate weepers, the makers-of-scenes in airport terminals. She did promise vaguely to come for us soon, but I can't exactly hear her saying that, nor does even a ghost of her Shalimar hang in the car that ferried us to the airport.

Joey was hired to fly along, to squire us through plane changes. He right off got wasted on scotch in the bar while Lecia and I wolfed peanuts and sipped Shirley Temples. Our square-bottomed stools were covered in black Naugahyde. They swiveled, bumping into each other like big padded metronomes marking off the morning. On the bar before us, our twin Barbies sat, backs ramrod straight. They had on matching prom dresses in baby-blue crinoline with silver sashes. But we'd lost their white plastic sandals in transit, so their arched feet stuck out bare.

Joey's first act on the plane, after he'd buckled Lecia and me into our seats across the aisle, was to barf volubly into his airsick bag. Lecia and I then dug down in our seat pockets, so our Barbies could do their own make-believe barfing, which troubled the old woman cat-a-corner from me. She sighed disapproval. She shook her head so hard at me her cheek wattles shook above the triple strands of blue-tinted pearls. We moved from Barbie barfing to Barbie fart-jokes and kept those up at top volume clear to Albuquerque, where I announced that my Barbie batched her prom dress with diarrhea squirts. She'd be forced to wear a TWA napkin to the prom, with a rubber-band belt, and minus any underpants.

In Albuquerque, we boarded the wrong plane. Airlines discourage that sort of thing, naturally. They post a fellow at the gate to read your ticket before you even step on a runway. It says right on the front where you paid to fly to. But somehow, against odds I can't fathom, we all wound up in Mexico City, illegally, of course. Maybe Joey even booked us there on purpose. Mother had planted in his noggin her romantic notion of disappearing to

Mexico. He may have fancied living cheap in some beach shack flapped over by palm trees, with an Aztec princess bringing him rock lobsters and tortillas patted out with her own small hands.

The *federales* who met us at the customs gate had other ideas, especially when it turned out that Joey had dropped his wallet—with all evidence of U.S. citizenship—in the airplane toilet. He claimed he'd been rising from the toilet and suddenly bent over sick. His bowels had just seized up. He didn't know what fell in the blue toilet water till after he'd zipped up. Then he patted around and found his back pocket light. All his ID had flushed away with an eardrum-sucking pop somewhere over the Sonora desert. He patted his pockets to show the small, official-looking crowd how it happened. Joey had that drunk man's myopic sense of how interesting this all was for everybody.

Meanwhile, the *capitán* shifted his weight from one shiny black boot to the other. He whispered to the customs officials. When he lifted one sinewy hand, two men with rifles at the baggage rack trotted over. Our luggage was called for and disemboweled—dresses, jeans, nylon pajamas. My torn-legged panties got waved a second like some tattered flag of surrender. Joey looked like a smuggler, or like some Mexican national crossing the border without papers. But his bigger crime—or so I guessed from where Lecia and I stood by the coffee machine with three stewardesses who'd taken hold of us—was his lack of seriousness. He just couldn't stop giggling.

They kept him, of course, the customs officials. They had to. The miracle was that Lecia and I were let go. The airline folks even took it on themselves to phone Daddy, telling him they'd tote us back to Texas.

Anyway, I never got to ask Joey if he was kidnaping us, or himself running off, or what. My last sight of him was in that customs holding area, where his face under fluorescent lights resembled the washed-out green of a martini olive. For some reason, they'd made him take off his shoes and one sock. He stood on one leg like a stork, arms held out. Periodically, he exploded with laughs so his big toe dipped down to touch the dirty linoleum.

In the airport employees' lounge, a waiter delivered us an oval platter of huevos rancheros while Lecia told the wide-eyed stews how Joey planned to sell us to some men he knew down there, the extremity of which tale caused me to kick her under the table. Those ladies were paying the check, and I didn't aim to piss them off before it came.

But Lecia knew the furthest limits of credibility. She always had. The women hung on her every word. Their perfectly manicured hands patted our uncombed heads and squeezed our skinny shoulders through our dress plaid. Eventually, they waved us onto a night plane heading for Harlingen, Texas.

I woke to clouds. A whole Arctic wasteland of them bubbled up in the round plane window where Lecia's sleeping head was tipped. The clouds seemed to have seized up in violent motion, like some cauldron that got frozen mid-boil. A full moon shone across them. It cut a wide white path straight to us, the beauty of which flooded me with some ancient sense of possibility. Maybe there was hope for me yet, even from the vantage point of being a kid, hurtling across the black sky with my sister, whom I would never know the heart of again. (When mystics talk about states of grace, surely that's the feeling they mean—hope rising out of some Dust Bowl farmer's heart when he's surveying the field of chewed stems that locusts left.) This hope lacked detail. From it came neither idea nor impetus. I only felt there was something important I had to do, held by the clear light of that unlikely, low-slung moon.

Then it was gone. The man in front of me clicked off his overhead light. He tilted his seat back so deep his bald head seemed to plop in my lap. He can't have been that close, but that's how it felt. I stared at his head, which was white as a worm. He reached up to unscrew his wind-vent.

The stale air that blasted across his scalp and into my face somehow carried the familiar backdraft of doubt. Surely hope was for boneheads. Surely any goodwill God held for my future was spent. Hell, I'd wished my own sister dead a few days back. I glanced over at her glossy blond head tipped in sleep. The rough red blanket was pulled clear to her chin. *Just like a kid,* I thought. I wanted to shake her shoulder and tell her how much I loved her, but she would have said to pipe down.

I glared hate rays at the bald man's head. The monk's fringe of black hair circled his pate like some greasy halo. Earlier, I'd wedged my bare-assed Barbie between the seat cushion and the arm-rest. Now I grabbed her legs like a club and drew back. No thought for consequence, I brought her down on that guy's bare scalp with every ounce of force I had, popping her head off.

The fellow jerked up and let out a whoop. He held his skull with both hands, twisting around to see what had whacked him. I slipped the headless doll under Lecia's red blanket and quick faked sleep on the arm-rest. When he started dinging the stewardess bell, though, Lecia startled up. She blinked and rubbed her eyes, so I blinked and rubbed mine. Meanwhile, the stewardess tripped over that blond and pony-tailed Barbie head. It skittered up the aisle, then swerved under a seat, never to be recovered.

Lecia and I meandered back to Daddy through an underworld of airport personnel. Pilots, baggage handlers, stews and off-duty janitors washed us and fed us. We traveled gratis, without corporate okay. And not only were we never menaced or pinched, beaten or buggered, we never stared with longing at a deck of cards or chocolate doughnut that some stranger didn't ante up for it. Their particular faces have been worn featureless as stones, but those uniforms I walked next to at waist-level prove that hope may not be so foolish. (Sure the world breeds monsters, but kindness grows just as wild, elsewise every raped baby would grow up to rape.)

On each leg of the trip, the planes got littler and more ragged. In Houston, we reached a green camouflage plane with shark's teeth painted on its nose and a big X of gray electrician's tape on the cargo bay. It was parked outside a tin hangar beyond view of commercial aircraft. The pilot wore bifocals. The cubby that he wedged Lecia and me into behind the cockpit was built for flight plans, maybe, or a thermos. We doubled our knees up under our chins. We must have looked, when the pilot turned around to say hold on tight, like a pair of groundhogs poking up from some hole.

The plane cut a tight circle, its headlight just brushing over thick fog. The pilot flipped some ceiling switches and talked back to radio static. We bumped around a lot taxiing. The wings shimmied against bracings thin enough for a backyard swingset. Still, Lecia's profile was calm studying the plane's dials, though the engine racket when we surged was like a vacuum cleaner we had to sit in. The pilot reached down at knee level and pulled back with effort, as if his very strength were hefting the plane's nose off the runway. After considerable bucking around, we pulled into a cloud.

And that was the cloud that held us—with only an occasional deep drop to tease my stomach—all the way to Jefferson County. The pilot used pink Kleenex to scrub at the window steam. But the fog pressed against the windshield was a thick membrane the headlights couldn't puncture. Even I could see we were flying blind.

Nor did visibility get better with landing. We stood on the wet runway with our Barbie cases. No terminal building or parking lot presented itself. Only a tower beam swept over our heads—a fuzzy cone of yellow light wheeling.

Then from an unmeasured distance, headlights flipped on. A car was parked right on the tarmac. I set down my Barbie case. Through the mist, I made out two shapes walking toward us, each in the riverbed of those twin lights. One was small and slight with a cowboy hat. The other had big hands dangling off a long frame. This second shape broke and ran for us, heavy work boots scuffing on the concrete.

There was no clear boundary Daddy ever crossed over, no second he assembled fully before us out of fog. He just gradually got brighter and denser till he was heaving us both up in his arms. He'd been drinking black coffee during his shift, the coffee that poured like tar from the foreman's beat-up percolator. That coffee brought my whole former Daddy back. I knew the solvent he used to strip grease from his hands, and the Lava soap applied with a fingernail brush. His chin bristles scraped my neck. And he must have been sweating from damp or work or worry, for the Tennessee whiskey he'd stood on the tarmac sipping was like fresh-cut oak coming off him. I could feel Lecia's arms on the other side of him hugging, and for once, she didn't swat me away, like my hug was messing hers up. For once, our arms reached around the tall rawboned bulk of him to make a cage he fit right into.

His partner was a small, birdlike man named Blue, which was appropriate for he was all over the color of flint. Blue was soundless, odorless, and completely without opinion. He was one of those clean, featureless men who can move for decades on the periphery of a pool game buying his fair share of beers without ever uttering a full sentence.

Blue had bought Lecia and me each a doll, curly-headed, near as tall as ourselves. Lecia's was blond, mine black-headed. Under the sedan's dome light, mine stared from its box on the wide back seat with an indifference bold enough to edge over into insult. A copper wire garroted her head in place. Her wrists and feet were likewise strapped down. Highway lights started streaking over the cellophane mask above her perfect features. She gazed out sullen. Her cold blue eyes announced that she wanted some other girl, not me. Well, I wanted my very own mother, and I'd have told her so, too, if the thought didn't put a lump in my throat. Instead I told her—out loud, I guess—"People in hell want ice water." Daddy said, "Say what?" And I told him I'd kill for a glass of ice water.

Surely Daddy said more to me in the car. But any other words were wiped clean from my head. He sounded real country talking to Blue while we drove. "Now you take old Raymond there . . ." he was saying to Blue. But it came out, "Nah yew tike ol Ryemon thar . . ." And slow, like he was addressing a deaf man.

In the house, Daddy slipped his jean jacket over a kitchen stool. We were fixing to eat, he said. Lecia unstacked the white melamine picnic plates on the plywood bar. They looked crude as Flintstone plates after our Colorado china. Each had three plastic compartments so you could keep your butter beans out of your greens, and the greens' pot liquor from sogging up your cornbread.

Daddy stood at the stove working with a long wooden spoon inside a pot of something muddy. He dribbled water from the silver kettle into the pot, and I heard it loosen up. In a few minutes you could smell garlic and pork back, and then came the steamy idea of sheer celery slices in a mess of red beans and rice. "This here'll be even better tomorrow," he said. He'd also made a wheel of cornbread in an iron skillet, the bottom-crust burnt first in hot lard on the stovetop the way I liked. Lecia cut hers off and flipped it across the butter dish at me. There was a dish of raw green onions we ate between bites. And I nearly finished the whole cereal bowl of collards, spoon after slotted spoonful. "Pokey, you know what I'd do to them greens?" Daddy said. He didn't even wait for me to say what, just doctored them with vinegary sprinkles from a jar of yellow Tabasco peppers. He kept looking up to tell Lecia he loved her with all his heart, but mine was the plate he fussed over.

We didn't even have to beg to sleep with him, just bounce twice and say please once before he said okay. First, he lit the gas stove in the bedroom with a *whump,* then smoothed my socks over the top, so they'd be warm come morning. Lecia buttoned our dresses up on hangers while he stripped off his khakis. His legs were white and skinny poking out of blue-patterned boxers. The pinched fingernails he ran all along his pants crease, to sharpen it, made a stuttery noise in the cloth, *rrrrr.* After, he draped them over a chair back and hit the light.

Lecia and I lay down in the vast bed with Daddy in the middle. He slept on top of the covers because he couldn't stand anything binding his feet. And from the second Lecia and I slid our legs under the sheet on either side of him, he was crying.

It's a fine trait of Texas working men that they cry. My daddy cried at parades and weddings. Watching the American flag slide up the pole before a Little League game could send tears down his leathery face. That night, I stoppered my ears against it. Still, I could make it out under the seashell noise of my own skull. Sniff and sniff and a deep-chested moan of grief rising from him. Through the window, the refinery towers burned, sending out black strands of smoke against the acid-green sky, so many threads weaving around each other. I finally unplugged my ears and the sobs rushed in with gale force. I squeezed his broad hand in both my smaller ones till I thought the finger bones would snap like twigs. I only let go when he needed to reach under his pillow for a red bandana to wipe his nose on.

Long after I thought he'd drifted off, his cracked voice rose up to ask if we'd say a prayer that Mother would come on home.

He had to say it, of course, for such a request struck us wordless. I'd never heard Daddy pray. He'd only gone to church for funerals, when he was toting somebody in a box. "Lord," Daddy started, "please bring these babies' momma back—" Then he broke down crying some more. We patted on either side of him till he quieted and Lecia threw in a big hearty amen.

I lay awake a long time listening, Daddy with his arm over my shoulder, Lecia behind him. We warped together like planed lumber. At least, that's the thought I had. We were just like the three curved boards for the hull bottom of some boat that only needed gluing and caulking together.

When Mother did come back, she arrived unannounced in a rented yellow Karmann Ghia sports car with Hector behind the wheel. She unfolded from the car's low-slung seat. Her alligator heels sank in the spongy ground, leaving holes like a crawfish makes. For weeks, I'd practiced the cool indifference I'd greet her with if she ever came back. But when I saw that beaver coat hem swirl around her calves like so much sea foam, all my resolve washed away. I slammed out the door and bounded toward her. I would have reached her first, too, had not Lecia shoved me down in the flower bed crowded with English ivy.

They'd come to pick up some clothes, Mother told Daddy. No more was said in the way of plan or explanation. If he knew she was coming before, he hadn't let on. He leaned on the far porch while she stooped down to hug me, that coat soft as any bunny and exuding Shalimar. "I miss you, baby," she said. She eyed Daddy over my shoulder the way you'd check the chain length of a tethered hound before you stepped in his yard. He didn't flinch under the gaze. He stayed rock still, but gave her wide berth. Eventually, she and Hector set about dragging dresses by armloads to the car, trailing hangers all down the yard and walk.

If the pope had advanced on us, outfitted in embroidered robes with acolytes behind wagging gold incense burners, the neighbors would have been held in less thrall. No sooner had that low yellow car halted in its tracks than every family on the block started from their various houses, prepared to stay a while, wearing windbreakers and winter jackets and rain slickers in case the fat clouds overhead broke open. They pulled their lawn chairs out of garage storage, aimed them to face us, and sat watching like we were some drive-in movie projected across the soft gray horizon. The misty rain that speckled the air didn't stop them. Mrs. Dillard just unfolded her clear plastic rain bonnet from its tuckaway pocket and tied it right under her chin, so her hairdo wouldn't get sticky. Mrs. Sharp wielded the massive black umbrella they toted to football games.

The men who weren't working stood together under the eaves of the Carters' garage, smoking, the red coals of their cigarettes visible when drawn on. They were watching too. Don't think they weren't. The kids scampered behind their front-yard ditches like nothing special was happening, all but Carol Sharp, who crossed the street to stand right at the edge of our yard. I gave her the finger in full view of everybody. That set her loping back to tattle, her Keds slapping against the wet asphalt.

I walked back and forth along the ditch's slope till it struck me that I'd once seen a cow dog patrol its territory with the exact same level of concentration I was bringing to bear. Mother and Hector toted some more dresses out the house. They were made of silk, colors of whipped cream and beige and palest tangerine shimmering in the gauzy air. I could just imagine the neighbor ladies reckoning their worth—"Why, one a them alone's worth Pete's whole paycheck . . ." I hated them at that instant, hated their broad heavy bottoms slung low in those stripy garden chairs. I hated their church suppers, their lumpy tuna casseroles, their Jell-O molds with perfect cubes of pear and peach hanging suspended. I hated their crocheted baby booties and sofa shawls, the toilet-paper covers shaped like poodles everybody worked on one summer.

For the first time, I felt the power my family's strangeness gave us over the neighbors. Those other grown-ups were scared. Not only of my parents but of me. My wildness scared them. Plus they guessed that I'd moved through houses darker than theirs. All my life I'd wanted to belong in their families, to draw my lunch bag from the simple light and order of their defrosted refrigerators. The stories that got whispered behind our supermarket cart, or the silence that fell over the credit union when Daddy shoved open the glass door—these things always set my face burning. That afternoon, for the first time, I believed that Death itself lived in the neighboring houses. Death cheered for the Dallas Cowboys, and wrapped canned biscuit dough around Vienna sausages for the half-time snack.

I picked up one of the coat hangers that had dropped on the ground, cocked my arm, and hurled it across the street at the Carters' house. It sailed like a boomerang, that hanger, but didn't even cross the street. Daddy called out to me then. "Pokey, come on in here." He'd moved just inside the screen, his profile sharp through the fine mesh.

Hector slammed down the Kharmann Ghia's hatch. Mother kept looking back at us, at Lecia and Daddy and me, behind the screen. I could feel us pulling on her like magnets. Her face went soft. On either side of her lipsticked mouth were deep parentheses of fret. I didn't hear what Hector said to her. I was too busy in my head pulling on Mother to stay with us, using a prayer full of thee's and thou's. Lecia later told me that Hector had told Mother to get her ass in gear, or some such.

What happened next points to Hector having said at least something that bad, for Daddy fast closed the space between himself and the yellow car. He reached inside and dragged Hector out by the shoulders, though Hector tried hanging on real hard to the wheel to prevent that happening. My stepfather was standing, though, before Daddy threw the first punch. I keep a very distinct image of Hector's thin-lipped mouth drawing itself into an "o" of surprise as it dawned on him that he was fixing to be hit. Hard, and more than once if necessary.

I would like to say the film clip I've shot for myself stops there, for I have seen men fight in the parking lots of certain bars. And always after the first collision of fist with face, or the first spots of blood down a shirtfront, I turned away, thinking myself too tenderhearted to watch. On that day I watched steady, for Daddy's pounding on Hector made me truly glad.

After he'd knocked Hector down once, he pulled him up to stand again, only to knock him down again. He practically dusted off Hector's shirt and adjusted his collar before clocking him the second time. Hector went down again easy, his legs swiveling under him like rope. He lay stretched there in the grass. Then Daddy did something I'd never seen him do before, which was to keep beating a fallen man. He sat down on Hector's chest and started swinging on him steady, pounding hard in the face without reason, for Hector had long since ceased to pose a threat to anybody. I watched Daddy's back muscles get very specific through his thin blue workshirt the way a boxer's would on a heavy-bag drill. He kept it up till I heard what must have been nose cartilage crunch.

That noise seemed to stop him. His shoulders dropped. He sat there on Hector's chest winded a second. Then he stood, staring down at his own bloody hands. He turned them over like objects of great curiosity, as if they belonged to another man and had been sent to Daddy solely for repair or inspection.

At that point I became aware Mother had been screaming. Her words—stored somewhere in my head all the while—came racing back like a tape I'd rewound. "Get offa him, Pete, you're killing him, Baby. Oh God. Lecia, Mary—somebody stop him—" She shut up as soon as Daddy stood. She didn't want to rouse him any worse. He looked at her across that yellow car roof and sighed. "I'm sorry," he said, and seemed to mean it, though when he glanced down at Hector again, the fury must have rushed back through him again, for he raised his boot and stomped down on my stepfather's rib cage. I heard ribs crack with a noise like icy branches going down in wind.

Hector rolled on his side, and I feared he was curling up like a tumblebug would if you'd squashed him too hard playing. But after a while, I saw his mouth suck for air.

Still, all the pity that surged through me that day was for Daddy, for the world of ugly he'd kept inside that came pouring out on my stepfather. In fact, seeing Hector's face like a slab of veal just pounded with one of those wooden kitchen mallets pleased me no end. Lecia and I moved outside to study him better. It amazed me that he wasn't dead. His breath was light and rattly. When he rolled over to spit out gouts of blood, you could hear tooth chips hit the sidewalk.

The few times I'd seen Daddy heave up a coffin with other men, he always toted more than his share of weight, doing so with that slow-paced, sweating dignity a funeral requires. That was the bearing Daddy brought to handling my stepfather that day. He helped Mother fold him into the seat with utmost gentleness.

When he turned to climb up on the porch, his face was blank and sweaty. There was a fan-shaped pattern of blood sprayed across his chambray shirt. "Y'all get on in the house," he said, but his voice lacked any edge. He brushed past me.

I watched the Karmann Ghia head down the street—a streak of canary yellow against the gray tract houses that acted as backdrop. Then I heard the pipes groan in the kitchen when Daddy cranked on the faucet to wash up.

Mother never said that she was coming back to us that evening. Per usual, nobody said spit. But I sensed that she would come back, eventually at least. She had a soft spot for Daddy whipping up on a man who'd spoken to her in disrespect. And back then, heat still passed between my parents. You could practically warm your hands on it.

That evening she dumped Hector at the nearest emergency room, checked out of the room they'd just checked into, and headed straight back to us on Garfield Road. She'd spent or been cheated out of every cent of her inheritance. So she came back not just broke but deep in debt. And she stayed. She stayed with Daddy till his death, stayed well into her own dotage.

The neighbors were folding up their lawn chairs, closing their umbrellas to head back indoors. I shoved into my own house, into the cool dark of its wax-papered windows, feeling something like peace. Daddy's public ass-whipping of Hector proved to me that my stepfather was a bad man. Our time with him had been a bad time. That was over now, Daddy had ended it. He'd drawn a big line in our lives between that bad time and our future. He was shirtless when Mother came back, and they slow-danced into the bedroom laughing.

When the sheriff stopped by after dark, Mother went to the door naked under her black silk kimono. Daddy wasn't home just then, she told him. Anyways, there'd just been a domestic disruption—that was the phrase she'd used. She was a terrible flirt, and her eyes while she talked to the sheriff were amused. He took his Stetson off and stood there on the porch while june bugs pelleted the screen and neighbors behind their windows drew back their Priscilla curtains.

Lecia and I hung over the sofa back, still gleeful from the triumph of Hector's exile and Mother's coming back. I'd never seen her eyes so green, deep green, green as the sea past the farthest sandbar where the waves start to head out away from the beach to all the unnamed archipelagoes. Her arms were long and white coming out of the vast black sleeves of that kimono. She clutched it closed at her sternum, the black heavy silk bunching up like an orchid. The sheriff was already backing down the porch when Mother's last words on the subject were spoken. Here's what she said before the door closed on that rectangle of night, closed on the red silent siren light whirling across our window, closed like a tomb door sealed over the subject of Hector entirely, for she never mentioned him again: *silliest thing,* she said, *no big deal,* she said, then, *nothing we couldn't handle.*

III. Texas Again, 1980

. . . you were saved not in order to live
you have little time you must give testimony

be courageous when the mind deceives you be courageous
in the final account only this is important

and let your helpless Anger be like the sea
whenever you hear the voice of the insulted and beaten

let your sister Scorn not leave you
for the informers executioners cowards—they will win
they will go to your funeral and with relief throw a lump of earth
the woodborer will write your smoothed-over biography

and do not forgive truly it is not in your power
to forgive in the name of those betrayed at dawn

beware however of unnecessary pride
keep looking at your clown's face in the mirror
repeat: I was called—weren't there better ones than I . . .

—Zbigniew Herbert, from "The Envoy of Mr. Cogito"
(translated by John and Bogdana Carpenter)

CHAPTER 14

Seventeen years later, Daddy had a stroke while sitting on a stool bellied up to the American Legion bar. It was ten on a summer morning. He'd been pounding shooters of whiskey he washed back with glasses of tap beer, which trick he'd performed daily for the seven years since he'd retired from Gulf Oil at the age of sixty-three. I say retired. Technically, he had a part-time job running errands for Lecia's husband, David. The Rice Baron, I called him, for he owned working rice farms that nudged his income up towards the fifty percent tax bracket. David bought Daddy a little white pickup for mail-runs or for getting tacos come lunchtime, whatever needed doing. When Daddy, who supplemented his Legion alcohol-intake by sucking from a whiskey bottle he kept ratholed under his truck seat, got too weaving drunk to operate the pickup at all, somebody rang my brother-in-law, who dispatched one of the field hands to ferry Daddy around on some fabricated job till his head cleared and his hands started back trembling, a sign that his blood-alcohol level was edging down toward normal. Then he got re-deposited at the white truck.

During all this, Mother was usually laid up in bed wearing something filmy. She'd quit teaching art in public school, allegedly to spend more time with her rickety and rheumy-eyed husband. Instead, depression had walloped her. She stayed in that giant bed she'd built decades before, with a bearing I still think of as imperial. She'd stopped drinking under threat from Lecia and me, but stayed drugged to the gills on Valium and related pharmaceuticals and whatever book she'd drawn from the literal tower of them stacked on the floor by her nighttable.

Her reading tended toward religion and philosophy, the books ranging from the profound—Sartre was still a favorite; so was Gandhi—to the crackpot. She'd studied hatha yoga and macrobiotics, macramé and est. Her basic trouble at the time of Daddy's stroke was that she saw no good reason to get up and put on clothes.

Back then, I talked to her long distance from Boston most every night. After prime time, she lay in a torment that barbiturates only blurred the edges of: *Football, fishing, and fucking*—she'd say—*that's all anybody down here thinks about. I swear to God I'm going to blow my brains out.*

My live-in boyfriend at the time—a recent Harvard grad from an old Long Island family—praised my patience with Mother. He took the long hours I spent on the phone with her for kindness. His family estate had a name, an aged and doddering staff, and a formal library where silver polo trophies shone between rows of leather-bound editions. He spoke to his mother on holidays, from one end of a long glossy dinner table (a formality I envied and, when we later married, failed to master). In truth, I stayed on the telephone those nights from an old fear: I didn't want Mother to kill herself.

By the time I'd landed in Boston at twenty-five, that phone line was the only umbilical cord that joined me to Mother. Daddy and I had long since faded from each other.

My weird travels had first taken me from him. I'd started leaving home on short jaunts at fifteen—Houston, Dallas, Austin, Mexico—shopping for books mostly, or drugs. Mother puckered her mouth with worry hearing how I'd smoked opium at a surf contest on Padre Island. But I'd first filched Tom Wolfe's *Electric*

Kool-Aid Acid Test from her knitting bag. And her curiosity about the drug ultimately leaked through: *What was opium like?* Together we conspired to lie to Daddy about my whereabouts, lies Daddy helped by not prying overmuch.

I'd left his house for good at seventeen. I'd climbed into a camper truck with surfboards strapped on top and driven with a bunch of kids to California, where (before I managed to snag a job in a T-shirt factory) I lived in a car and ate whatever I could steal from local orchards or grocery-store Dumpsters.

Such squalid facts never reached Daddy's ears. When I landed back home, tanned, string-skinny, and eager for the comfort of the Minnesota college I'd talked into taking me, he liked pretending I'd never crossed over the state line. "How was the beach, Pokey?" he wanted to know.

He took me to GI Surplus to buy me a winter parka. I hold a distinct picture of him picking through the rack of olive-drab coats with orange liners, each one sloped down on its hanger, as if shouldering in itself a burden. Daddy was a suspicious shopper. He peered extra close at the quilted stitching. He ran a lot of zippers up and down.

The college was a private liberal-arts school that had ginned out a few left-wing presidential candidates. The specter of my coed dorm—one of the nation's first—must have prompted Daddy that day into his one, veiled lecture on sex. Here's how it went: "I reckon you know by now not to let any a them little boys mess with you, Pokey." He was squinting down at a parka's size tag while he spoke. It had Korean ideograms on it. I said I reckoned I did. "They mess with you, you call me." He turned me around to measure the coat's shoulders against mine. "I get on them like ugly on ape."

This concern from Daddy for my virtue, however casual, just added to the vague backwater of guilt I carried about him. I'd long since left the world where my virtue warranted defense, which is to say, Daddy's world.

So at the cash register in GI Surplus where Daddy shelled out

$19.95 for the parka, I felt a flush of guilt. I said no to the suede mittens he wanted to throw in. It was better wearing bobby socks on my hands that first winter.

Still, on my first visit home from college, he not only spooned my supper plate high, but actually used his pocketknife to saw my T-bone into a grid of tiny bites.

Lecia—who'd stayed in town for college and who, therefore, garnered not a glance from Daddy when she breezed through the house every day—teased him about it. "Jesus, Daddy, why don't you just chew it up for her and spit it right in her mouth?"

Daddy couldn't stand my growing up, specifically since I grew up female.

For no sooner had I bought my first training bra (Vassarette 28A stretch), than my invites to the Liars' Club began trailing off. Puberty was hard won for me. I was a late bloomer. My nickname in the neighborhood was Blister Tits, which I earned in part because Lecia at age twelve already harnessed her boobs into a Playtex 36C. But bloom I eventually did, at least enough to alter the deportment of men Daddy hung out with. If, during a crap game, Ben Bederman let slip the word "cocksucker" in response to having rolled snake-eyes, he'd go pale apologizing to me special, something he'd never done before.

The last fight I saw Daddy have pretty much cinched my going to any Liars' Club functions ever after.

I'd hitched home during college for Easter break. Daddy took me to the Legion, to shoot pool supposedly. But I half suspected that the long-standing flirtation he carried on with the woman barkeep was really a full-blown affair. (Mother actually put the idea in my head, afterwards tacking on this heart-breaking sentence, "All that was over between me and your daddy way back.")

Lucy was a small Cajun woman with enormous breasts and a trace of mustache. When we came in that afternoon, she hugged my neck before drawing our beers. She even scooped me a bowl of the cheddar Goldfish they usually didn't break out till dark.

Lucy collected things—souvenir spoons, porcelain dolls. She had an assortment of wiglets, braids, and falls that she wove in complicated whirls with her own dark hair. She'd also filled the back wall of the bar with those old cat clocks whose black tails hung down twitching while their eyes rolled side to side. But the clocks were out of sync in a way that preyed on your nerves. Mother always said if you weren't a drinker heading into the Legion, that woman's wall-eyed clocks jerking at odds with one another would start you off.

I plugged quarters into the pool table, and the balls dropped with a fine thunder. I racked them extra tight, my fingertips wedged in the plastic triangle so not one loosened a notch when I finally raised the rack. A second later, Daddy broke solid but easy. The balls whacked around in sharp angles. They slowed up, and finally stopped with nothing sunk. I went to powder my hands. The can lid left a pattern of dots on my palm like white braille till I rubbed it in.

A pool game mixes ritual with geometry. The slow spaciousness of the green felt mirrors some internal state you get to after a few beers. Back at school, I'd been trying to read the philosophy of art, which I was grotesquely unequipped to do but nonetheless stuck on. I loved the idea that looking at a painting or listening to a concerto could make you somehow "transcend" the day-in, day-out bullshit that grinds you down; how in one instant of pure attention you could draw something inside that made you forever larger. In those days the drug culture was pimping "expanded consciousness," a lie that partly descended from the old post-industrial lie of progress: any change in how your head normally worked must count as an improvement.

Maybe my faith in that lie slid me toward an altered state that day. Or maybe it was just the beer, which I rarely drank. In any case, walking around the pool table, I felt borne forward by some internal force or fire.

My first shot sank a ball. Then I made the most unlikely bank shot in history to drop two balls at once after a wild V trajectory. Daddy whistled. The sky through the window had gone the exact blue of the chalk I was digging my cue stick in, a shade solid and luminous at once, like the sheer turquoise used for the Madonna's robe in Renaissance paintings. Slides from art history class flashed through my head. For a second, I lent that color some credit, as if it *meant* something that made my mind more buoyant. But that was crazy.

Then it hit me that my joy came purely from being in the Legion. In fact, I'd hitched twelve hundred miles to shoot pool there, with that cue warped to shit, on the table whose perimeter was scarred with cigarette burns. And I'd done so without even knowing it. I'd stood solo at the on-ramp of the Oklahoma turnpike for hours with my wind-chapped thumb stuck out and my cardboard sign saying DALLAS nearly torn from my hand every time a gust sucked a dust-devil up off the plain beyond me, and all that while I'd stared back at the ridge wishing for some vehicle to rise up and carry me the fuck out of there, I had no conscious idea of what was tugging me south. The trucker who finally rolled up at dusk and swung open his door, saying climb on up, wondered why I'd hitch so far alone, in such sharp weather. *Going home* had been answer enough.

But it was more than that. Something about the Legion clarified who I was, made me solid inside, like when you twist the binocular lens to the perfect depth and the figure you're looking at gets definite. Maybe I just liked holding a place in such a male realm.

That bar also delineated the realm of sweat and hourly wage, the working world that college was educating me to leave. Rewards in that realm were few. No one congratulated you for clocking out. Your salary was spare. The Legion served as recompense. So the physical comforts you bought there—hot boudain sausage and cold beer—had value. You *attended* the place, by which I mean you not only went there but gave it attention your job didn't deserve. Pool got shot not as metaphor for some corporate battle, but as itself alone. And the spiritual comforts—friendship, for instance—couldn't be confused with payback for something you'd accomplished, for in the Legion everybody punched the same clock, drew the same wage, won the same prize.

A truck loaded with chicken cases waggled off the road shoulder outside the Legion, fishtailing and sending dust and diesel fumes through the screens. The racket roused up a cowboy who'd been passed out at a round cocktail table in the back corner. We hadn't seen him before. He'd been sleeping bent over by the accordion-shaped room divider where an army of folding chairs tilted. A straw cowboy hat sat beside him. His face was buried in folded arms, which were sunburnt the unlikely crimson of an oil-rig worker's. His back heaved up and down as with sobs. Daddy walked over and regarded him a minute. *Don't cry, buddy,* Daddy finally said. *I hate seeing a fella cry.* The guy lifted his crimson face. He wasn't crying, he said, he was trying not to throw up. *Well, I don't like watching them throw up either,* Daddy said. The guy eventually swaggered bowleggedly off to the men's room.

When he came out, there were comb marks in his wavy brown hair. His name was Dole, like the pineapple company, and he happened to be from Buna, Texas, where Daddy was born. After a few no-shits, he and Daddy started buying each other beers, talking about who all Dole knew in Jasper County, which turned out to be pretty much everybody you could know. Dole also knew Black Angus cattle, cutting horses, and enough about pool to challenge Daddy to a money game.

Lucy kept me company the rest of the day. She'd been harboring secret plans for my personal appearance and set about executing them. She teased my hair with a rat-tail comb, lacquered it stiff, then wound it up tight like hers. Hairpins dug into my scalp. From a tackle box under the bar, she drew out frosted blue eye shadow and a black cake eyeliner she wet with her tongue. I closed my eyes when she came at me.

When I finally opened them, she still had the mascara wand raised in her hand. I blinked a few times. My eyelashes had noticeable weight. In the back mirror, I looked like somebody's kid sister trying to get in a roadhouse without ID. Lucy went on to whip up a blender of brandy alexanders for the purpose of putting tallow on my flat little heinie. She plunked a few extra filberts in my lowball glass of foam.

By the time her soap opera came on about two, I was affably drunk. The cat clocks' offbeat tails twitching overhead didn't faze me a bit. I was the bodhisattva of brandy, the crown princess of alexander.

I woke with my damp cheek flat to the bar. I'd somehow crossed from my original joy into drunkenness, and beyond that into a sugar coma. Hours had passed. My bird's nest of hair tipped sideways. It seemed to be drawing my worrisome headache far beyond the parameters of my skull. I looked around while Lucy poured me a collins glass of water. The stools beside me had been untipped. A shallow paper bowl of Goldfish sat before each one. At back tables, folks stared intently at the domino tiles they'd lined up into short walls. I drained my glass and slid it back to Lucy, who arched a thin brow penciled the color of coffee and caught me up on Daddy's pool game.

The neat stack of dollars on the table's edge had once belonged to Dole and now belonged to Daddy. The cowboy had responded to this by getting sidewinding drunk. He stabbed at the balls in hard, mean little pokes. He was also shooting too high, his cue-stick sailing upwards in an arc so it whacked the hanging metal lampshade a few times, sending it sideways. And he didn't bother to sight along the stick or hunker down so his eye could work out angles. He just sucked his front teeth and jabbed, pissing away every shot.

Daddy was probably just as drunk, but that only made him walk straighter. He took aim with the slow concentration of a man underwater. Nearly every ball he stood behind eventually moved slow to the pocket he'd picked for it. When Dole started making sissy shots—trying to jump one ball over another or shooting behind his back, Daddy said let's wrap this deal up, which the cowboy snorted at. "You took my money," he said.

Daddy just grinned. "Hell, brother, you set the stakes."

Suddenly Dole was at the bar next to me, pounding on the sparkling Formica with his meaty fist. His features seemed scrunched in the center of his round, red face, crowding each other for room. "Beer here, barkeep," he said.

"You're eighty-sixed," Lucy said. "Cut off. No more for you."

"What for?"

" 'Cause I said. That's what for." She'd had both hands on the bar when he strode over. Now she dropped one out of sight with a move so smooth I wondered if she kept some ballbat or other equalizer under the counter.

Dole jerked his thumb over at Daddy. "What about Tonto back there?"

"Tonto's still drinking," Daddy said. But, in fact, his glass sat empty. He was slipping his cue back in the wall rack even as he spoke.

I was deep in my own headachy admiration of Daddy's equanimity when *poof,* he appeared at my side. Then Dole was saying we should all go fuck ourselves, and Daddy was balling up his fist to catch that cowboy under his jaw with an uppercut. Dole arched back a few paces, then looked down at his shirt.

It was, of course, a cowboy shirt. Seeing its little embroidered violets (his ex-wife had done crewelwork) speckled with blood where his buck teeth had bitten down on his own bottom lip obviously pissed him off. If he'd stopped to think, though, Dole might have backed off a step, apologized, squirted club soda on some napkins to sponge off his shirt. That would have ended things, for Daddy had dropped his arms to his sides. But Dole made a tactical error. He grabbed the pool cue he'd leaned against the bar and swung it in a whistling arc at Daddy about eye-level, in a motion so wide and slow only a moron would have failed to catch that cue midair and sucker-punch Dole in the throat with it. Which is what Daddy did.

Dole cooperated by falling down. He lay on the linoleum in an x-shape. Lucy fetched his Stetson to balance on his big belly. "That was better than *Gunsmoke,*" she told Daddy.

He never took me to the Legion again. Nor to any bar. Nor fishing nor hunting nor out to throw dice nor to the Farm Royal for chicken-fried steak nor to Fisher's Bait Shop on Christmas Eve morning, nor anywhere that my mere female presence might provoke some goofball into mouthing off, in which case Daddy would have to tear him a new asshole. No policy to this effect got announced, but that's how it worked out.

So over the years, Daddy and I grew abstract to each other. We knew each other in theory and loved in theory. But if placed in proximity—when I came home, say—any room we sat in would eventually fall into a soul-sucking quiet I could hardly stand.

He started off every visit by piling a plate up for me as you would for a linebacker. Meanwhile, I'd urge him to retell some old story everybody else had long since gotten sick of. I'd recorded a few for an oral-history project in college, and that set a precedent. But any story eventually trailed off into quiet. He'd say he had to go check on his truck (translate: sit alone in the dark garage sneaking pulls off a bourbon bottle), or the phone would ring and I'd fly to answer it.

Liquor had eaten away at Daddy. He got mean-mouthed those last few years before the stroke. Mother bore the brunt of it, but it cropped up with other folks too. At my brother-in-law's farm he'd pulled a knife on a field hand from Oaxaca who contended that the tacos from Daddy's favorite vendor weren't authentically Mexican. Another time, a farm partner from Arkansas who'd ridden horseback across a rice levee during dove season found himself looking down the business end of Daddy's twelve-gauge. "Old man," the partner claimed to have said, "I own eighteen percent of every stalk of rice growing out there." To which Daddy said that the fellow was fixing to own a hundred percent of some buckshot in his ass too if he didn't back that horse off that levee and head right on down the road. In a supermarket line, Daddy cold-cocked a young marine; he went across the counter of the gas company at some surly clerk.

Daddy turned on me just once, the summer of his stroke. I was trying to finish my grad-school thesis and was, as usual, broke. Lecia and her husband had lured me down with a quick-money scheme that involved my trucking live crawfish from Breaux Bridge, Louisiana, to a new crawfish farm out in Winnie, Texas. They were Rolex-wearing young Republicans, and constantly tried to infect me with the entrepreneurial spirit that powered them both.

Maybe they also wanted to humble me with the task, for the crawfish may stand as the most ignominious-looking creature you can find yourself in service of, being black and shiny with all its jointed skeleton on the outside. It makes a wet clicking noise like a giant cockroach. So if at a dark truck stop you pause to hose down a flatbed truck with eighty-pound sacks of crawfish piled three deep (crawfish die when they dry off, it turns out), the sacks emit damp sucking sounds that conjure in your lumbar region a prehistoric fear and can set clamoring through your head images of insect hordes cresting hill after hill toward you. I drove at night, before the sun's heat could too quickly dry the burlap I wet down and draped over and around and between the sacks for moisture. This made for slow going.

Still, by late morning, I was usually done unloading and was scrubbing my hands with lemon to get the fish stink off. That left whole afternoons for me to type my critical paper, which I was supposed to be doing in Mother's studio. But I spent most days dozing, writing postcards or thumbing old *Artforum* magazines. I'd also affected smoking strong French cigarettes after a trip to Europe, and went through quite a few packs of those.

One night Mother startled me awake standing by my bed. Her shadow slid across me, and I jerked upright into the icy blast of a window air-conditioner. She held some big object against her belly like a child. She was crying. "Can you help me with your daddy?" she said. "He won't let me plug this vaporizer in by his bed. And he can't hardly breathe." I slid out of the covers and pulled on a hooded sweatshirt. Her hair was silky white, a glow in the dark room. "Won't *let* you?" I said. The concept of permission as applied to Mother was foreign. She answered with a tired sigh. I took the sloshing vaporizer, which was the old hot-steam type she'd used for our croup as kids.

Daddy was sitting on the edge of that oceanic bed in his boxer shorts barking out a dry cough. His head hung down between his broad shoulders like a wounded bull's. On his right thigh was a plum-colored bump where he'd caught some shrapnel during the war. "Daddy?" I said, and he roared up for me to get the fuck out, which assault seemed to blast all available oxygen from the room. Maybe my hair flew back in cartoon astonishment. Then he wound down again into a gasping cough.

He'd never talked to me that way, and I froze in it. After a while he seemed to forget I was standing there. He lay back down. He wasn't exactly coughing, but his breathing had a jagged gasp in the middle of it. When I started nosing around behind the dresser for an electrical outlet, he roared up again. "What you want in here?" More coughs, the tendons on his neck stood out in sharp relief. I turned on the dresser lamp. The room was icebox cold, but he was in a flop sweat, his face bright with fever. The bedclothes held moist wrinkles where he'd been resting. I told him I was fixing to plug the vaporizer in.

A bead of sweat hung from his nose. He wiped it with the back of his hand and squinted my way. "Your mother sent you in here, didn't she?" Then he started a rant against her the likes of which I'd never heard. She was the most selfish person he'd ever known. She'd ruined everybody she ever touched. Including me and my sister. We weren't nothing. Lecia with her Phi Beta Kappa in physics. Me with my MFA—Mother-Fucking Asshole's what that stood for.

Where he got the wind for all this, I can't guess. His voice came out in a guttural rasp, like the possessed kid in that exorcist movie. Daddy railed down to his last breath: I couldn't master my own rosy red ass, he said. Thermometers had degrees, he said. I still didn't know my butt from a hole in the ground.

I was crying by then. Once coughing had shut him up again, I started groping along the baseboard for an outlet. The lamp cord got jostled in the process, so the room plunged to black. He didn't say anything. When I plugged the vaporizer in, a chubby road of steam started puffing right in my face. It smelled of menthol chest rub. He waved his ropy arm in the mist. "Get that fucking thing out of here!" Daddy's whisper was both fierce and frail. I sat back on my heels. He doubled over coughing again.

And that's how we stayed for a while, like figures in a paperweight—me still as a deer with that warm steam going down my lungs somehow cool, him seizing up spastic for breath. "Mary Marlene"—*kharf kharf kharf*—"I'm gonna throw that fucking thing out the window"—*kharf, kharf*—"and you behind it," he said. The steam was making phantoms of us, clouding the room with eucalyptus. I finally said if he wanted the fucking vaporizer unplugged, he'd have to come over me to get it. Which, apparently, he didn't see fit to do.

When he finally curled on his side, breathing ragged, he looked like something dry you'd shake out of a shell.

Next day, I came in from my crawfish run to find Daddy upright at the table laboring slightly for breath. I kissed his scratchy cheek. His eyes showed nothing of the night before. He was cradling his white cat, Bumper, like a swaddled baby, cooing. "Confound the luck," Daddy said, meaning, *goddamn your fate.* His thumb smoothed the animal's throat, then rubbed along his jawbone where scent glands hid under fur.

Bumper was the sole survivor from a herd of mewling kittens that Daddy fed at the barn till the litter took sick and died. Poisoned, we later figured, judging by the mother cat's last seizure. Bumper himself lost every stitch of fur on his head. It grew back leaving bare patches, perfectly square, on his pointed face. Plus he walked with a weird shimmying gait, like his back legs wanted to list off in their own direction. Maybe he was swaggering around his testicles, which were big as golf balls. His meow stayed so dim and soprano, though, you couldn't hardly hear it. So he'd learned to bump the screen with his ass if he wanted in or out. Hence his name.

The Lone Star I took from the fridge matched the one sitting in front of Daddy. "I don't know how you drink one of these salted," I said and popped the top. He said he didn't rightly know. I drew my stool across from his. On the varnished plywood that stretched between us lay scattered foil sample packets of penicillin. "Dr. Boudreaux stop by?" I said. He said yep and commenced to tamping down a Camel.

"Bet he didn't want you smoking for a while," I said.

"Didn't say nothing about it," he said. Bumper slithered from Daddy's lap to the floor with a liquidy plop. He rolled over for me, his legs sprawling off his round belly. Daddy kept that cat so loaded up on Friskies and wet food, Bumper was round as a bear.

"Know what he weighs?" Daddy said. I couldn't guess. "Seventeen pounds," he said. Every morning Daddy dropped the struggling cat on the bathroom scale, peering down at the little window till the red needle stopped swinging. He logged each day's weight on a scratch pad by the phone.

I played My Hand's a Spider on the cat's belly a minute. He batted back with slow, soft paws. "He wants stretching," Daddy told me. He'd trained the cat to get stretched before coming in or out. This involved holding the cat's hands and feet, pulling gently while he arched his whole length. All this time, you had to say (I shit you not, the cat would only come in or out once these words were spoken), "Gosh, what a long cat." Afterwards, Bumper body-blocked the glass door and trotted out. A wave of heat rolled in.

When I turned back to Daddy, his cigarette's thread of smoke was coiling right into his eyes. I hadn't planned to tell him to quit drinking that day. But something in how Daddy never blinked at that curl of stinging smoke, something of that small discomfort, cut right to where I loved him most.

I told him drinking was killing him. That I loved him and didn't want him dead. I was neither less blunt nor more articulate than that.

After, I took a sip of beer. Neither of us spoke. My head bent down as if to catch a blow. But no barrage of denial or rage came flying at me. What I got was way worse. Daddy shrugged. "I don't give a shit," he said. His voice and gaze were steady enough that I heard the declaration for non-negotiable fact, an opinion cut into the very grain of what he was.

I studied the kitchen floor, gold and ivory crosshatch like Italian tile. Lecia had paid her handyman to install it that very morning. She was prone to flashy presents. The new stove, microwave, and console TV that took up half the living room were from her. She'd even shelled out my graduate tuition first term, doubtless thinking it her duty. That lie of responsibility was part of the wedge that lay between us as sisters. I had a sudden urge to call her. Instead, I nodded at the linoleum. "You think the new floor's nice?" I said.

"It don't bother me," Daddy said. The gray ash that had been growing off his Camel finally broke and fell on the new tile, where it lay like a caterpillar. He ground it with his shoe, the same type of heavy black work shoe he'd worn my whole life. I could practically turn blindfolded to the page in the Sears catalogue where a pair of them floated in the pale-blue ether among the tasseled loafers and Weejuns that never garnered so much as a glance from Daddy.

I knew where he got those shoes resoled, and how often, and could myself, with his shoeshine kit and a soft cloth, buff them to a mirror glaze. I'd done so under his close instruction for quarters as a kid. I knew his height and weight (six feet even, one hundred and sixty-five pounds), and how he liked his steak (burnt black, with salt and black pepper and Worcestershire). But for the life of me, the contents of his skull that afternoon were closed to me. He was unknown to me, and unknowable, though I sensed inside him during that time a darkness so large and terrible that perhaps his last gift to me was trying to shield me from it, and his last failure was that he couldn't entirely do so.

"I'm going out to check on my truck," he said, and drew up to full height before shoving through the glass. He walked on the path of square stones heading out to the garage. The white stones made a chessboard diagonal through the red gravel. Daddy was careful to set his black shoe dead center each one. I watched the triangle of his khaki back grow smaller till he disappeared through the door.

By the time Daddy's stroke slumped him onto the Legion bar a few weeks later, so his beer dregs rivered down the gold-speckled Formica, he was a gargoyle of himself. For nearly a decade he'd sat on that oxblood-covered bar stool as if skewered to earth by it. It was just one in a line of such stools, like dots in an ellipsis heading off toward oblivion, each occupied by a veteran of some other war.

At the hospital, I stepped on the black rubber pad that swung open the magic doors. The lobby was deserted. I'd volunteered as a candy striper in that hospital a few bleak Sundays during the oil boom. Back then, babies were getting born by the fistfuls, and old people were sicker than ever. You couldn't find a seat in the lobby not crawled over by some saggy-diapered toddler.

Ten years later, the place was a wasteland. I passed rows of darkened Coke machines, empty nursing stations, vast wards with beds stripped to mattress ticking. A lone janitor outside intensive care was shoving one of those rotating waxers around with an attention I thought of as Zen-like.

Mother sat in a plastic peach-colored tub chair outside Daddy's room boldly smoking a long brown More cigarette beside a No Smoking sign. "I told them to go ahead and arrest me," she said. Lecia rolled her eyes at this. My sister was heading home to fix supper for her husband and four stepkids. She had car keys in her hand and a list of things I had to know. Daddy couldn't talk, wasn't continent, and might or might not understand what you said to him. "Maybe you can get him eating," she said. "He's pretty much turned up his nose at everything they've brought."

People tend to say how small a sick man looks in a hospital bed. But Daddy looked bigger than ever, even in the oxygen tent. He'd stayed long-muscled and wiry from decades of climbing oil towers. His hospital gown's thin blue cotton looked overdelicate on his raw-boned frame. Somebody had slicked back his hair with Brylcreem. The green oxygen-tank hissing made the only sound in the room. The heart monitor sat squat and disconnected in the corner, its screen a muddy brown. But for the tube running from an upended bottle into the back of Daddy's hand, he might have been carved of gray marble. He looked like a soapstone statue of my daddy sleeping, or like the elegant casket tops of pharaohs I'd pored over in the Egypt section of our encyclopedia as a kid.

I slid my hand under the tent plastic to take his large dry hand. His lips were flaky. His eyes were swollen to reptilian-looking slits. I lifted the tent plastic another notch and poked my head in. The air inside was thin and cool as mountain air. "Daddy?" I said.

The night nurse popped her head in the door and told me to get out from under there, I was killing him. She came over to fiddle with his feeding tube and feel his pulse.

The door had just hissed shut behind her when Daddy's eyes opened a notch. He raised his arm up stiff the way a cartoon sleepwalker would. With one trembling finger, he poked the plastic oxygen tent as if to touch my face. Then his arm dropped heavy. "Looooo," he said. The left side of his mouth was drawn down in a sharp parody of being sad. "Hello, Daddy," I said. I sounded cheerful enough to teach *Romper Room.* "Goddamn," he said. Then, "Yamma." I told him Mama was talking to the nurses. He used his good hand to feel down his bad arm like a blind man, exploring each finger. He pulled it across his middle as if to park it there. But the arm slid back to his side, dead as a fish.

I drew the supper tray over and lifted the plastic lid. "Presto," I said. Did he want any of that? He wrinkled his nose. "Shit," he said. He went back to studying his bad hand, like it held the answer to some question he couldn't quite formulate.

I finally stuck a bendy straw in a carton of milk, and he sucked that down. Afterwards, I wiped his wet chin with my sleeve. "Ah looo," he said. He stared at me steady, like a swami sending brain waves. "Hello, Daddy," I said. I held up a cup of orange juice covered with Saran Wrap, and he wrinkled his nose.

From curiosity, I pulled open the metal drawer of his bed table.

A single can of Lone Star rolled into view. I shut the drawer, and in that brief interval, Daddy's eyes had closed. I sneaked under the oxygen tent to be sure. "Daddy?" I said. But he was like Brer Rabbit, just playing possum.

Mother let me drive home. Dr. Boudreaux had spent an hour going over Daddy's condition with her and Lecia. He'd dismantled a plastic model of the brain for her. The report to me was way more concise: "His head's all fucked up," Mother said. There was something called an "immediate-recovery period" of a few weeks after a stroke, while brain swelling went down. In that time, Daddy could just snap out of it, start talking and walking like before. Or maybe he'd turn into one of those chicken-chested old men you see in rest-home hallways, tied to their chairs and listing for decades.

The Leechfield I drove home through that night had eroded into a ghost town. I'd somehow not noticed this before. Streetlights had been shot out in strings. Our car kept moving into black intervals of road, then bursting into light again. Lawns grew wild. For-sale signs stuttered by too fast to count. All the necessary stores were boarded up—pharmacy, cleaners, hardware. Gone was the jewelry store with its Ferris wheel of lockets and birthstone rings; gone the coffee shop. The fancy clothes store—where all the cheerleaders worked after high school—went bankrupt when the proprietor was arrested in a motel room with two such cheerleaders and a Ziploc baggie of cocaine.

I set down in my journal the businesses we passed that night: nail-sculpting salon, knickknack shop, trophy store, aerobic-dance studio, K-9 dog-training school. There was a diet center that sported a plywood cutout of a pink pig wearing a brick-red polka-dot dress. The bubble coming from the pig's mouth held this phrase: A New Way To Lose Weight Without Starving To Death. Where the filling station used to stand was a parking lot lined with industrial ice machines. So driving by, I read ICE ICE ICE ICE ICE. You could also get chemotherapy in a modern cinder-block building, which didn't surprise me since the town formed one of the blackest squares on the world cancer map. (It's still right up there with Bhopal and Chernobyl.)

Once we hit the hurricane fence that ran alongside the rubber factory, Mother started talking. Money was a problem, she said, being as they didn't have any. She thought he'd bought some supplementary insurance. That reminded her to fish Daddy's wallet from his jeans jacket in the backseat.

She unfolded the wings of it and started picking past onionskin gas receipts and ticket stubs. There was a cocktail napkin with the point spread from a baseball game on which the lights had long since gone dim. Strangest of all, she found two documents of mine—the one college report card where I pulled down straight A's, and a Xerox of my first published poem. The poem was about Daddy's sister. It had been unfolded so many times and smoothed across so many damp bar tops the parchment warped and buckled. The middle creases were cloudy with blurred ink. The notion of his toting that around nearly broke me in half crying, so Mother started bawling too.

We blubbered in a wild chorus behind bobbing headlights all the way home. Maybe all my snubbing kept me from seeing clear. Or maybe, as Mother always contended, I just drove too damn fast, for when the car finally surged in the garage, there was a dull thump under the rear axle, a hollow sound like a dropped cantaloupe.

I threw the car in park and crawled around in the exhaust fumes looking for what I'd hit. By the back tire on the shotgun side, there was a blood smear. It looked black as an inkblot in the red taillights. Of course, Bumper didn't come when called. He was nowhere in evidence. Mother later believed she saw some animal's white hindquarters slithering off into a field of saw grass and blackberries in back of the garage. But there were snakes galore in those weeds, Mother said. Maybe even nutria rats.

She found him bloody and panting shallow on the back porch at dawn. She wrapped him in a lemon-colored bath towel and fetched him to the animal hospital. We only had a hundred dollars between us and planned to put him to sleep. But the vet offered to try some surgery for free. He put pins in the cat's hips and wired his broken jaw shut. For years the doctor had heard outrageous tales in bars about this animal's unlikely survival. The old cat might just make it.

CHAPTER 15

One morning, an orderly with arms like a wrestler's scooped Daddy up, bent his limbs around so he'd fit in a wheelchair, then rolled him from intensive care to a regular ward while I walked alongside. I carried a warm jar of piss that had a tube running out and leading under Daddy's hospital gown. Mother brought his metal flip chart, where somebody official had declared Daddy's condition "stable" in block letters.

After that, the men from the Liars' Club came practically every night to shuffle at Daddy's bedside. They came straight from work, unfed, but refusing to dip into any pizza box you tipped open or to take any wrapped sandwich you held out. They arrived alone or in awkward pairs, holding their silver hard hats at belt level, turning them around in their hands like so many prayer wheels.

Once, when Daddy had shit the bed, I found Ben and Shug talking about an upcoming Yankees game, talking volubly as if the room didn't stink like a barnyard.

Ben cried that night in the hall. His big meaty hands covered his face. And after that, he only came late, when Daddy was dozing and Mother was gathering up the day's magazines and leftover soda cans. Ben took his post in a precariously tipped tub chair outside Daddy's room nearly every night for hours at a pop "in case something happened."

But nothing ever happened. Whatever vacuum the stroke had dug inside Daddy's skull held its place. He was pitched way back behind flat-staring eyes, too deep for any mere human presence to register on him as much more than shadow. Some mornings if he'd slept straight through, he'd spark up when you came in. You could suddenly *see* him seeing you, almost feel him bearing toward you from where he lay, though the form of his body never altered one iota.

Such times, he might come into a word like "juice," squawking it out in his new crow's voice. Only a few such words ever got spoken, though, before his eyes fogged over again, and his head dropped back on the pillow.

On the anniversary of D-Day, Mother and I watched a TV special. The first young GIs scaling the wall on the French coast got picked off by German bullets like so many insects. Daddy had been an infantryman there. He'd waded out of a landing craft with his rifle held up out of the surf. The film footage must have overlaid with images fixed in his head, for watching he roused as if jolted up by stong current. He cried out, "That's Omaha Beach!" with perfect clarity. He pointed at the screen and fought to rise to a full sit, but his own body pinned him down. Mother had to push the button to tilt the electric bed up. "That's Normandy!" Daddy hollered. A while later, he started calling what first sounded like nonsense, then took on the cadence of the old Latin mass. But I finally figured he was saying names, surnames, in fact, the ones I'd seen scrawled in the ragged address book he carried all across Europe. He was still calling those names in a whisper when the light went out of him.

Mother tapped on the nursing station window, eager to announce Daddy's miracle turnaround. But the night nurse just kept painting her nails with sheer lacquer. Whole chunks of brain function stayed intact after a stroke, she told us. Usually times that had a strong feeling attached, as D-Day would. That was also why Daddy could still cuss like a sailor. He'd stored words like "motherfucker" in the region of the brain where a man's most basic expressions—those rising out of rage or grief or stark fear—were kept.

The next morning, I brought an stack of old *Life* magazines I found in the back closet. Sure enough, Daddy could name a B-17 fighter plane and an M-1 rifle. On the maps, he could tell Italy from Poland, and he placed a shaky finger on the thin face of General Montgomery when I asked who'd pinned the medal on him after the Battle of the Bulge. He frowned at General Patton—"Riding crop. Mean-assed. Bad."

But when I tried to steer him from those glossy pages smoothed across his bed tray to naming the implements on that tray, he lost it. "What do you call this, Daddy?" I held up a fork. He mimed eating with his good hand. "That's right. You eat with it, but what's its name?" He looked off to the side, as if some invisible straight man there could confirm what a bonehead I was. After a second, though, his head's machinery must have started to scramble. His eyes tilted up as if he were searching for the right word. Meanwhile, in my own skull I leaned hard on the right word—*fork fork fork*—like a mantra. His eyes flashed. The good side of his mouth warped up in a half smile. "Bacon!" he said, as if some switch had been thrown. In my best nursery school voice, I said bingo, Daddy.

Being in that hospital room for half an hour at a pop took all I could muster. Not that I did anything else of value. Crawfish season had ended. My typewriter's machinery was a well of dust. I went on a few awkward dates to cowboy bars with fellows Lecia and David scared up for me.

After one such debacle, I lay awake with a wicked case of the whirlies induced by tequila, resolving to devote myself to Daddy all day, to by-God master whatever it took.

Next morning, I tried shaving him. With his own daddy's old boar-bristle brush, I lathered up his neck, which was leathery as a Christmas turkey's. But my hand shook holding the plastic razor. It felt light and insubstantial next to his throat cords. My first stroke nicked him deep enough to draw blood; a thick drop cut through the white soap. Daddy didn't flinch at this. His breathing pattern didn't quicken. Still, Mother had to finish.

Afterwards, I held my moon-shaped compact up to his face. He ran his good hand over his smooth chin. "Purty," he said. The left side of his mouth twisted up in a sharp half smile. With the other half drawn down, he turned into one of those split masks, comedy and tragedy. "Purty goo," he said. I left the hospital to buy a quart of malt liquor in a paper bag. Inside the cavernous movie cineplex, I drank this fast, then watched three matinees in a row. I sneaked from one theater to another, never paying extra, half daring the pimply young usher to turn his flashlight on me and ask for a ticket stub.

A few days later, Dr. Boudreaux came to stand on our porch in the purple dusk. He held his brown Stetson formally in two hands like a suitor with a box of chocolates. He had on a short-sleeved blue shirt going dark at the armpits. The neighborhood kids broke up whatever loud game they'd been playing to stare gaggle-jawed at Dr. Boudreaux while he wiped his feet on the mat before stepping inside. A real doctor was a thing to witness. They stood at the end of our driveway even after he'd come inside.

Suddenly, I knew that Daddy was dead, knew it by the train sound rushing in my ears and by the way the room suddenly telescoped, so Mother and the doctor got little.

No, Dr. Boudreaux said. It wasn't that. Some folks might call death a blessing. He didn't believe that was so. But anyway, Daddy wasn't any deader than he'd been at suppertime. That was the good news.

It's the money, isn't it, Mother said. The insurance from the new refinery won't cover the hospital. Or home nursing after he gets home.

You know if it were up to me, Dr. Boudreaux said. He paused and hawked something from the back of his throat. His hands were small and girly. He folded them in his lap. He said the union lawyers might be a help.

But Mother didn't seem to be listening. She'd moved to the

door to shoo the kids away from their staring. They scattered like buckshot. She stepped back in.

Dr. Boudreaux said it wasn't his decision. Hell, he'd treated plenty of folks on credit, times when a strike drug on.

Outside the kids divided into two teams for a game. You take Barbara, and we get Bob, a voice said. No fair, if we take Barbara, we get Bob and Robbie too, the other voice said. You cheating sack of shit, the first voice said. Then I heard a slap and the sound of two small bodies falling on the grass to the cheers of other kids.

You'll never get a bill from me, Charlie, Dr. Boudreaux said. And then the doctor's white Buick backed away from us like an enormous ship.

Next morning, the hospital called to say an ambulance was hauling Daddy home. Somebody needed to come down and settle his bill. That set Mother's sarcasm loose in the beige phone receiver. (Etymology: *sarkazein,* to tear flesh.) She told the phone that the fucking ambulance could deliver Daddy buck naked to the aluminum lounge chair in the front yard. As for paying, Mother wanted to point out that debtor's prison had been abolished long ago. They couldn't get blood from a stone.

I've heard it said that caring for an invalid is like caring for a baby. And I suppose it's the same basic deal, but a baby rewards you each day with change, sprouting a tooth or discovering that the object randomly waggling before its eyes is, in fact, its own hand. But an invalid is a hole you pour yourself into. Every day he fixes you with a glance more gnawed-out tired than yours, more hurt. If life is suffering (as the Buddha says), some endless shit-eating contest, then the invalid always wins, hands down.

Maybe real nurses grow accustomed to a sick person's pain. I tried to ignore Daddy's uncircumcised penis lying swollen along his thigh, plugged with a cloudy tube and red from the steady irritation.

One day when Mother was turning him to change his sheets, she found small red spots on his heels where they'd rubbed the sheet fabric too long. Days later, the spots were water blisters, which eventually broke and started to ooze. Over time, those bedsores ate oval holes into Daddy's heels nearly half an inch deep. His very bones were trying to cut their way out of him. Or that's how the visiting nurse put it. She showed Mother how to pack the wounds twice a day with wormlike strips of gauze soaked in antiseptic and tamped down in the sores gently as you could with the back end of a tweezer.

Other bedsores broke out not long after, on his bony lower back, at the winglike tips of the shoulder blades. Just keeping those wounds cleaned out and dressed, and feeding Daddy, and fighting by phone and mail with the insurance company for various reimbursements kept Mother busy like I'd never seen her. Plus he messed the bed a lot, so there was laundry by the bushel basket every day.

But his speechlessness was the battle I was least fit for. If you'd been able to tell me unequivocally that Daddy had no more brain wattage than an eggplant, it would have been easier. Instead, I tended to feel around in his aphasia for signs of the old self.

"That was Lecia on the phone," I said.

"Purty goo," Daddy came back.

"She's worried sick about their taxes on their motels this year."

"Loooo," Daddy said.

"You want some of this ice cream? It's vanilla."

"Bad bad bad."

"It's not that bad, Daddy. Try some. I'll fix you a dish."

"Yamma," he'd say.

"Yessir, Mama ate some too."

I couldn't go on this way too long without making up somewhere I needed to be. I wanted to treat him with dignity—needed to do so, even—but his circumstances defied the only forms of dignity I knew. Maybe I was suffering from a failure of imagination: I couldn't make up new forms of dignity unrelated to articulate speech or the body's force. Plus Daddy could pout like a two-year-old. If Mother were trying to roll him over to change his bed, and he wanted sleep, he'd clamp hold to the bed railing with his good arm and fight her.

Sometimes it even seemed he shit the bed on purpose right after, to get even. Surely that can't be true. Maybe the air on his butt only motivated his bowels those times. Still, she often had to clean him twice in a row, while he crossed his good arm across his thin chest and sulled up, refusing to help.

The speech therapist who came a few times was equally clueless about how cogent Daddy might be. "I tell you, Charlie," Harold told Mother over coffee one morning, "you need to learn some equanimity, honey." He was a soft-spoken black man who drank his Sanka real blond and wore a ring that opened up as if for magic powder. His cyanide ring, he called it.

"Equanimity, my ass," Mother said. "I can't tell if he's in there or not."

Neither could I, which ultimately made me a piss-poor nurse. The one time I fed him all by myself, I nearly killed him, albeit slowly, and with none of the double-barrel grandeur of a real mercy killing.

I'd brought him a pint carton of shrimp gumbo from the Farm Royale. Those days, Daddy was subsisting on milkshakes Mother cracked whole eggs into, and small plastic cups of chocolate pudding. But the gumbo worked some voodoo on his appetite. Once I'd lifted the plastic lid, a curl of garlicky steam rose up. The gravy was thick and brown as bayou water, with a few plump shrimp bobbing under the surface, and translucent scallion greens and nibbets of rice floating at the edges. I imagined that steam forming a misty and serpentine finger that rose to tease at Daddy's nostrils. His mouth popped open—pink and naked as a baby bird's, for we'd long since taken his dentures out.

For nearly an hour, I shoveled that gumbo into him. He'd grind away till I told him to swallow, which he did with effort, needing water through a bendy straw to wash it all back. Then he'd nod for the next mouthful. Getting him to eat felt like a moral triumph, the way having a strange dog come wagging up to you can make you proud, or how a random toddler choosing your knees to climb at a party can seem some innocent and, therefore, final testament to your good character.

I was scraping the bottom of the carton when I noticed one side of Daddy's jaw swollen up like a squirrel's. He'd been stashing away the shrimp he couldn't swallow. He'd leaned his far cheek into the pillow to hide it. The ragged gray wad of shrimp I spied between his lips was approaching the size of a golf ball. I cupped my palm under his lip and told him to spit it out. He'd choke falling asleep with that in there, and his eyelids had already drooped to half mast.

In fact, while I stood there saying *spit,* he corked off entirely. His mouth lolled open another notch. The chewed-up shrimp had only to shift sideways about three quarters of an inch before his windpipe blocked off. I shook his shoulder: nothing. "Daddy!" I yelled; his eyes stayed closed, glued, sealed. I finally took aim with my index finger at his mouth's breathing slot. Maybe he'd stay asleep, I thought, if I poked gently enough across his tongue, which felt warm and foreign as a slug.

Then he bit me. Even before his eyes creaked open to thin slits, he clamped down with his slick gums hard enough to hold me by that finger. Like some terrier who'd caught me snitching his biscuit. We stood that way a minute—my finger in his mouth, his black eyes glaring out with no glimmer of recognition. And when I grasped that iron-boned jaw with my other hand as you might grab a horse's to force it to take a bit, his good hand wrapped around my bicep so tight that in the morning I found the bruised imprint of each finger.

Also the next morning, I overheard the visiting nurse asking what in God's name had Daddy got in his mouth. But he just gave a loose-shouldered shrug, all the while staring at the wall like she'd lost her mind while she scooped the old shrimp out with a tongue depressor.

The only other evening I spent alone with Daddy I had to get drunk for. Lecia and the Rice Baron had taken me to their country club summer dance, where I'd stomped through the Cotton-Eyed

Joe with various doctors and insurance salesmen, intermittently downing whole goblets of a sinister rum punch. A fellow I called Gomez finally drove me home in a convertible black as the Batmobile.

Daddy's eyes lit up when I peeked in on him. "Hey, Pokey," he said, his words clear as ice. Then, "You fun?"

Mother had left the TV on with the volume cranked down. Why I'll never know, for that summer the local station played nothing after midnight but reruns of old dog races. The old tube spilled out an aquarium-blue light.

The whippets were pale and lizardy. Their spines sloped down from high haunches, which left the impression that they had spike heels on their back feet. They were being corraled into individual starting pens while I watched. It depressed me no end, I told Daddy. Not only did a whole slew of other people know the outcome of that race before we even saw the gate fly up, but the dogs themselves were probably long since dead. Daddy puckered his mouth into a sour pinch that said he knew exactly what I meant. Those dogs were deader than doornails, I told him, dead or else lying before somebody's gas heater farting up a storm. He nodded his head like it made him tired to think.

Daddy's face had shrunk. All his skull's hollows—temple and jaw and cheekbone—held shadows the color of shale. Maybe I nodded off. Maybe I was woozy and drunk enough to hallucinate over Daddy's face a death's head, but for a split second that's what I saw in his pillow's trench. Then he sneezed, and I said bless you, and he was back to himself.

I pushed the button to shut the TV off. The picture shrank to a little blue star that hurtled backwards through the swampy dark.

Then I started shuffling through a shoebox of cassette tapes on the floor till I laid hold to the one with "Pete Karr" on the label in red Magic Marker. I wanted nothing so much as to hear Daddy tell a story, to unreel a story in my head like so much sheer, strong fishing line casting me back to times I'd never lived through and places I'd never been except courtesy of his voice.

I held that tape over the aluminum bed rail, in what I guessed was Daddy's line of sight. "You remember this?" I asked.

"Yep," he said. He grinned on half his face and gave a sharp nod.

"Mind if I play it?"

"Gone," he said, which I took to be "Go on," as in, "Go on ahead, honey, and play it if you want." I popped it in, then pressed the rectangular button so the brown tape started turning.

This all started on the nineteenth day of July in nineteen hundred and twenty. Started at a barrelhouse called Bessie Mae's back the woods. Place you could get barbecue and strawberry soda pop. Home brew if they wasn't any government men around. . . .

Course it actually started when Buck Neelan rode the train down into the logging camp. Buck was what you call a sport. Didn't work nor nothing. Liked to gamble. Liked to fool with other fellas' women.

A man name of Nan Crocket and his brother, Ugh, was working with my daddy that summer when Buck come around. He fooled around and got it in his head that Nan was messing with one of his girlfriends. Hell, Nan was married. Didn't mess with nobody that I ever knew. Think what actually brought it about was Nan beating Buck at Bouray. Which was the card game of the day . . .

Anyways, Buck finds Nan up there, catches him with a straight razor. Cut old Nan down. Cut him bad. My daddy had to run him over to Evadale to the doctor. Get him sewed up. Hell, it was three weeks or better till Nan come on back to work. Took him that long to get his strength back.

Poppa asked Nan's brother, Ugh, what Nan was planning to do about it. And Ugh says, "I don't know what Nan gone do, but I know what I'd do."

Nan come on back to work. And that rocked on a year or more. . . .

Then one Saturday morning here come Nan by the house. Poppa was hard of hearing. They'd always come to the gate and holler for Momma. She knowed everybody in camp by voice. "Ruth," Nan hollers. Them bird dogs was yapping like they fixing to eat him up.

"Come on in, Nan. They ain't gonna bother you," Momma says. "Tom's setting in the kitchen."

Daddy was setting at that table with a glass of cornbread crumbled up in buttermilk when Nan come in. See, Nan was supposed to work with Poppa in the morning. "Don't want you expecting me and me not be there . . . I'm fixing to go out to Bessie Mae's tonight."

"What you want with Bessie Mae's?"

And Nan tells him he heard through the grapevine that Buck Neelan's coming through. Poppa tells him, "Nan, you go on ahead. Tell Ugh come give me a hand in the morning. But get your ass back down here tomorrow evening." My daddy knew what was fixing to take place. . . .

Nan walks into Bessie Mae's that night. Sees old Buck Neelan way down to the other end. Buck's sitting on one a them screw-top piano stools thumping on that piano. Wore a black derby hat at that time with a satin band. Buck's a-thumping, and they's two women leaning on either side the piano singing.

Well, Nan walks in and that singing flat stops. 'Cause they was all looking this way. But old Buck's looking yonder way. Them women stop singing and back on up out the way so Buck knows they's something wrong. . . . He spun around on that stool. 'Course when he swung around, he was looking right down the barrel of that old .45. Wham! Wham! Hit him just as square in between the eyes as you could measure. Blowed a hole back of his head you could put a orange in. Blowed him off that stool.

Nan stuck the gun in his britches and walks on out.

He come on over to the house hollering for Momma. You can hear the bed squeak where she's giving Poppa a shake. He asks her what the hell's the matter. She tells him Nan Crocket's out by the gate again.

"Hell, Nan don't have to talk to me. I done know what's the matter. He done killed Buck Neelan's all." But Poppa gets on up. He come easing right along them porch boards where me and A.D. supposed to be sleeping. Kept our bunk beds out there all summer. Course we'd heard them dogs start worrying around before Nan even hit the gate. Moon was big around as a skillet. So we seen Poppa come outside in his drawers.

"Tom," Nan says, "they tell me Mr. Bishop's coming after me." Beaver Bishop was the sheriff of Jasper County at that time.

"Aw, Mr. Bishop's ass," Poppa said. "Why didn't you just come on

in here and lay down the couch. Then you'd a been here if Mr. Bishop is coming." *Nan said that'd be okay too.*

That Monday morning Beaver Bishop calls to say the circuit judge'll be coming up to our end of the county in a week or so. Wonders was Nan fixing to run off before then. Poppa tells him, "Hell, Nan ain't going nowheres."

Sure enough, a week or so later, a black Model T come pulling up in front the sawmill. Was a great big fellow driving it. Hands big around as pie tins. Had the prettiest head of red hair you ever seen on anybody, man or woman. I mean a big mess of it curly. Wore a black suit like a undertaker. Drove that Ford right up to where them rough trees was stacked yea high and still running sap so strong you couldn't get a whiff of your lunch bucket less you went upwind.

"Nan Crocket," he says, "you know I can send you to the penitentiary for killing people?"

"Yessir," Nan said. "But they can also haul me to the cemetery for Buck Neelan whittling on me." Last thing Nan says, ain't nobody ever did him nothing but Buck.

And that was the end of it. Never will forget it. They was a killing ever now and again. They always come to my daddy with it. I can see Poppa right now. That silly-assed hat stuck on his head. I can see him. . . .

I woke to the brown tape unwinding silence.

I'd gone to Houston when Daddy's old commanding officer came to call. The man we knew as Captain Pearse had retired a colonel out west. The D-Day stuff on TV got him tracking down guys he'd served with. Soon as he heard Daddy was sick, he booked flights down and a room in the Holiday Inn. Lecia was there when the rented Pinto pulled up a few days later. She said Pearse had probably done a lot of sit-ups in his life. He was wearing one of those yellow golf shirts with an alligator over the heart. He actually pulled off kissing Mother's hand when she came out on the porch to greet him.

Daddy saluted him with a sharp right hand. "Captain Pearse," he said, his speech clear for the first time in weeks. And Pearse said at ease, Sergeant Karr. Then they were both wiping the wet off their faces, holding each other like a pair of frail old ghosts.

Pearse sat on Daddy's bed well into the evening, paging through old pictures. Once again, Daddy's war talk came out clear. The effort tired him, though. He finally dozed off while the colonel was still peeling the foil top off some pudding.

By phone, I heard the colonel's fine tenor voice. "Your daddy turned down a battlefield commission after the Bulge," he told me. "He didn't like the idea of drinking at the officers' club. Anybody above the rank of sergeant was what he called a *poodle*." After I hung up, Pearse drank black coffee from Mother's bone-china cups till the small hours. He told her more war stories we'd never heard.

Daddy was wounded twice, for instance. Once, a German soldier stuck a bayonet through his forearm, leaving a scar I'd seen a thousand times and never once asked about. Another time, a bridge they'd mined blew early and buried Daddy so completely in rubble that Pearse presumed him dead. They hadn't even bothered digging for him. But a few days later, Daddy came riding up the road in another fellow's Jeep. He had a big bandage wrapped around his head, and a grin a yard wide. In fact, Pearse thought the old head wound might have led to Daddy's stroke. If so, the army might help us with some of our costs. Pearse had testified in a few cases like that, and both times the family got help.

That's how I wound up in Mother's attic. We needed army medical records proving Daddy was head-injured in combat. I'd put off climbing up there for weeks, claiming I needed a good rain to cool things off. In truth, the attic scared me.

An attic in East Texas is especially bad. The hot damp in such places accrues over years; all manner of organism can breed. Cardboard gets dappled with green mildew in patterns that put you in mind of chrysanthemums on antique wallpaper. You can hear roaches scuttle through papers in an East Texas attic, can practically feel their threadlike antennae reaching toward you all whispery. Plus you face the slight danger of stumbling across a snake.

The summer before, Lecia's attic had been infested with them.

We'd heard thumps on the ceiling one night. Something heavy was falling from the inside attic rafters, without the scuttling sounds afterwards that a raccoon or rodent would make. Armed with flashlight, she was supposed to poke her head up there, scout around, and report back so she could let her exterminator know what he was in for. The fluffy pink insulation showed no small-animal scat, only what looked like old nylon stockings somebody had peeled off and strewn around. Then the flashlight beam in her hand went level, and they were snakeskins. The house sat close to a bayou, and moccasins had been nesting up there.

So by the time I finally pulled down the spring-hung ladder in Mother's garage, a spike of cold fear ran through me. Thunderheads had been bearing down all morning in a heavy, iron-gray bank. When the rain came, the whole sky seemed to rip open with a sound like silk tearing. Fat drops pelted on the palm fronds. The honeysuckle and wisteria vines on the redwood fence shivered under it. The patio bricks sent up thin ribbons of steam. I'd sprinted from house to garage and still my T-shirt stuck to my chest.

I pulled the light string dangling from the peaked roof. On the day Daddy had run that electrical cord along the top beam with a staple gun, I'd stood by holding the very lightbulb that still hung there, only webbed in spider silk now. He'd let me screw it in back then, so it had lit in the cage of my fingers. I hadn't been there since. Nobody had, I figured, except to bench-press boxes up. The stale air was sweltering wet. But nothing fluttered, neither bat nor pigeon nor death's-head moth. Among the skeletal lamps and rusty kitchen appliances from the Eisenhower era, no corpse sat up. I breathed in the heat, breathed it out. My heart went scamper-scamper.

After a few minutes, I waded away from the light and deeper into the boxes, which held, once I started opening them, detritus of the most generic nature—books, records, Mason jars, dime-store vases. A yellow carpenter's kit with miniature tools gave the only hint of my childhood. There was an old hurricane lamp still smelling dimly of kerosene, and a sewing machine you powered with a wrought-iron foot pedal. There were endless empty pieces of Samsonite luggage, hatboxes without hats, garment bags containing no garments.

Finally, a camel-backed trunk I spotted under the far eaves gave me a twinge. It didn't thrum or spill light from its cracks. Still, somebody had slid it back there locked and on purpose. I poked my screwdriver in the hasp and whacked down on it with my old toy hammer. The lock broke open with a snap. I knelt there sweating a minute. An old storybook illustration of Pandora took shape in my head, how from her box demons the size of dragonflies went spiraling up the page while her small hands flew to her cheeks and her cupid's-bow mouth assumed the standard oval of Victorian surprise.

The trunk lid I raised hit the sloping roof. I let it drop shut, then grabbed the leather side handles. My back and quadriceps muscles strained to drag the whole trunk from its hiding hole. Then I sat down again under the dusty bulb cross-legged and puffing.

Flipping back the lid unleashed no winged demons, only the smell of wet newsprint, like a paper you'd picked off a dew-soaked lawn. The top tray held a scattering of sepia photos and letters tied with twine. I also found four jewelry boxes lined up neat as soldiers. Two were covered in black velvet, one in royal-blue satin, another in a deep raspberry grosgrain. Each clicked wide to show some version of a wedding ring.

The family jewels, I figured. I squatted on my haunches to lift the whole tray, to tote it down to the kitchen. Mother had fixed iced tea before I'd gone up. I could picture the swollen crockery pitcher beaded with frost in the dark fridge, little pinwheels of lemon floating in the brown tea.

The instant I stood, though, what lay in the trunk bottom startled me into dropping the tray. It fell heavy on the tops of my bare feet, as if some huge fist had smashed down on it dead center. The wedding rings and snapshots and letter bundles went spilling around. At the same time, I stumbled back into a swollen box of Christmas decorations. The box edge caught me behind my knees, which buckled. My hands shot down to stop the fall. They plunged up to the elbows in a rat's nest of tinsel and colored lights. Glass balls in thin containers crunched under my weight like boxed eggs blown hollow. A spiky plastic star raked a scratch up the inside of one arm.

But all this barely slowed my panicked, backward-scrambling motion, for lying in the trunk bottom was Grandma Moore's prosthetic leg. The mortician had left the thick stocking stretched on and tied off in a silly top-knot where her thigh should have been. The same stiff black shoe was stuck on the rigid foot, which was carved toeless, like a doll's stub. Maybe a coiled rattler weaving its head and shaking out a rasp would've panicked me more, but I doubt it.

Mother found me standing in the cool green light of the icebox. She bore her laundry hamper of linens into the kitchen behind me. The bleach smell preceded her so I turned from the open fridge door. I'd been scooping out the heart of a deep watermelon round, using my bare hands to claw out chunks, letting the sticky juice go down my chin, swallowing the black patent-leather-looking seeds along with the fruit, which was sweet and cold in a way that made my back fillings ache. If this pose struck Mother as odd, she didn't say. She just wanted to know did I find anything useful in the attic.

But when I asked about that line-up of wedding rings, whose they were, the whole tenor of the room altered. (The only metaphor I can find for such a change is musical: where one note had been playing, it suddenly grew into a chord involving lots of black keys.) The look in her eyes was one I'd seen in the narrowing pupils of certain caged animals. "They're yours, aren't they?" I finally said, which option hadn't even breezed through my head before. Again, the quiet between us held. "Don't start hounding me about those rings now, Mary," she said. Her voice was flat. She set down the mountain of laundry. "I just can't take it."

She took to her bed. From the kitchen, I could hear her rummaging through the fruitcake tin where she kept pharmaceuticals. What was she looking for? I wondered. Some powerful pagan god, name of Valium or Thorazine or Halcion, was the only answer I came up with.

Mother's particular devils had remained mysterious to me for decades. So had her past. Few born liars ever intentionally embark in truth's direction, even those who believe that such a journey might axiomatically set them free. Several times, I'd flown to Texas ready to push against the figurative door of the past. But the resistance I met was both invisible and fierce. Even when Daddy could still speak, he wouldn't. He'd put on I'm-just-a-dumb-ol'-cracker face. "Shit, darling, I can't remember none of that."

Lecia could confirm what I dredged up. But like me, she lacked basic facts, the whys and wherefores of Mother's past. In her world, though, people who whined about their childhoods were woosies, ne'er-do-well liberals seeking to defraud the insurance industry out of dollars for worthless therapies. "Unconscious mind, my ass," she said. "Get over it." She went back to scrubbing Comet off some sink porcelain. (She worked her butt off all day and had a full-time, live-in cleaning lady, but spent hours every night in rubber gloves. Her house was as gleamingly sterile as most operating theaters.)

Nonetheless, truth was conspiring to assemble itself before me. Call it fate or grace or pure shithouse chance. I was being guided somehow into the chute that led down the dark corridor at the end of which truth's door would fly open.

After I found the wedding rings, Mother became stonily resolute about not discussing them. Or her past. "I can't take care of your daddy with you beating on me about all this," she said. She pressed on her temples with both hands, as if her skull might explode from internal pressure unless she kept it squeezed tight. "I have two headaches, one behind each eye, each one the size of a Kennedy half-dollar."

I talked long-distance to a former therapist who had me write out all my questions for Mother on a spiral pad. I read them back to him: *Whose wedding rings were those? Who were the two kids Grandma Moore showed me school pictures of? After she died, why did you go nuts? What were you doing with the knife that night? Why did you tell Dr. Boudreaux you'd killed us? What happened to you in the hospital?*

He pointed out that they weren't *cruel* questions. In my family lingo, though, they were. More than mean, they might prove lethal. The night I approached Mother with my spiral pad, she locked herself in the bathroom for hours. That left me to pace the dim hall outside like a lioness wondering if she was in there holding a Gillette super-blue blade to her wrist. "Call the police when she does that," the therapist said the next day. But until he gave me an ultimatum, I wouldn't knuckle Mother to talk. He refused to take my calls. He hung up on me three days running, saying he couldn't help me if I wouldn't take some risks.

"You're not gonna give up on this wedding-ring business, are you?" Mother finally said. I said no ma'am.

We set out to get drunk. Our favorite Mexican waiter scribbled our order for two pitchers of margaritas on his green pad with no sign of judgment. His busboy son then promptly delivered a basket of steaming chips along with sinus-opening salsa in an earthenware bowl.

The wedding rings were Mother's, of course. She confessed that right off. She'd first married at fifteen. No, she hadn't been pregnant at the time. Grandma Moore just wanted her out of the house. The first baby came a few years into that, a boy. Let's call him Tex for the sake of simplicity.

After Tex's birth, my teenaged mother began to long desperately for escape from Lubbock, particularly from the hawklike vigilance of her very critical mother-in-law, whom we might describe metaphorically as a broomstick-wielding German housewife with a gaze merciless as the sun's. So when the young husband graduated from college—let's say in business—his wife urged him toward a job in New York City. In 1942, the family set off from Lubbock, a dust trail blowing up behind their Ford, baby boy cooing in a willow basket in the backseat.

Once there, my young mother became enraptured by the whole shining and steel-girdered metropolis. Tex's navy-blue buggy got lugged down subway stairs and shoved along the wide corridors of various museums. She wanted to paint the human form, which desire puzzled her husband. Why would she want to sit around staring at naked strangers? Quarrels erupted. The whole endeavor was put on hold with the arrival of a new baby girl, blond and green-eyed like Mother. Let's call her Belinda.

After the birth of Belinda, the wicked mother-in-law flew north on her leathery wings and assumed control over the household. The young wife responded with an act shameless enough to border on scandal: she took a job, full-time, doing mechanical drawing for Bell Labs. Pearl Harbor had been bombed. The husband's employer was military; now the wife's job was adjudged essential to the war effort. The mother-in-law pouted, but didn't want to seem unpatriotic. She grudgingly cared for the children while Mother worked.

And it was from that job that Mother returned home one evening to find her entire house empty, her family gone.

It was winter. Imagine it. During the short walk from the train, a dry snow falling fast had accumulated on Mother's hair and the shoulders of her charcoal coat in a pattern of flakes I picture like a lace scarf, like the white mantilla a girl wears at her First Communion.

Mother crossed the threshold into an empty house. The radiators were cold. She followed the pale plumes of her breath from room to bare room, throwing light switches to no avail. Even the phone was dead.

The neighbors had seen the moving truck pull away that day, the loading of it supervised all morning by the old woman. The young husband arrived by car after lunch to pick her up with the kids, toddler Tex standing in back, the infant girl in the old lady's arms.

I was crying by this time, and so was Mother. Our waiter was poised behind the hostess desk, motionless as a figurehead. He stared politely away from us, into the drafty and cathedrallike mall space, our unstudied menus tucked in his armpit. At a side table, the busboy was filling salt shakers with a small plastic funnel and deep attention. The salt poured from the giant bag like swift liquid while Mother dabbed at her eyes. She slipped a paper napkin flat under her lower lashes to blot any mascara.

The neighbors let Mother sleep on their foldout couch. They also fed her and took her out to a bar down the block. She wasn't yet old enough to have voted. "And that's the first night I got drunk. Oh, I'd taken a drink before, but they got me pie-eyed."

Next day at her husband's office, she found his desk drawers cleaned out. A few unsharpened pencils rolled around among the paper clips. The boss wore a watch fob across his portly middle. He wouldn't tell her where the young husband had gone, claiming those whereabouts were top secret, a matter of national security.

Still, she stayed numb and dry-eyed. Surely her kids were nearby. The war made searching for them hard. Nights, the whole Eastern seaboard got blacked out after curfew. Buses and trains were booked with GIs, so travel was nearly impossible. "Even if you had ration stamps, which nobody did, there wasn't any gas."

Her parents had also moved from Lubbock proper to a farm in Morton. They didn't have a phone. Letters meandered slowly back and forth. When Grandpa Moore threatened to shoot the young husband, he did so by postcard. And the Lubbock branch of the husband's family had likewise vanished, leaving no forwarding address, no bank records, nary a trace.

Like a forties movie where calendar dates get torn off in a flurry, some months passed. Mother blankly plodded through. "I'd tell myself the kids would show up next week, or my parents would track them down soon as they could find a detective to hire. Everybody who could do anything was off in the war." She took a studio apartment in Manhattan and signed up for night classes in painting at the Art Students League, after which she drank till blackout. Days, she worked hungover at the labs.

Six months after the kids disappeared, Mother's daddy dropped dead unexpectedly. "Cerebral hemorrhage," the death certificate read.

The call came in to Bell Labs while she happened to be at the switchboard, filling in for a friend who'd gone to the women's room. Mother felt awkward accepting the call for herself from the operator. Then the very dry voice of her aunt Audrey came worming through Mother's headset, right into her ear. "Your daddy passed away last night," it said, and Mother responded by yanking all the cords she could lay hold to from the switchboard, grabbing wires with both hands and just pulling blind, so every call hooked through that switchboard broke off suddenly into the monochromatic hum of dial tone.

Mother got a Defense Department waiver to ride trains to Texas for the funeral. But troops bumped her off in Chicago, where she was stuck for days. Bumped again in Amarillo, she hitched a ride with a truck driver who carried her to the aunt's white-picket fence.

Grandma Moore had slipped into something like madness. She'd locked herself in the back pantry where they shelved canned peaches and dusty jars of chowchow. Mother peeked in, and Grandma looked up from her lace shuttle, her face on its delicate bones showing not the least surprise. "Everybody's saying your daddy's dead, Charlie Marie." She'd been doing a floral pattern and went back to it. Her lips pursed. "But he isn't dead. He's just real, real cold." Mother remembered the dry sound of silk thread sliding through, the knot creating a perfect clump of lilac on a lace branch.

In the parlor, the fair-haired aunts were nonplussed by Grandma Moore's decline. They were crisis vultures. "Somebody else's trouble just thrilled them to death," Mother told me. After supper, they hid from their husbands to smoke out on the gazebo.

Mother was bringing out glasses of fresh lemonade when she overheard what must have been the family wisdom on her loss of those children. "Charlie Marie must have done something awful to run that man off," one said. "And him taking the babies," another said. "Where there's smoke there's fire," piped in a third.

The kids were found wholly by chance long after the funeral, when Mother had gone back to New York and Grandma Moore had returned to her version of sanity.

My grandmother was finishing an egg cream from the wrought-iron chair of a Lubbock drugstore when her insurance man stopped by. He asked about my mother's whole-life premium, which had gone unpaid for some time. "Her husband sends us money orders for his policy. But he's not covering Charlie's," he said. "You want to let her policy lapse, or what?"

Within five minutes, Grandma had the young husband's address. Within two days, my mother had flown from New York City to the small Western town—let's say it was Reno, Nevada—where the husband lived.

The town constable picked her up. He drove her to the house where her kids were ensconced. The young husband had just remarried, it turned out, claiming his children's mother had run off years before to parts unknown. Maybe she was even dead. "Hell, I didn't even realize I was divorced, much less dead," Mother said, which caused the constable to cock an eyebrow. He knew—because she'd told him—that the black alligator handbag on Mother's lap held a court order from a New York judge assigning her full custody of the two children.

The house was a sprawling ranch with a winding brick walk that led to a broad, brass-knockered door. The young husband had done well. That door swung open on the evil mother-in-law. The constable blushed and stuttered explaining his mission to her. She finally stepped back a few paces to let them enter.

A small boy hid behind her apron, and a blond toddler girl was idly stacking blocks on the immaculately vacuumed Oriental rug.

Mother stooped down and held out her arms to the girl, who stood, shrieked, and fled behind the long sofa, cowering. Just the crown of her blond head bobbed up shining.

"That was the first time I thought," Mother said. In the small table space between us were many stemmed margarita glasses, the crusted salt missing on each where her mouth had sipped, or my mouth had. We'd long since stopped leaving lipstick marks. "I just got the papers and hopped on a plane when I heard they'd been found. I didn't think. I had a studio apartment back then, on Jones Street." Tears made her face slick, but her voice stayed flat, as if those tears had a source in the gray eyes of a different woman, one whom Mother knew only in passing.

The mother-in-law was a broad battleship of a woman. She walked behind the sofa, the boy still scuttling to hide himself in her voluminous skirts. The old woman hefted up the weeping toddler girl, who quieted to snuffles.

Mother collapsed in a ladderback side chair. She bent over her handbag with the court order unfolded on top and wept. The constable stood like a soldier under orders before the long silk draperies. "I knew then they were better off there," Mother said. "With their daddy, I mean, and whoever the woman was. I didn't even have beds for them. I didn't have anybody to watch them while I was at work. I hadn't *thought,* just hadn't *thought* about any of that." Mother says the word *thought* like she's stomping out something, or as if the weight of it fell on her like a blow.

Then Mother did what seemed at the time the Right Thing, though had she Thought, she may have Thought Twice about how Right the Right Thing would wind up being, for surely it drove her mad. She sat in that ladderback chair and tore up the papers giving her sole custody of the two minor children, Tex and Belinda. She tore them up under the smug smile and predatory eye of the monolithic Mother-in-Law. The constable showed visible relief. But the kids were still skittish, which was partly why Mother didn't even hug them good-bye, for they would have winced in her arms. "I couldn't have stood that," she said.

"What'd you do then?" I asked.

"Then I flew back to New York and started looking for somebody to marry who'd help me get my kids back."

The room around us had vanished completely. We were held close in this timeless bubble of bad neon. "But after I got married, whoever it was"—she waved her hand at the various husbands—"would lose interest in getting me my kids. And I'd get sick of them and run off. Your daddy would have taken them, finally. Your daddy was the only one. . . ."

In fact, after Mother and Daddy married, she wrote for the kids, but they were too big by then. "They didn't want to come," Mother said. The stepmother sent a letter to that effect. "Then it was like a big black hole just swallowed me up. Or like the hole was inside me, and had been swallowing me up all those years without my even noticing. I just collapsed into it. What's the word the physicists use? Imploded. I imploded."

Those were my mother's demons, then, two small children, whom she longed for and felt ashamed for having lost.

And the night she'd stood in our bedroom door with a knife? She'd drunk herself to the bottom of that despair. "All the time I'd wasted, marrying fellows. And still I lost those kids. And you and Lecia couldn't change that. And I'd wound up just as miserable as I started at fifteen." Killing us had come to seem merciful. In fact, she'd hallucinated we'd been stabbed to death. "I saw blood all over you and everything else. Splashed across the walls."

As to why she hadn't told us all this before—about the marriages and the lost children—her exact sentence stays lodged in my head, for it's one of the more pathetic sentences a sixty-year-old woman can be caught uttering: "I thought you wouldn't like me anymore."

The next day Lecia hired a detective to find the lost kids, who were kids no longer, of course, being well into their forties by then. They were also damn eager to be found. Within weeks of our first phone call, they arrived at Mother's house, bright and fresh-faced and curious as all get-out.

That reunion's their story, really, one I could not presume to tell, except to say it marked a time when our house began to fill with uncharacteristic light.

Mother and I didn't foresee that result in the Mexican café. We wobbled to our feet. Our table was littered with pitchers, cocktail napkins soppy wet and shredded, a forest of stemmed glasses. Lime rinds rested in the smoldering ashtray. I looked down at it all, weaving from what seemed a great height. Salt from the various tortilla baskets had spilled across the checkerboard cloth. All afternoon, I'd been using my butter knife to scrape the crystals up into white lines, arranging them in geometric shapes, like some code you might find on a cave wall. For some reason the designs pleased me no end, like some unreadable testament we were leaving. I hated to think of the busboy sponging them up.

We were grim-faced crossing that restaurant. We leaned together like cartoon drunks. Our high heels barely held us up. We bumped table edges and sloshed and apologized and righted ourselves and went back to our single-minded forward lurching. Bright piñata shapes I hadn't seen before loomed from strings above us—bull and clipper ship, crucifix, five-pointed star.

In the dusk outside, the low sun made me squint. It was hot. We spread newspapers on the car seat before sliding across. The chrome inside would blister you. I used a blue Kleenex to pinch the ignition. Once I cranked it, hot air blasted from the the slatted AC vents. I shifted to reverse. The sky above us was going from musky yellow to purple. Colors of a cut plum, Mother said.

I pulled onto the freeway thinking of Daddy in that aluminum bed like some old ideogram of himself. Since Dr. Boudreaux had told me to prepare for his death, I always drove home picturing an ambulance parked in the driveway; a corpse on the inside stretcher with white sheet draped over its features. But five years would pass before Daddy died, paralyzed, light enough for me to lift into his wheelchair, an act that always made him giggle and coo like a baby. He was oddly happy at the end. He adored the white cat Bumper, who came home from the vet still mute and miraculously wired together, to coil on Daddy's sunken chest purring, or on the laps of nurses we hired till our money ran out.

That day in the car, I only knew we were late getting home to relieve Daddy's nurse. In the slap of tires on the road's melted tar, I heard the ashy voice of my own fear hissing *Daddy's dead, Daddy's dead.*

Mother was crying softly beside me. She slipped on her sunglasses. The white oil tanks sliding off the lenses still seemed primordial to me. As a kid, I'd thought they were dinosaur eggs and worried about what might hatch out of them. They cast humped shadows across the refinery yards. We drove past them. The fence running alongside us went from the industrial hurricane's diamonds to barbed wire that sloped in parallel lines from post to post, behind which were broad rice fields, rich green stalks leaning every which way, almost heavy enough to harvest.

Then the fence vanished, and the dissected fields gave way to a foggy riverbank spilling morning glories. Dark was closing in. We hit a long stretch of roadside bluebonnets that broadened to a meadow. Here and there in the flowers you could make out small gatherings of fireflies. How odd, I thought, that those bugs lived through the refinery poisons. Beyond Mother's tired profile, the fireflies blinked in batches under spreading mist like little birthday cakes lighting up and getting blown out.

I didn't think this particularly beautiful or noteworthy at the time, but only do so now. The sunset we drove into that day was luminous, glowing; we weren't.

Though we should have glowed, for what Mother told absolved us both, in a way. All the black crimes we believed ourselves guilty of were myths, stories we'd cobbled together out of fear. We expected no good news interspersed with the bad. Only the dark aspect of any story sank in. I never knew despair could lie. So at the time, I only felt the car hurtling like some cold steel capsule I'd launched into onrushing dark.

It's only looking back that I believe the clear light of truth should have filled us, like the legendary grace that carries a broken body past all manner of monsters. I'm thinking of the cool tunnel of white light the spirit might fly into at death, or so some have reported after coming back from various car wrecks and heart failures and drownings, courtesy of defib paddles and electricity, or after some kneeling samaritan's breath was blown into stalled lungs so they could gasp again. Maybe such reports are just death's neurological fireworks, the brain's last light show. If so, that's a lie I can live with.

Still, the image pleases me enough: to slip from the body's tight container and into some luminous womb, gliding there without effort till the distant shapes grow brighter and more familiar, till all your beloveds hover before you, their lit arms held out in welcome.